And Blessed Is She

SERMONS BY WOMEN

Edited by

David Albert Farmer
and
Edwina Hunter

JUDSON PRESS ® VALLEY FORGE, PA

"And blessed is she who
believed that there would
be a fulfillment of what
was spoken to her from God."

(Luke 1:45, Inclusive Language Lectionary)

And Blessed Is She: Sermons by Women
© 1990 by David Albert Farmer and Edwina Hunter
Judson Press Edition, 1994
Judson Press, Valley Forge, PA 19482-0851

Bible quotations in this volume are from *The Holy Bible*, King James Version and from the Revised Standard Version of the Bible, copyright © 1946, 1952, 1971, by the Division of Christian Education of the National Council of the Churches of Christ in the USA. Used by permission. All rights reserved.

Library of Congress Cataloging-in-Publication Data
And blessed is she : sermons by women / edited by David Albert Farmer & Edwina Hunter.
 p. cm.
Includes bibliographical references and index.
ISBN 0-8170-1216-8
1. Sermons, American—Women authors. I. Farmer, David Albert, 1954-
II. Hunter, Edwina.
BV4241.A685 1994   252'.0082—dc2094-20709

Printed in the U.S.A.

95 96 97 98 99 00 01 8 7 6 5 4 3 2

Contents

Preface

This book was in the planning stages for several years. As Dr. James W. Cox's teaching fellow during graduate school in the early eighties, I met several women who elected his basic course in preaching. The women students were always in the minority in those classes, but the quality of their work, usually, was exceptional. As I began to know some of them I became increasingly aware of the struggle and pain many of them endured in order to find their way into ministry of any kind—pulpit ministry in particular.

George Sweazey, in *Preaching the Good News*—our basic text during those years—wrote of a difficulty faced by developing preachers who are women: the shortage of role models. "The one handicap the women students have is their delivery. The reason for this is obvious—they have no models."* Not only are models for delivery limited, but also homiletic literature—especially sermons—by women is lacking. Since I taught the practice preaching laboratories, I learned very quickly that these were indeed serious problems.

Sweazey's insight and the experience of trying to assist women in improving or enhancing preaching skills initially planted in my mind the idea for a book such as this. When Harper & Row agreed to publish the book, they asked me to find a woman in the world of preaching to participate in the project. I feel very fortunate that Edwina Hunter, professor of preaching at the Pacific School of Religion and a former parish preacher, agreed to join in.

---

* George Sweazey, *Preaching the Good News* (Englewood Cliffs, NJ: Prentice-Hall, 1976), 302.

The purpose of the book is to offer in print a collection of sermons by women. Those who are interested in preaching in general or its history, and those who are interested in women's studies may find the material useful; but this book has also been prepared for women who consider preaching style and methodology as part of their work. It is important to note here that readers will have to establish critical and evaluative responses to the models offered on their own. This book, through historical and contemporary samples, offers an interesting collection of what has been, and what is, in the world of women preachers—without analysis or criticism.

Further, this book is not an attempt to be comprehensive. We do not offer a complete selection of sermons representing *all* the great women preachers in our American religious past. Nor do we attempt to examine the work of *all* of today's most noted women preachers.

Unfortunately, the work by women preachers in the past has gone largely unnoticed and, thus, unpreserved. This combined with the fact that there have not been nearly so many women preaching as there have been men makes it difficult to find appropriate sermons. None of the primary historians of preaching known to me, for example, have recalled a single contribution by a woman.

Thankfully, in contrast, the sermonic material by contemporary women is too extensive to deal with in any comprehensive manner—especially in a single volume. The end result, as far as this book is concerned, is a broad sampling of all that is available.

The sermons you will read and the stories of the women who preached them are all fascinating. You will be in touch here with strands of American tradition heretofore largely untapped and, thus, unavailable to most of us.

The format of the book is simple. I introduce women preachers of the past, and then seven women are presented with biographical sketches and samples of their work. Where possible archaic language, spelling, and expressions have been preserved. Professor Hunter offers a section that introduces the preaching of women in contemporary America followed by sermons of fifteen women and their reflections.

I am grateful to those who have assisted with this project—especially those whose suggestions helped get it going: Dr. Elizabeth Achtemeier, visiting professor of homiletics and Bible, Union Theological Seminary, Richmond, Virginia; Dr. Bill J. Leonard, professor of church history, the Southern Baptist Theological Seminary, Louisville, Kentucky; and Dr. James Smylie, professor of church history, Union Theological Seminary, Richmond, Virginia. Also, President Neely McCarter and Dean Barbara Brown Zikmund of the Pacific School of Religion have provided ongoing encouragement for the project.

In addition, I express appreciation to the following persons:

To Ms. Page Lilly, archivist/librarian, the Shaker Library, Poland Spring, Maine; and to Dr. Kermit J. Pike, director of the Library of the Western Reserve Historical Society, Cleveland, Ohio—for their assistance with the sermon by Mother Lucy Wright.

To Ms. Patricia M. King, director, and to Ms. Elizabeth Stenton, assistant to the director, the Arthur and Elizabeth Schlesinger Library on the History of Women in America, Cambridge, Massachusetts—for their assistance with the sermons by Olympia Brown and Anna Howard Shaw.

To Mrs. Julie Fewster, Rochester, New York—for her assistance with the sermon by Helen Barrett Montgomery.

To Dr. Charles Duarte, executive secretary of the International Church of the Foursquare Gospel; and to Ms. Lannae Graham, reference archivist, the Billy Graham Center, Wheaton College, Wheaton, Illinois—for their assistance with the sermon by Aimee Semple McPherson.

To Major Lloyd F. Stoops, literary secretary, and to Ms. Judith Johnson, archivist, of the Salvation Army Archives and Research Center, New York, New York—for their assistance with the sermon by Evangeline Booth.

To Dr. Rosemary Skinner Keller, professor of religion and American culture, and Mr. Al Caldwell, librarian, Garrett-Evangelical Theological Seminary, Evanston, Illinois—for their assistance with the sermon by Georgia Harkness.

David Albert Farmer
New Orleans, Louisiana
May 1989

I. WOMEN PREACHERS OF THE PAST

Introduction

David Albert Farmer

The truth is that women have been doing preaching, or at least what looked very much like preaching, almost since the founding of America. And, perhaps, more women are preaching today—with more freedom—than ever before. Indeed, there have been significant breakthroughs for women in opportunities for theological education and for service in many of the major denominations. But women who preach still are not widely recognized in mainstream Protestantism—and certainly not in Catholicism—as the equals of male preachers, and the greatest evidence of the fact is the limited opportunity for women to preach. Though a few have been welcomed into American pulpits with as much enthusiasm as men, most women preachers have had to struggle to find—if they can at all—a place in American churches where they can have any significant ministerial role, a preaching role in particular.

In the history of preaching in America, the trend has been for women who felt a call from God, or who desired to preach for any other reason, to find their way out of mainstream churches and into a sect where they were not viewed as "radical"; where their preaching gifts were not merely tolerated, but enthusiastically recognized; and where there was little or no "tradition" to restrict their religious expression in any way. This surely has been the path of least resistance. Those women who insisted on ministerial rights and credentials within the mainstream have had a much more difficult time of it, and their story is still being told.

That anyone can, with assurance, point out the woman who first preached formally in any American pulpit is doubtful. Certainly, the first women who preached did so outside mainstream American religion. Women likely "preached" in places other than sanctuaries of churches at first, but they preached. Barbara Brown Zikmund, a church historian and dean of the Pacific School of Religion, has concluded about preaching women:

There is no simple way to document chronologically the struggle for the right to preach, because various Christian groups resolved this issue at quite different times. The Quakers, Universalists, Unitarians, and Congregationalists resolved it earlier than most Methodists, Presbyterians, Lutherans, and Episcopalians. Part of this discrepancy had to do with church polity and part of it related to the connection between preaching and priestly functions in ordained ministry.[1]

The attitudes of New England Puritans in early America mirror, in many respects, the popularly held views toward women and religion. The churches were societal bodies that operated in much the same way as other institutions—local government, for example. The men, generally, were more educated and informed about current events; thus, men, rather uncritically, were given roles as leaders and decision-makers.

This carried them into positions of ecclesial dominance and authority—as had been true in England. Ironically, by the 1630s, more women than men were members of the churches, a trend that would continue. In spite of this, women were still not permitted to hold any kind of leadership positions—let alone be blessed or received as preachers. Rosemary Keller, professor of religion and American culture at Garrett-Evangelical Theological Seminary, explains:

Keeping women in their socially prescribed place was essential to the maintenance of the Puritan order, and most women probably accepted their subordination without question. Yet the social order was strained even during the first generation of Puritan settlement because a considerable number of women applied the implications of radical spiritual equality in St. Paul to themselves.[2]

Anne Hutchinson, evidently, was one of the earliest and best-known women to challenge the prevailing idea that women must not speak out in matters of religion. She began expressing her concerns in private meetings she held at her home. She taught her religious ideas to both men and women in this setting, and the crowds became so large that she had to conduct two weekly meetings. No one dared call what she did preaching, but her presentations, at the very least, reflected sermonic elements. In particular she challenged the belief in salvation by works, which she perceived to be a commonly held doctrine. Anne Hutchinson insisted, in contrast, on a salvation by God's grace alone. And she pointed out that—in all of the area around Boston—only her pastor, John Cotton, emphasized grace as it should be.

In 1637, she was brought to trial because, as the charge went, she was holding meetings in her home for the purpose of publicly criticizing the clergy of Boston. But that charge became incidental to the theological inquiry that emerged. Without a doubt, her theology was questionable in the minds of religious and political leaders alike.

Mistress Hutchinson was preaching a very easy and acceptable way to salvation, they thought. To do nothing, to have nothing, but to wait for Christ to do all, even to save a sinner from his sin—what a smooth path to Heaven.[3]

As the trial progressed accusation after accusation was made, but she was undaunted. She told her judges:

I am in the hands of the eternall Jehovah my Saviour, I am at his appointment, the bounds of my habitation are cast in Heaven, no further doe I esteeme of any mortall man, than creatures in his hand. I feare none but the great Jehovah, which hath foretold me of these things, and I doe verily beleeve that he will deliver me out of your hands, therefore take heed how you proceed against me, for I know that for this you goe about to doe unto me, God will ruine you and your posterity, and this whole state.[4]

But Mrs. Hutchinson, judged to be a heretic and a trouble-maker as well, was banished from Massachusetts. She fled to the freer religious atmosphere of Rhode Island and finally died in 1643 during an Indian massacre in New York.

In marked contrast was the experience of women in the Society of Friends. There was no official ministry in Quakerism; anyone who felt moved by the Spirit of God was free to express herself or himself. As one historian of Quakerism put it:

To educated and uneducated, old and young, men and women, the call may come to yield to the requirement to speak in a meeting for worship. . . . [Quaker] history has made it clear that the gift of ministry is not confined to any particular kind of person. There is no ordination other than evidence that a divine gift has been bestowed. . . . From the very beginning Quaker women shared the vocal ministry with men. To show that women could receive as genuine a call to this service as men, Friends had only to point to results.[5]

This has meant, practically, that there were numerous Quaker women who were preachers. In fact, the earliest Quaker missionaries from England to New England were two women: Ann Austin and Mary Fisher.

In England, Quaker men and women were public witnesses, missionaries, and preachers. And the women along with the men were whipped and imprisoned when they challenged the status quo by, for example, speaking out against the "hireling priests" and in particular those ministers who were generally more respected in society primarily because they were university trained.[6]

In seventeenth-century America, only Quakers—among all the Christian denominations or sects—accepted women as preachers or even welcomed their opinions on matters relating to the Christian Community.[7] Quakers, however, as a group were not widely accepted. When some of them crossed the Puritan authorities in Massachusetts, the reaction was negative—and finally grew violent. Authorities in that state would banish both women and men who challenged any of the theological views of the Puritan establishment, and many who violated their banishment were hanged. Nonetheless, within Quakerism, the freedom of women to preach remained a reality. Several of the early voices for women's rights as well as those to speak out against slavery would be Quaker women preachers including Lucretia Mott and Susan B. Anthony.

By the end of the seventeenth century, religious revivals were breaking out, and some of the evangelists turned out to be women. In time, these revivals would merge with the First Awakening. "The one minimal evangelical role open to women in the late seventeenth century was preaching within the private circle."[8]

The eighteenth century was not much different than the seventeenth century for women preachers. The greatest freedom was still among sectarian groups; most notably, the Quakers whose system affirmed the right of women to speak in the power of God's Spirit, but which, again, recognized no professional ministry for men or women. Gradually the intense opposition the Quakers had known in New England was subsiding.

In 1774, Mother Ann Lee arrived from England to found Shaker societies in the United States. She was the leader of the group and often preached in Shaker worship services. With heavy reliance upon the leading of the Holy Spirit and immediate revelation for testifying or preaching, Shaker "sermons" (as in the sermon by Mother Lucy Wright that follows) tended to be brief and exhortative or instructive. Mother Ann was illiterate and was not able to write down any of her sermonic thoughts, nor were her sermons transcribed. Still, her influence was great.

Outside the sects, women preachers who had any opportunity at all largely were evangelists. Perhaps the best known among these came in late eighteenth century and were Freewill Baptists. Mary Savage preached such a series of sermons in New Durham, New Hampshire, in 1791; from New Durham she moved out into several surrounding villages where there were no churches. Someone recalled that the "melting power of her exhortations was irresistible."[9]

One of Mary Savage's Freewill Baptist contemporaries was Sally Parsons who also was an evangelist in New England during the 1790s. At an annual meeting of some of the Freewill Baptists in 1797, Sally Parsons's ministry was praised—especially for the encouragement she had given to struggling churches. A collection was taken to help her. Enough money was raised so that she could buy her own horse, bridle, and saddle for her travel.[10]

Into the nineteenth century, the most well known of these female Freewill Baptist evangelists was Clarissa Danforth. She was called the "sensation preacher" of the decade (1810–1820).

In 1818, Clarissa began an evangelistic ministry in Rhode Island that "resulted in many revivals, and the organization of several churches." She easily crossed over denominational lines, and "almost all houses of worship in that region were opened for her, and ministers and people in multitudes flocked to hear her." In less than a year after she arrived in Rhode Island, "the great revival commenced in Smithfield . . . and continued with great power for sixteen months, and extended into all parts of the state, and into all societies."[11]

The nineteenth century saw more women preachers than any previous generation had seen. Most of them, however, were not a part of any mainline church; most were not ordained. Neither did they serve as pastors, but these women did preach even in the face of the severe criticism from the more established denominations.

E. Glenn Hinson, church history professor at the Southern Baptist Theological Seminary in Louisville, Kentucky, credits Quaker preacher Lucretia Mott as the leader of the movement to bring about equality for women in the pulpit.[12] In 1848, Elizabeth Cady Stanton organized the Seneca Falls Women's Rights Convention. During this meeting, Lucretia Mott led in drafting the Seneca Falls Declaration of Sentiments. The declaration insisted that women had been denied their freedom by the very government that supposedly guaranteed freedom for all; this oppression was seen in all facets of society including religious life. The resolution's propositions included this one: "That the speedy success of our cause depends upon the zealous and untiring efforts of both men and women, for the overthrow of the monopoly of the pulpit."[13]

The women who preached in the nineteenth century typically were associated with the

Quakers, Freewill Baptists, Free Methodists, as well as factions connected with the holiness and deeper-life movements. All of these . . . emphasized direct communion with God, the leading of the Spirit, and the call to ministry over and above clerical counsel, church bylaws, and ordination. As was the case with the Anabaptists and other free church movements in history, the high priority placed on spiritual gifts left the door ajar for women in ministry.[14]

The holiness groups played an important part in the development of opportunities for preaching among women. Holiness groups broke away from mainstream Methodist churches. They believed they were reviving the original teaching of John Wesley and especially stressed sanctification.[15]

In this company were prominent wife-husband teams such as Phoebe and Walter Palmer. Phoebe Palmer wrote a book, *Promise of the Father* (1859), that advocated—largely on biblical grounds—the right and responsibility of women to speak in public and to preach. She was not ordained, but she became well known as an effective lay preacher in Methodist camp meetings.[16]

Also in the holiness tradition was evangelist Margaret (Maggie) Newton van Cott who, in 1869, was the first woman granted a license to preach by the Methodist Episcopal Church. She was a widow who was on the "sawdust trail"[17] for thirty years. In one of her busiest years, she preached over four hundred sermons and had a part in bringing seventeen hundred people into the membership of various churches. She was compared in terms of powerfulness and effectiveness to her contemporary Dwight L. Moody.[18]

Perhaps the best-known Black women preachers of the nineteenth century were (Isabella) Sojourner Truth and Amanda Smith. "Isabella" was born a slave in New York. The mother of five children, she was emancipated in 1827. She had spiritual visions, and it was after one such vision that she changed her name to Sojourner Truth. She began preaching—focusing largely on her own religious experiences. By 1843, in addition to her religious work, she was a prominent speaker against slavery and came to be respected as a strong voice for women's rights as well as for racial equality.[19]

Amanda Smith—an evangelist affiliated with the African Methodist Episcopal Church—also was born into slavery. As an adult she became heavily involved in the very emotional camp meeting revivals. Her first husband abandoned her; her second husband died. After his death, she felt a call to preach. With no less opposition than her white counterparts, she faithfully answered the call.[20]

The first ordinations for women in the United States came about in the nineteenth century. There were types of ordination from early in the 1800s, particularly by the Disciples of Christ churches.[21] But the first "full ordination" took place in 1853. Antoinette Louise Brown—later Mrs. Blackwell—was ordained by a local congregation, the First Congregational Church of South Butler, New York, on September 15. (A church organized according to congregational government and commitments would be the "highest authority" in a matter such as ordination to ministry.) A Wesleyan minister, Luther Lee, delivered the ordination sermon entitled "Woman's Right to Preach the Gospel."[22]

The first woman to be ordained in a tradition requiring endorsement beyond the local congregation was Olympia Brown in June of 1863, by the Northern Universalist Association in Canton, New York. Her biographical sketch and a sermon follow.

Mary Baker Eddy's *Science and Health* was first published in 1875, which is also the year Christian Science was institutionalized. Mrs. Eddy did effective preaching in this church that she founded.

In 1879, the Salvation Army came to America. Catherine and William Booth, former Methodists turned holiness preachers, had founded this organization in London. While preaching the gospel, they sought to provide for the needy and rehabilitate society's outcasts. The organization was patterned after an army, and women could move up in rank just as men could. Women ministers/officers were often in positions of leadership over men and by the end of the century would outnumber the men in these roles.

The first woman to be ordained in the Methodist Protestant Church was Anna Howard Shaw, M.D., in 1880. Shaw and her work are discussed in detail in the introduction to her sermon included in this book.

Frances Willard was a very well-educated Methodist woman, at one time, a college president. She is most known for her temperance work; in fact, she was one of the founders of the Women's Christian Temperance Union. What may not be so well known is that she aspired to be pastor of a Methodist church, though she never had the opportunity. In 1880 the Methodist General Conference denied ordination to women and took the drastic step of revoking all licenses to preach that had been granted. In response—no doubt—she wrote a book, *Woman in the Pulpit*, which was published in 1888. It was, among other things, a defense of ordination for women.[23]

When *Woman in the Pulpit* was published, there were an estimated 350 Quaker women preachers and as many as five hundred women evangelists. Nuns and female Salvation Army officers were not listed; however, there were approximately twenty women serving as pastors in the United States, and to those groups who had previously ordained women could be added Methodists, Baptists, and Unitarians.[24]

By 1890, the Cumberland Presbyterians had ordained their first woman to ministry. She was Louisa M. Woolsley. The year after her ordination, she published a book, *Shall Women Preach? or The Question Answered*. In four years of preaching, she delivered some 912 sermons, which played a part in bringing five hundred members into churches. Opposition to her grew in some quarters, and she left her denomination—affiliating with a Methodist church.[25]

B. T. Roberts was founder of the Free Methodist Church in 1860. Originally the group had not ordained women, though women were received as preachers and revivalists. Roberts strongly supported women in ministry roles. At a denominational meeting in 1890 he fought diligently to pass a resolution permitting the ordination of women, but there were not enough votes. The next year, his book, *Ordaining Women*, was published; in it, he argued vigorously, on biblical grounds, for the equality of women.[26]

Also in 1891, Juanita Breckenridge Bates received her Bachelor of Divinity degree—the first woman to receive this degree from Oberlin Theological Seminary. She served as pastor of the Congregational Church in Brookton, New York, and was ordained in 1893.[27]

Most women seeking opportunities for preaching and ordination in mainline denominations were opposed. As an example, Southern Baptist women who would preach were having a tough go of it around this time, and they still are. Credentials for ministry were virtually out of the question. The *Biblical Recorder*, the Baptist state newspaper of North Carolina, in February of 1892, had an editorial, "Once for All," which urged Southern Baptists to refuse the use of their facilities to all women speakers. And John Albert Broadus, well-known professor of preaching and one-time president of the Southern Baptist Theological Seminary in Louisville, Kentucky, did not help their cause with the publication of his pamphlet, "Ought Women to Speak in Mixed Public Assemblies?".[28]

The Brethren Church had formed in the early 1880s as a split-off of the German Baptist Brethren. The new group moved quickly to grant ministerial privileges to women. Their first woman minister, Mary M. Sterling, was ordained in 1890, and by 1894, the General Conference and most district conferences had given formal approval to the practice of ordaining women.[29]

In 1894, the constitution of the Church of the Nazarene was adopted. The document specifically provided for the ordination of women.[30]

The twentieth century has seen further firsts in the story of women preachers though great struggles and barriers remain. In 1901, the first Northern Baptist woman was ordained to ministry. Evangeline Booth was commissioned as a commander in the Salvation Army in 1904 and given responsibility for directing all the group's work in the United States; as her biographical sketch indicates, she would become, in 1934, the first woman general of the Salvation Army. In 1908, the first Nazarene woman was ordained. The Mennonites ordained their first woman to Christian ministry in 1911. Northern Baptists elected—in 1921—the first woman executive of any of the mainline denominations; Helen Barrett Montgomery, whose story and sermon are included in this book, also was the first woman to have published an English translation of the Greek New Testament, *The Centenary Translation of the New Testament*, in 1924. Zealous evangelist Aimee Semple McPherson, founder of the Church of the Foursquare Gospel, preached the first radio sermon by a woman in 1922 from San Francisco. (More information about Mrs. McPherson follows in the book text.) Georgia Harkness, in 1940, became the first woman to hold a professorship in theology at a theological seminary; she was appointed, as her biographical sketch indicates, by Garrett Bible Institute to teach applied theology. The first woman ordained in the northern branch of the United Presbyterian Church received her credentials in 1956; in the southern branch, 1964. The Methodist Episcopal Church decided, in 1956, to grant full privileges for ministry—including ordination—for women. The first woman minister's ordination in a Southern Baptist Church took place in 1964—though the denomination as a whole still formally opposes ordination of women. In 1970, the Lutheran Church in America and the American Lutheran Church first ordained women ministers. And, in 1974, the Episcopal church ordained eleven women to the priesthood at one time.

Great strides have been made as to opportunities for women to preach, but there is still resistance in some denominations. Even when a woman has been ordained to the ministry in a given denomination, it has not meant and does not imply unanimous approval or acceptance of the practice by the denomination as a whole. Georgia Harkness, in her *Women in Church and Society*, reports: "Contrary to the glowing expectations of their predecessors, the opportunities for women ministers did not increase in the twentieth century, but in its early decades began to decline."[31]

Her book was published in 1972. At that time, she said:

Though no exact statistics are available, there are probably fewer women serving parishes today than there were at the turn of the century, though the number with some theological education is larger because for many years the major Protestant seminaries have admitted women without protest. But to have a theological degree does not ensure that one will preach, or be ordained, or even enter a religious vocation as a profession.[32]

Nonetheless, many women have preached, and a look at some of their sermons follows.

1. A Golden Chain

Lucy Wright

(1760–1821)

In eighteenth-century England, the United Society of Believers in Christ's Second Appearing was born. Because of their worship practices, this religious sect came to be called the Shakers. An English newspaper writer described the early group in this way:

They took their rise from a prophet and prophetess who had their religious ceremonies and tenets delivered to them in a vision, some years ago. They hold theirs to be the only true religion and all others to be false. They meet constantly three times a day, at the house of someone of their society, and converse in their own way about the scriptures, a future state, other sects of religion . . . until the moving of the spirit comes upon them, which is first perceived by their beginning leisurely to scratch upon their thighs or other parts of their bodies; from that the motion becomes gradually quicker, and proceeds to trembling, shaking, and screeching in the most dreadful manner; at the same time their features are not distinguishable by reason of the quick motion of their heads, which strange agitation at last ends in singing and dancing to pious tunes. . . . These fits come upon them at certain intervals, and during the impulse of the spirit they disturb the whole neighborhood for some considerable distance, and continue sometimes whole nights in the most shocking distortions and commotions until their strength is quite exhausted, from which uncommon mode of religious worship they have obtained the denomination of Shakers.[1]

Nine persons associated with the English Shakers sailed, in 1774, to the shores of America for the purpose of establishing the sect here. A part of this group was Ann Lee who was the foundress of the Shaker Church in America. The first Shaker family[2] was organized in 1776 at

Watervliet, New York. This initial community and subsequent Shaker communities were set up according to the teachings of Mother Ann Lee. The ideals that evolved for the Shakers, and which were desired for all of society, are: equality of the sexes in all areas of life, equality in labor, economic equality, freedom of speech for all, religious toleration, justice, and practical benevolence. These ideals meant celibacy for all, spiritual leaders of both sexes, communal sharing of all material goods, daily manual labor for everyone, opportunities for intellectual and artistic development, simplicity of dress and style of living, and an emphasis on worship of the one, eternal Father-Mother God. As one early summary of Shaker history and belief described a unique feature of Shaker doctrine:

They recognize the Christ Spirit, the expression of Deity, manifested in fulness in Jesus of Nazareth, also in feminine manifestation through the personality of Ann Lee. Both, they regard as Divine Saviors, anointed Leaders in the New Creation.[3]

The centrality of Mother Ann Lee cannot be overstated. The persons she chose as her successors, then, were quite significant. "That responsibility of leadership fell, in the male line, to Joseph Meacham . . . ; in the female order it was Mother's wish that the lot fall to Lucy Wright."[4] Practically, Meacham was the recognized leader of the Shakers once Ann Lee had died. However, it was his vision of the "Gospel Order" that further emphasized the role of women and designated Lucy Wright as the female leader of the sect, the first Mother in the Revelation and Order of the first organized Church in Christ's Second Appearing, corresponding to the first Father, Joseph Meacham.

According to the Creative Principle in God, there must be a Mother, as well as a Father of Church Order; for the analogy of all existence declares that wherever there is a Father, there is also a Mother or rearing agency to bring forth and perfect the offspring in the life and likeness of the parentage.[5]

Lucy Wright was born on February 5, 1760, in Poontoosuck Plantation, Massachusetts. This was a frontier area, and numerous struggles were a reality, part of the way of life. An opportunity for education, for example, was a struggle. Nonetheless, Lucy managed to develop her skills of reading and writing well.

From her youth, she was religiously inclined. She recalled that she would often prostrate herself before God "in low humiliation, seeking His mercy, favor and protection, from all the snares of evil."[6]

She was aware of the revival generated by the New Light Baptists, in nearby New Lebanon about 1777. Their emphasis was eschatological, and some were prophesying and having visions of the immanence of Christ's second coming and, with it, God's judgment.

Some two years after this revival broke out, Lucy Wright was married, at the age of nineteen, to a merchant, Elizur Goodrich. Influenced by the millennial gospel of the New Light Baptists, he was very open to the similar emphasis of the United Society of Believers in Christ's Second Appearing, and he soon became a disciple of Mother Ann's. Lucy, though sympathetic, did not follow at first. Lucy would need more time to make her own decision. Once she had become convinced, Lucy Wright and Elizur Goodrich agreed to dissolve their worldly marriage in order to be married "to the Lamb"—a Shaker way of expressing a relationship of unity with Christ not possible for those tied to "marriage of the flesh." Lucy resumed the use of her maiden name. In addition, as Shaker rules required, they sold all their property and possessions in order to support the Shaker cause.

Mother Ann had great confidence in Lucy Wright from the beginning. She commented that Lucy's commitment to Shakerism was equal to gaining a nation.[7] Lucy's earliest assignment was to be the leader in the care of Sisters at Watervliet; however, when Mother Ann's health began to decline, she called for Lucy Wright to be her caregiver.

Lucy served as Mother while Joseph Meacham served as Father. When he died in 1796, she assumed leadership of the sect and continued for twenty-five years. Under her leadership, a mission was undertaken that resulted in the establishment of seven Shaker communities in Indiana, Kentucky, and Ohio. She authorized the 1808 publication of a book that presented the basics of Shaker theology; it was written by Benjamin S. Young and entitled *The Testimony of Christ's Second Appearing*. She wrote to Young and his evident collaborator, David Darrow:

I have felt and experienced considerable [sic] with Father Joseph in relation to writing, and making more fully known to the world the foundation of our Faith—We always felt the time was not come—But now I feel satisfied, the time is come and the gift is in you and with you to accomplish this work. . . . I hope and trust you will consider well and not get anything printed but what you are willing to Live by and die by.[8]

Mother Lucy was also known for her contribution of bringing greater order and greater variety to Shaker worship and for her emphasis on education of children.

She died at the Watervliet community at sixty-one years of age. She was buried beside Mother Ann Lee.

This family appears at present to be visited with a considerable degree of suffering and affliction.* You have, in general, very heavy and severe colds; but this need not deprive you of the possession and enjoyment of the gifts of God, for outward affliction will not deprive a soul of the comforts and blessings of the gospel.

You must all labor to keep order, for it is your protection. The orders of God seem hard to a carnal mind; but I should say there are not many if any here present, so young but that they may see and feel the necessity of keeping good order. To my sense believers are held together in union by a *golden chain*— This chain is composed of the gifts and orders of God, and every order adds a link in the chain; and if you break any of these orders, you break this chain, and are exposed to be led astray; but while you are careful to keep the gifts and orders of God you are surrounded with this golden chain and are secure from evil; you are on safe ground and nothing can injure you,

---

* This sermon, Lucy Wright's last public discourse, was given at Watervliet, New York, January 21, 1821.

unless by disobedience you break a link in this chain, and expose yourselves to the enemy without; for the enemy cannot come within, to injure anyone.

You may see the necessity of order and union, by viewing the kingdoms of this world; for if they had not a kind of natural union and order, they could not stand, but would soon tumble to pieces, and destroy each other, till there would not be a man left on earth. And this I think may serve as a suitable comparison between the kingdom of Christ and the kingdoms of this world.

How miserable a person must feel without friends; all people want union and friendship, and if we cannot conduct in such a manner as to gain friends we find a hard travel indeed.

Union is more valuable than all earthly things, and you ought always to be careful to support a just union and relation together in the gospel. You ought to be very careful how you speak to each other, speak kind and loving one to another according to the simplicity of the gospel, and neither give nor take offence.

I do not feel to speak much at this time, but I hope you will remember what I have said, and if you observe it, you will certainly be under blessing.

2. The Path Is Plain

Anna Howard Shaw

(1847–1919)

Anna Howard Shaw was born in Newcastle-on-Tyne, England, on February 14, 1847. Her parents were English Unitarians. The family moved to the United States when Anna was four years old. After living in Massachusetts for several years, the Shaw family moved to an unsettled area of Michigan, near Big Rapids; here they endured the rigors of pioneer life. Among the hardships there was the inaccessibility of a public school. Anna Shaw began to find every opportunity for reading and study; she was self-taught. When she was fifteen years old, she began teaching others.

At twenty-four years of age, Miss Shaw became a part of a Methodist Episcopal church. Here, her ability as a speaker was first recognized. In addition, her interest in preaching and ministry was established. In 1873, she was granted a license for local preaching by the district conference. This license was renewed annually for eight years.

Shaw entered Albion College in Michigan in 1872. After completing studies there, she began theological studies at Boston University in 1875. She graduated with honors in 1878. Financially supporting herself during these years created the dilemma of finding sufficient time for all her involvements and adequate funds to underwrite them.

During the final year of her theological study, Shaw was pastor of the Methodist Episcopal Church in Hingham, Massachusetts. Following graduation, she became pastor of the Methodist Episcopal Church in East Dennis on Cape Cod, where she served for seven years. For six of these years, she preached Sunday mornings and evenings in her church and on Sunday afternoons in a congregational church.

While serving in East Dennis, Shaw applied to her denomination for ordination. She passed the examination with higher distinction than any other candidate that year, but because she was a woman, she was denied ordination by the New England Methodist Episcopal Conference. She appealed to the general conference that met in Cincinnatti, Ohio, in 1880, but the denial was upheld. In response, Miss Shaw applied for ordination to the New York Conference of the Methodist Protestant Church's General Conference. Permission was granted, and on October 12, 1880, Anna Howard Shaw became the first woman ever to be ordained by the Methodist Protestant Church. Her ordination was contested later, however, and ruled out of order in 1884.

Shaw was trained not only in theology, but also in medicine. Concerned about the sickness she saw in Boston's slums, she decided that the study of medicine was important. After completing medical studies, she was awarded an M.D. degree by Boston University. Shaw completed her medical studies while serving as a pastor. She is generally thought to be the first woman to achieve both ordination *and* medical licensure.

Increasing concern about women's rights caused her to resign her pastorate in East Dennis in order to become a lecturer in Massachusetts for the Women's Suffrage Association. "Shaw's vision of Christianity underlay her strong advocacy of women's rights."[1] She was such an effective speaker that she was soon nationally recognized. She preached the opening sermon at the Women's International Council of 1888 meeting in Washington, D.C., and she was president of the National American Women Suffrage Association from 1904 through 1915. Deciding to slow down, she resigned in 1915. However, as soon as America entered World War I, President Woodrow Wilson appointed her chairwoman of the Women's Committee of the National Council on Defense. Dr. Shaw died soon after the war ended.

Shaw was acclaimed a great preacher and public speaker. She was described in this way:

She is one of the most eloquent, witty, and popular speakers in the lecture field. She is possessed of the most remarkable personal magnetism, a fine voice, and power of pointed argument. Much of her strength and force of thought and expression are believed to result from the experiences of her pioneer life in Michigan, and her power of moving audiences from the touch with humanity which came to her while practicing medicine in the city of Boston, during her studies to be a physician.[2]

Text: St. John III, 14, 15

And as Moses lifted up the serpent in the wilderness, even so must the Son of man be lifted up:
That whosoever believeth in him should not perish, but have eternal life.

All doubtless are familiar with the history of the Hebrews while in bondage in the land of Egypt, of their deliverance by Moses and their wanderings in the wilderness.* The period in their wanderings to which the text refers is that immediately after their conquest of the Canaanites which resulted in the complete destruction of them and their cities, and during which the Hebrews had again resumed their wanderings and journeyed from Mount Hor by the way of the Red Sea to compass the land of Edom. By the way of the Rea Sea here does not mean that branch of the Red Sea over which they had already passed: but another branch lying [farther]† east. The Hebrews

---

* Editor's Note: This sermon by the Reverend Anna Howard Shaw was probably first preached on September 30, 1877. This was the first sermon written by Shaw in order to get a license to preach from the presiding elder; it is a transcription of her handwritten manuscript, which is now a part of the Dillon Collection at the Arthur and Elizabeth Schlesinger Library on the History of Women in America, Cambridge, Massachusetts.

† Brackets throughout the historical section indicate the correct spelling of an originally misspelled word or the insertion of a word by the editor(s) for sense.

became very much discouraged on account of the frequent disappointments, and delayes on their way. They began to murmur and speak against the Lord and against Moses, saying,

"Wherefore have ye brought us up out of Egypt—to die in the wilderness, for there is no bread here, neither is there any water, and our souls [loathe] this . . . light bread." And the Lord sent fiery serpents among them; and they bit the people, and many of the people died. Therefore they came to Moses saying, "We have sinned for we have spoken against thee; pray unto the Lord that he take [away] the serpents from us." And Moses prayed for the people. And the Lord said unto Moses, "Make thee a fiery serpent and put it upon a pole: and it shall come to pass that every one that is bitten when he looketh upon it shall live." And Moses made a serpent of brass, and put it upon a pole, and it came to pass that if a serpent had bitten any man when he beheld the serpent of brass, he lived.

It has been difficult to assign a name to the creature termed in the Hebrew: *nachash*. It has different signification, but its meaning here is most difficult to ascertain. *Seraphim* from the same root is one of the orders of angelic beings. As it is written in Isa. VI. 2.

Above it [the throne upon which the Lord sat] stood the seraphim; each one had six wings; with twain he covered his face; and with twain he covered his feet; and with twain he did fly. Then flew one of the seraphim unto me having a live coal in his hand, which he had taken with the tongs from the altar.

But as it comes from the root, *saraph* which means "to burn," it has been translated "fiery" in the text.

It is likely that Saint Paul alludes to the seraphim in Hebrews 1:7. "Who maketh his angels spirits and his ministers a *flame of fire.*" The animals mentioned by Moses may have been called "fiery" because of the heat, violent [inflammation], and thirst occasioned by their bites. And if they were serpents (which still exist in that part of Arabia), they were of the prester, or dipsas, species whose bite, especially that of the former, occasions a violent [inflammation] through the whole body, and a fiery appearance of the countenance.

The poet Lucan has expressed the terrible effect of the bite of these serpents in the following manner.

> Ahns a noble youth of Tyrrhen blood,
> Who bore the standard; on a dipsas trod;
> Backward the wrathful serpent bent her head,
> And, fell with rage, the unheeded wrong repaid.
> Scarce did some little mark of hurt remain,
> And scarce he found some little sense of pain.
> Nor could he yet the danger [doubt] nor fear
> That death with all its terrors threatened spread,
> And every nobler part at once invades;
> *Swift flames consume* the marrow and the brain,
> And the *scorched entrails* rage with burning pain;
> Upon his heart the thirsty poisons prey,
> And drain the sacred juice of life away.
> No kindly floods of moisture bathe his tongue,
> But cleaving to the parched roof it hung;
> No trickling drops distil, no dewey sweat,
> To ease his weary limbs, and cool the raging heat.

The effect of the bite of the prester, he describes in this manner.

> A fate of different kind Naridius found,
> A burning prester gave the deadly wound;
> And *straight a sudden* flaim began to spread,
> And paint his visage with a glowing red.
> With swift expansion swells the bloated skin,
> Naught but an undistinguished mass is seen
> While the fair human form lies lost within
> The puffy poison spreads and heaves around,
> Till all the *man* is in the *monster* drowned.

Other writers are of the opinion that the serpents were of the flying kind, and might have been called "fiery," by reason of their color. The season of the year in which the [Hebrews] were under this calamity was the season when these creatures were on the wing to visit the neighboring, and adjacent countries, and might have been directed into the [Hebrews'] camp.

That they were very numerous can not be doubted. And for this and [various] reasons it appears to my mind that they may not have belonged to any of these species but might have been miraculously produced by God to punish the Hebrews. [Their] recovery was supernatural. Why may not the production of the serpents have been the same?

The effect of the [serpents'] bite was such, as to change the [character] of the person. As the poison spread through the system he seemed to lose all control of his reasoning powers and became more and more ungovernable until he grew rabid, the venom still preying on heart, and brain consuming them, and his form expands into an unsightly shape. Until at last the fierce struggle is over, and he is left in a state of stupor in which he dies.

The effects of evil habits on the human heart are such that if indulged in cannot be stayed; it is [morally] impossible to practice habitually one sin, and maintain the purity and elevation of [character] in other respects. The conscience becomes hardened, and it is silenced with more ease when our wishes urge us to other sins. Sinners grow worse and worse not as their capacity is enlarged and their means to do evil are increased, but as the habit of vice acquires strength; until at last their nature becomes so corrupt that out of it proceeds all actual transgressions. It is an [excessive] indulgence which forms the habit of guilt and degrades and bows them to misery; every new transgression adds strength and vigor to their already corrupt propensities which they feel will one day sink them to ruin. And by sin they are subject to death, and all miseries temporal, spiritual, and eternal. The sinner is a slave; he is not free who cannot govern himself, who cannot do what he sees and feels to be right. This bondage consists in his being the unresisting slave of passion and appetite, and his inability to control himself by reason and [conscience]. He is at the mercy of every temptation yet he [groans] in vain for the power to resist. You have all seen in numberless habits of vice the wretched victim mourning over his sins, sighing to return to innocence, and resolving in the bitterness of his soul never to offend again; yet at the first temptation, rushing to misery which he sees is surely approaching.

Who has not seen the struggles of an intemperate man to burst away the chains which his appetite has [imposed], striving for a time in tears then rushing with frenzied violence to an indulgence which sinks him below the brute. Yet a life of sins is a life of restlessness, and anxiety. Men tire of sin, and pleasure, but they know not where to end; they do not [resort] to it from love but from a habit which it is too painful to resist, or to be saved from a weariness of life, or from the reproaches of [conscience]. Yet they look forward to it with a restless desire which only serves to [embitter] their present life, and they can only look back upon it with sorrow and remorse.

And what are the effects of evil? You see it in the haggard countenance—that [emaciated] and sinking [frame]—that [loathsome] train of disease and want and all the numberless forms of wretchedness which guilt has created. And is this all? Glance into the depths of that soul, and there you will see the bitter regret with which a life of sin is remembered, and the ragings of a wounded [conscience]; and still farther go to the bed of death, and see there the horrible anguish which rends the soul that stands trembling on the brink of the grave, and can look up only to an offended God and forward to his judgment.

In the comparison between the lifting up of the serpent, and that of Christ we learn that as the serpent was lifted upon the pole or ensign, so Jesus Christ upon the cross. The object of God's command was not because there was any healing power in the serpent, nor in the simple act of looking; but that they might through obedience to God's command exercise faith in his power to heal them.

The fiery serpent saved the Hebrews from the effect of the [serpent's] bite. Jesus Christ saves us from our sins not in our sins—from our sins. There is this difference: the serpent saved from the effect of the evil, Jesus Christ from the evil itself.

The object of natural sight for physical cure was to my mind that as it is necessary before we can exercise faith in anything we must have something upon which our faith may rest. And presenting the object before the eye it formed a basis upon which to rest their faith in the promise of God. And so it is that with the spiritual eye, we are enabled to look to the crucified [redeemer] and trust him to save our souls for it is an acceptance of the divine and glorious truths which compose his [doctrine] that cleanses from sin. The belief of the truth itself is of no other advantage than its effects in delivering from sin and changing the mind into the divine image: for this kind of knowledge is that kind which changes the mind from darkness to light, and delivers it from the reigning power of sin to the love of holiness, and to the obedience of the just.

All were free to look at the serpent and be saved. There was no decree by which they were compelled to look. Each must exercise his own free will. It is the same spiritually. God never compels any of his creatures to seek their [soul's] salvation, but he has provided a way and pointed in his word to Jesus as their [redeemer]. "Behold the Lamb of God which taketh away the sins of the world." "Who hath loved us and [redeemed] us and washed us from our sins in his own blood." "Though your sins be as scarlet they shall be as white as snow; though they be red like crimson they shall be as wool."

The invitation is universal, "Ho! Everyone that thirsteth; come ye to the waters of life. He that hath no money come ye buy and eat; yea come; buy wine, and milk without money and without price." God in mercy has by Jesus Christ promised eternal life to all, who by a patient [continuance] in the ways of well doing seek for glory, honor, and immortality, but they who do not comply with the conditions can have no claim to the reward.

As each must look for himself and as there was no human or possible cure except in obedience to [God's] command so must every man work out his own [soul's] salvation. No one can do it for him. As it is written, "Work out your own salvation with fear and trembling."

The [remedy] was simple and easily comprehended by all and within the reach of all. So is salvation placed within the attainment of every individual of the human family. The path is plain, so plain that the [wayfaring] man though a fool need not err therein. We are clearly instructed in our duty, and promised support under all its conflicts. We are invited, persuaded, commanded to obey his laws that we may be happy. Yet we are treated as the subjects of a moral government; and when he shall judge the secrets of men by Jesus Christ he will reward them according to their works.

The command was to look, and to obey it was simply an exercise of the will. It did not require any strength to turn the gaze toward the serpent. Neither could we all purchase the cure.

One bite was fatal, and by refusing to look they would have as surely died as though no serpent had been provided.

The command given to us is the same, and to obey it is simply to submit our will to the will of God. It does not require any severe mental or physical exertions, just a simple letting go of self and clinging to Jesus. I read a [narrative] a short time [ago] which I think will illustrate this. A poor man whose mind had been much troubled by the question, "What is saving faith?," dreamed a dream which he thought explained it to him fully. He thought that he stood on some desolate spot on the very edge of a steep cliff. Far below him at the bottom of the cliff the sea dashed violently. He stood with only half a footing on the edge of the cliff when something—he knew not what— whirled him over the precipice, and he felt himself falling, and falling downward into the ocean beneath; but suddenly he could not tell how, he thought he [caught] hold of a crag on the side of the cliff as he was falling past it, and there he hung with one hand grasping a small piece of rock. He hung a few seconds when he felt the crag was crumbling in his fingers. What was he to do? The next second he must be dashed to the atoms. All at once he turned and looked behind him and saw a figure dressed in pure white coming toward the cliff and walking on the water; the figure came nearer and nearer until he was very great. He could see the expression of his coutenance, that it was kind and gentle, and as their eyes met, the figure whispered softly upward "Let go! Let go!" He let go and fell into its arms, and was saved. The poor man understood his dream then. The crag was self-righteousness and every false refuge that crumbles in the grasp of the sinner. . . . The words, "Let go," were the same as, "[Believe] on the Lord Jesus Christ, and thou shalt be saved."

Faith is the letting go of all other dependence and falling into the arms of Jesus. O! friend out of Christ. God help you to "let go."

As God provided no other [remedy] than this looking for the wounded Hebrews, so he has provided no other way of salvation than faith in the blood of his son.

All who looked at the brazen serpent lived, and all who did not died. So they who believe on the Lord Jesus Christ as their savior shall not perish, but have eternal life for he has promised eternal life to as many as believe on him. And in what beautiful language does our blessed Lord himself invite us to come to him. "Come unto me all ye that labor and are heavy laden and I will give you rest." "Take my yoke upon you and learn of me for I am meek and holy of heart, and ye shall find rest to your souls, for my yoke is easy and my burden is light." How can we refuse to accept such an invitation when we think of the blessed Jesus who left the glory of heaven and [descended] to earth clothed in our humanity, suffering shame and poverty for he had no where to lay his head, and leading a life of persecution; put to the ignoble death of the cross, that we through his sufferings and death might receive eternal life. I say, when we think of all this how can we refuse to go to him. O! let us then while in this moral state cherish faith in God and in all his promises and prepare to dwell with God in heaven for Jesus will be there, and his spirit is a spirit of love. The whole atmosphere of heaven is love. Contemplate the future world as . . . the very contemplation of it will serve in some measure to fit us for it. Dr. Doddridge has described the future world in the following beautiful strain:

> No more fatigue, no more distress
> Nor sin nor death shall reach the place
> No groans shall mingle with the songs
> That warble from immortal tongues
> No rude alarms, no raging foes
> To interpret the long repose,
> At midnight shade, no clouded sun,
> To veil the bright, eternal noon.

3. Baptism

Olympia Brown
(1835–1926)

Olympia Brown was not the first woman to be ordained to the Christian ministry in the United States. Antoinette Brown Blackwell was that woman; she was ordained by a local congregation—the Congregational Church of South Butler, New York—on September 15, 1853. However, Olympia Brown was the first woman in the United States to be ordained, and thus affirmed for ministry, by a denominational body; she was ordained in June of 1863 by the Northern Universalist Association at its meeting in Canton, New York.

She was born on January 5, 1835, in Prairie Ronde, Michigan. Her parents were strong in their commitment both to the Universalist denomination and to education. Olympia came to share her parents' concern for both of these. In an age when education for women was not yet widely held as particularly important, the Browns encouraged their daughter to press on once she had completed secondary school. Olympia took their advice and enrolled at Mount Holyoke Female Seminary in Massachusetts, but the religious perspectives that seemed to prevail there were too oppressive for this independent and forward-thinking young woman. In 1856, Olympia Brown enrolled in Antioch College in Ohio where she earned her baccalaureate degree in 1860.

While at Antioch College she heard a woman preacher for the first time. Ironically, it was Antoinette Brown Blackwell—the woman with whom she would come to be confused because of the name they shared in common, "Brown," and also because they both achieved "firsts" in regard to ordination. Olympia Brown was inspired and challenged by the experience of hearing Antoinette Brown Blackwell. This, in part, influenced her choice of ministry as a profession.

Desiring to receive the best possible education, Olympia Brown decided to apply for theological study. Though St. Lawrence University in Canton, New York, admitted her, admission was granted with reluctance.[1]

Olympia Brown graduated from St. Lawrence in 1863 just before her ordination took place. For the next year she did guest preaching and pulpit supply ministry in several Vermont churches while she was enrolled for studies in elocution at the Dio Lewis School in Boston. She was called to her first pastorate in July of 1864; she served the Universalist church in Weymouth, Massachusetts, until 1870 at which time she left to become pastor of the Universalist church in Bridgeport, Connecticut.

Three years into this service, Olympia Brown married John Willis but retained her maiden name. Mr. Willis was a businessman and not connected with professional ministry. In 1874, their son—Henry Parker Willis—was born, and in 1876, their daughter—Gwendolen Brown Willis—was born.

In 1878, Olympia Brown and her family moved to Racine, Wisconsin, where she became pastor of her third Universalist congregation. She served this church for some eleven years. According to Georgia Harkness, Olympia Brown had demonstrated that marriage, motherhood, and ministry could be combined successfully.[2] When she resigned, it was for suffrage work. She had been formally involved in the cause of women's rights since 1866. She had often been a spokeswoman for equal rights and actually had a hand in the formation of the New England Women Suffrage Association. Though the focus of her work had changed, Brown continued to preach when she could. Known for her logic and her powerful voice, Olympia Brown was a popular preacher and speaker, often in demand.

In the late nineteenth century, pro-suffrage advocates found themselves criticized by those who were using the Bible to support keeping women "in their place." Elizabeth Cady Stanton—a leader among those struggling to have the rights of women recognized—proposed the *Woman's Bible* as means of refuting the claims of those who were using poor biblical interpretation as a tool of injustice. This *Woman's Bible,* finally issued in two parts, was really simply a commentary (from the pro-suffrage perspective) on those passages of scripture that deal with issues related to women. Olympia Brown was part of the committee of twenty-three that produced the commentary.

I, indeed baptized you with water, but he shall baptize you with the Holy Ghost.

—MARK 1:8

The baptism of water and of the Holy Ghost.* What are they? What are the relations in which they stand to each other. What is their significance and importance?

These inquiries are not really suggested by the text. The discussions from this subject in the past have turned up on the form of water baptism—the most trifling and frivolous question which can possibly engage the attention of rational Human Beings. Questions of form rather than the spirit have engrossed the attention of theologians so completely that it has been regarded in the partialist churchs as a saving ordinance. Its true significance has seldom been dwelt upon and enforced. And people well informed and intelligent upon all other subjects have come up to the altar for baptism apparently believing that [thus] they were to be saved and without . . . any [recognized] understanding [of] the true meaning of the rite or the reasons of the occasion. The different denominations of Christianity have contended zealously in regard to the relative merits of immersion or sprinkling, the necessity or the propriety of the baptism of infants, or the danger arising from being twice baptized. But of the baptism of the Holy Ghost, the self-consecration and purity from the vices of the world which is sought by

---

* Editor's Note: This is an undated sermon by the Reverend Olympia Brown, transcribed from her handwritten copy, which is a part of a large collection of her works held by the Arthur and Elizabeth Schlesinger Library on the History of Women in America, Cambridge, Massachusetts.

those who are truly baptized in the spirit of their Lord, little has been said. . . .

In many of its bearings it is new and in coming to its consideration, we need at once a candor which shall lead us to recapture the real beauty and excellence of the rite though obscured by long cherished errors and gross superstitions and at the same time that freedom which shall lead to a fearless disregard for the authority of the past or the customs of the world. Thus, we shall be able to judge for ourselves independently, and learning the lesson . . . which reason and reflection would teach in regard to it, be able to fulfill our duty understandingly and sincerely.

While questions of form are trifling and frivolous, the real baptism of the Holy Ghost is at once important and essential to spiritual progress. The soul must be filled with the Divine Spirit, inspired by the lofty ideals which it presents . . . as attainable, elevated above . . . the trifling cares and perplexities of life and thus inspired. Thus consecrated to the good, the beautiful, and the true, it grows, it expands, it becomes more and more like . . . the perfect human being—more and more in the image of God: the perfect harmony of the universe is constantly "wooing all souls to the Divine pattern of their destiny." God by his Spirit, by the good influences which are thrown around men in the pathway of life, is always seeking to win them to the highest and the best. And it is only when reconciled to his will, conformed to his [love], and made like him that the soul enters into complete communion with God, that it is indeed baptized with the Holy Ghost.

The baptism of the Holy Spirit implies that there is the Divine life in the soul, the most sacred, exalted, and attuned life possible to human nature. [There] is a love of the good, a submission to the Divine will, and this gives constant joy, a sweet peace, and harmonious action of all the facilities a continued progress toward the highest. The germs of all excellence are indeed inplanted in the human soul, but these must be awaked to life, quickened and developed before there can be growth in goodness or great moral excellence. That seed which you plant in the ground in these spring days contains the rudiment of the future plant. But you understand very well that it must be quickened by the spring showers, refined and nourished before it will spring forth and grow into the beauty in the fashion of the well-developed plant. So the soul which [contains] in itself the elements of moral perfection must be quickened by the Divine Spirit, permeated by the love of God, baptized with the Holy Ghost before [it] can progress in its course. It is not bad in its nature [nor] incapable of goodness, but its wondrous powers are latent. Its capacities are undeveloped until it is brought within the influence of the Spirit of God from which everything good proceeds and is in harmony. As particles of steel with the influence of the magnet become polarized, each one becoming a minature magnet, so the soul is controlled when brought within the magic influence of the good and true—when moved by the Holy Spirit—and itself becomes another power, sending forth good influences and gaining new strength and harmony with every effort. You have seen those who were indifferent to their moral growth, intent upon the cares or the pleasures of the present, engrossed in the world or the things of the world. That man who [is] immersed in business cares only for the gratification of his avarice or his ambition, who regards not the welfare of his fellow beings nor the appeals of his conscience if only he can acquire wealth. That woman thinking little of the kingdom of God and true righteousness but anxious only for her body and what she shall profit. That young school person caring only for the present hour regardless of her future usefulness or happiness, content only to enjoy today but neglecting the use of the talent committed to her care. . . . [These] make up a great share of the people . . . whom we meet daily and with whom we hold converse. You see them every day squandering the best years of their lives in trifling in those things which are transient and pass away. They are not bad, not totally depraved, as our friends of the partialist denominations would tell. They are capable of all excellence, endowed with a power for growth and development beyond our present power to think or imagine, destined for the companionship of the angels, but at present they are not living their best and highest life. Their souls are not awakened. The good in them slumbers, waiting to be touched by the influences of Divine love. Selfishness and worldliness control them, mould their character, give direction to all their actions and will do so until . . . driven away by the purifying influences of the Holy Spirit and only the good and noble remain.

These need the baptism of the Holy Ghost that they may be aroused, taught to seek truth and virtue for their own sake, to love righteousness better than all the things of this world and the kingdom of God before every other object. This will at first require a struggle, sometimes a long and painful one. [Though] one is baptized with the Holy Ghost [and] without conscious effort [comes] a love of the good . . . [and the] earnest progress for the coming of God's kingdom, the demons tear down and rend the body from which they are cast out. Rebellion and sin are not overcome without fearful struggles. All have seen in the history of the world how obedience to other leaders than the representatives of liberty and order produced rebellion and war which was only put down by the most bloody battles hardly fought* and dearly won. We have seen how the nation arose in its might, met the enemy, and though brave and noble—soon fell by thousands; though our brave generals were cut down and the whole land bathed in blood and tears, yet the victory was achieved, and the right triumphed in the battleground of the soul. Worldliness and selfishness must be conquered. They may rebel against the law of God impressed upon man's higher nature, but when the human nature arises in its true dignity, and arrays itself on the side of Godliness, a victory will be gained though it comes at the cost of much long cherished self

---

* "hardly fought" here meaning fought with great effort.

love of many idle pleasures, many vanities, and follies. It may cost long and earnest conflicts. Possibly a bitter experience in the trials of the world will be the price that must be paid for the triumph [of] such ideas, the conflict from which even Christ was not exempt and which was so painfully real that he almost feared lest the disciples should be unable to follow him. As he said: "Can ye drink of the cup that I shall drink of and be baptized with the baptism that I shall be baptized with?"

Through struggles such as these which worked the forty days in the wilderness must human nature reach the grand height at which it is able to say calmly and proudly to the world, "Get thee hence, Satan, for it is written, Thou shalt worship the Lord thy God and him only shalt thou serve." Through sorrows like those of the man of Nazareth and sweat and tears like those of Gethsemane will humanity attain that sublime submission to the Divine will which shall in life or in death reecho the words: "Father not my will but thine be done." Through agony like that on the cross will man gain that Divine forgiveness which shall pray for his enemies: "Father, forgive them for they know not what they do."

When through such a baptism as Christ was baptized with, humanity shall approximate to such self conquest, such submission, such lofty charity and all conquering love, then will man be reconciled to his God, redeemed from sin, and salvation be accomplished. And this baptism is designed for all, sooner or later. The enemies to Godliness must be met; then conquest must be gained. All must drink of the cup and be aroused and be baptized into the baptism that he was baptized with.

Some may for a long time shrink from the conflict. They may rebel in sin, in all violations of law; [they may] rob, murder, be guilty of the most inhuman conduct, stifle the voice of conscience . . . , yet they can not forever kill the Divine spark within. It is immortal and cannot die. Sometime, either in time or eternity, it will be revived and the battle will come. Repentance will fill the soul with humiliation and the baptism with the Holy Spirit will wash away the sins of the past; and the contrite, humble, repentant reformed man will seek reconciliation with the Father.

In all his years of sin he has not been entirely weaned from virtue. He has only been temporarily careless and forgetful of her commands . . . as the soldier who has gone to fight his [country's] battles amid the din and uproar of preparation for the contest, in the excitement of the battle, or realities of the camp may for a time forget the mother that bore him or the wife that is far away watching and praying for his prosperity; but when the conflict is over his heart turns again to the peaceful and happy home he has left behind. He returns from his long exile to be received with joy; or if he dies upon the field, his days riot, his warlike pleasures are forgotten while in his dying moments his thoughts turn to those so dearly loved, and memories of home and hopes of heaven unite to call him to the good. So the soul which has for a long time exiled itself from virtue and lived forgetful of God and his commands is not entirely lost, but in some crisis of life or of death it returns to its first love, leaves the things of the world, and seeks reconciliation with God. It is baptized with the Holy Spirit and enters into rest.

The baptism of the Holy Ghost comes when the soul, filled with lofty aspiration, kindled by a desire for excellence, resolves to consecrate itself to the good, and then the human being begins to lay aside its old sins, interferences, idleness, irreverence, selfishness, arrogance, and puts on righteousness. Then it [is possible] to enter in at the straight gate. "Nearer my God to Thee, nearer to Thee," must be its prayer until the victory is gained and the soul [is reconciled] to the father. And this struggle and this triumph are for all the children of men; unto all the disciples of Christ was it said: "You shall indeed drink of the cup and be baptized with the baptism that I am baptized with." Christ is to be Lord both of the dead and of the living; to reign until all shall have been baptized into his Spirit and made one with him.

The baptism with water is but the symbol, the foreshadowing of the baptism of the Holy Spirit. It indicates a resolution to speak virtue and follow after righteousness as John the Baptist went before [Jesus] preaching repentance and baptizing with water, heralding the approach of one mightier who should baptize with the Holy Spirit. So each individual experiences repentance, and the baptism of water precedes and ushers in the approach of those holy influences which shall complete the work of salvation. The particular form in which it is administered is clearly unimportant and must be left to the circumstance and convenience of the time. In the time of Christ in a country where the climate is always mild and the people led an out of door [existence] and many of them a wandering life by the seashore, immersion was undoubtedly the usual form of baptism, but when people must depart from their usual place of worship and perform the ceremony in the most public manner, drawing together a noisy and irreverent company who attend from mere idle curiosity as they would attend any other show, then the solemnities of such an occasion are mocked. The good influences which might grow out of it are defeated, and the ceremony becomes powerless for good. It was to such a gaping, curious crowd who came to his baptism that the Baptist turned with such bitter reproof: "O Generation of vipers, who hath warned you to flee from the water and to bring forth therefore fruits meet for repentance?"

So [to] place especial importance upon the form of baptism is to make the ceremony more important than the preparation of the heart. Let the purpose be earnest, the consecration sincere. It matters not what the form of baptism. It can but be a source of new strength. It must confirm one in the good, for it is a declaration for the right and is like the oath of office, the pledge for Christian conduct. You may say that your resolutions are strong enough and binding enough without the pledge. . . . I look in vain for the man that does not need everything that can bind him to good and to hold him from temptation. You would not trust your neighbor with your money without a note of hand, not because you doubt his honesty always but because his resolution is strengthened by that pledge, and you have as little reason to trust your own good resolutions [unless] they are confirmed by a sign, a promise to deal justly and love mercy and walk humbly with God. The baptism with water may be made most effective for good, a power strengthening one in the time of trial.

Let it be but a sign of a devout purpose and a sincere resolution to follow after righteousness. Let the ceremony be performed in such time and place that it shall be associated with all that is Holy and sacred and as a part of the regular worship. And let there go forth from the hearts of all present an earnest prayer in behalf of the candidate that he may be kept from the evil and live a pure and holy life. At such a baptism there must be an inpouring of the Holy Spirit with the hearts of all present. As of old the heavens are opened, and the Spirit of God descends; and a voice says: "This, my beloved in whom I am well pleased."

4. Like a Tree Planted

Helen Barrett Montgomery
(1861–1934)

Born in Kingsville, Ohio, Helen Barrett's parents were teachers. Her father, Adoniram Judson Barrett, later became a school principal and subsequently a seminarian; then pastor of the Lake Avenue Baptist Church in Rochester, New York. Helen, who was called Nellie, was baptized in that church when she was fifteen years old. She had this remembrance of that event:

One cloud darkens the remembrance of that moving experience. . . . One old deacon put to me his unfailing enquiry, "My young sister, did you feel the burden of sin roll away?" Those were his exact words to me, a child of fifteen growing up in a Christian home! Trembling, I answered, "Yes, sir," and realized at once that I had told a lie in order to get into the church. It filled me with bitterness at the very moment when a gracious Father was welcoming me into the household of faith."[1]

After high school, Helen studied for one year at the Livingston Park Seminary; she entered Wellesley College in 1880 and graduated four years later. She taught school for three years before returning to Rochester to marry William A. Montgomery on September 7, 1887; Montgomery was a businessman who was active in her father's church. They were the parents of one daughter, Edith.

Mrs. Montgomery organized a Sunday school class for women, which became quite large over the years. She began as the teacher of the class, and—unless she was ill or out of town—continued the weekly teaching for forty-four years. Influenced by fellow Baptist Walter Rauschenbusch, and the so-called Social Gospel, Mrs. Montgomery devoted much of her time during the first twenty years of her marriage to civic and social causes. She was the first president of the Women's Educational and Industrial Union of Rochester. She was the first woman member of the local school board. She was president of the New York State Federation of Women's Clubs and for two years she worked with Susan B. Anthony to raise money, which made possible the admission of women students to the University of Rochester.

Helen Barrett Montgomery did enough preaching for her local church to recognize her gift and license her to preach in 1892. This commendation was adequate for her purposes, and she was not ordained.

Mrs. Montgomery developed—over the years—a keen interest in Christian missions. In fact, her many other concerns notwithstanding, missions became her passion. This led naturally into her selection as president of the American Baptist Foreign Mission Society, where she served from 1914 through 1924. With two other women, she founded the World Wide Guild in 1915. Local chapters were organized in many Baptist churches throughout the country and were effective providers of mission education for young women, many of whom would volunteer for foreign mission service as a result of their involvement in the organization. In 1913, Mrs. Montgomery took a trip around the world under the sponsorship of the Federation of Women's Boards of Foreign Missions. The group wanted a book with firsthand impressions of various mission sites; the book, *The King's Highway,* was published in 1915. During the years 1917 and 1918, Mrs. Montgomery served as president of the National Federation of Women's Boards of Foreign Missions.

In 1921, Helen Barrett Montgomery was chosen as president of the Northern Baptist Convention, the first woman to hold such a leadership position in any of the mainline denominations in America. In fact, it was a quarter of a century before a woman would again head any of the mainline denominations. She was busy! She once spoke 197 times in a two-month period.

Naturally, her interest and emphasis on missions continued while holding this position. In addition, she was able to utilize her translation of the Greek New Testament, which she had completed over several years. Her interest in New Testament Greek had begun during her student days at Wellesley and continued through the years. The American Baptist Publication Society was nearing its one-hundredth anniversary and wanted to publish a particularly striking book to help mark the occasion. The Society contracted with Mrs. Montgomery to use her translation, and in 1924 *The Centenary Translation of the New Testament* was published.

No woman had ever done this before. It was still considered presumptuous for anybody to do a new translation of Bible texts. Was not the King James Version good enough? Or, if one must be modern, the revision known as the American Standard Version? A whole new translation? And by a woman, of all people? Unthinkable! But the Montgomery translation was well received. While her work was scholarly, it was also done in the words of everyday life, carrying out the spirit of its writers. . . . It met with instant acclaim and has continued to be so popular that it has been reprinted dozens of times and is still published under the title *The New Testament in Modern English.*[2]

In 1929, Mrs. Montgomery delivered the initial John M. English lectures in homiletics at the Newton Theological Institution; her series— not surprisingly—was entitled, "The Preaching Value of Missions." The lectures were published in 1931 by Judson Press. They are not the basis for a homiletic; rather, they focus on biblical foundations for and a consideration of results of the centrality of missions in preaching. She said in the opening lecture:

The curse of religion today is churchianity, parochialism, small views of the meaning of the Cross, small enthusiasm for the gospel; the "crumb" Christians who are satisfied with the crumbs that fall from the Master's table when they might sit as guests at the marriage supper of the Lamb; the "mite" Christians, who are satisfied with dropping in their "mites," when they might be "hilarious givers" whom God loves. There is no correction for short-sighted views of Christianity like Christian missions.

Scolding accomplishes very little; telling people how worldly and worthless they are pleases a few of those who sit in the seat of the scorner, but leads to few reformations of character. But challenging Christians by the stories of utter nobleness, generosity, goodness, of those who have given of their utmost for the love of Christ, stirs heart and conscience.[3]

Helen Barrett Montgomery died at the age of seventy-three on October 18, 1934. She was living with her daughter in Summit, New Jersey.

Blessed is the man that walketh not in the counsel of the ungodly, nor standeth in the way of sinners, nor sitteth in the seat of the scornful.

But his delight is in the law of the Lord; and in his law doth he meditate day and night.

And he shall be like a tree planted by the rivers of water, that bringeth forth his fruit in his season; his leaf also shall not wither; and whatsoever he doeth shall prosper;

The ungodly are not so; but are like the chaff which the wind driveth away.

Therefore the ungodly shall not stand in the judgment, nor sinners in the congregation of the righteous.

For the Lord knoweth the way of the righteous; but the way of the ungodly shall perish.

—PSALM 1

The First Psalm is one of the most beautiful in all literature.* The picture of a tree planted by living waters that brings forth its fruit in due season, whose leaf does not wither, is a perfect simile of the true character, rooted in God.

Let us betake ourselves to some woodsy spot, and there, stretched upon the ground beneath some great tree, hear "all the broad leaves clap their little hands in glee with one continuous sound," while we meditate upon the likeness of a good man to a tree.

This tree of the psalmist is rooted, it strikes its roots deep, and in its rootage is the secret of its growth. So, too, the secret of human character lies in those deep roots, unseen, that lay hold of the eternal. The great arraignment of our generation is

---

* Editor's Note: This sermon was printed and circulated as a devotional pamphlet.

not that it is bad, but that its roots are shallow, so that the least storm blows it over. Trees of shallow rootage are easily blown over; after a heavy wind one may see uprooted apple trees with their roots spread abroad like a sail; but no matter how heavy the gale, the oak tree, with its deep anchored taproot, rides out the gale. Such a taproot is faith, laying hold on the eternal.

Again this tree is individual, and so are we. No two trees in the forest are ever alike. Nay, no two leaves on any tree are ever exactly alike. I remember when a little child to have spent an entire afternoon trying to match exactly two maple leaves. No, one tree differs from another tree in glory, one leaf differs from all other leaves in its expression of life. So, too, are we—unique, separate, individual. The profoundest mystery of personality is its uniqueness. Having made each one of us, God broke the mold; and never again will He repeat Himself. Each one, like the myriad leaves of a tree, is a thought of God, never again to be reuttered.

This gives value to human life. If I have the power of reflecting some facet of the divine glory, else unreflected, I cannot be weak or overborne.

Again the tree is like human life in its variousness. How many kinds of trees there are! The drooping willow, the square-shouldered oak, the graceful elm, the murmuring pine, the shimmering beech, the shady maple, the motherly apple tree. A thousand, thousand kinds, all different, each having its own beauty and its own usefulness. Not only are we individual, but we are such diverse individuals; as different as the oak and the cedar—but of this diversity is built the glory of humanity. To find what our true function is in life, this is worth the heart's deep searching. Is it for food or for beauty, for shelter or for blossoming loveliness, for winter storms or for sunny days? Each may fit himself into the divine pattern of humanity, sure that He who made so many leaves and so many trees has not made so many men without a purpose. Wherefore we should guard jealously our own individuality. When we fail to be ourselves, when we slavishly imitate another's gift, another's quality, we rob life of its richness; we impoverish in our small measure the universe.

The tree is like human life in its vital power. There is nothing so quietly powerful as a tree. Each spring with its unseen pulleys it hoists tons of moisture a hundred feet into the air with no creak of machinery, no strain, no effort. Yet to lift these millions of tons that the trees lift quietly every spring would involve us in a very whirlpool of busy-ness, and noise, and confusion. There is something of this same vital power in a good man. He grows as the tree does from his root in God and then pulls up with him mighty transforming influences that lift life resistlessly. The tree and the man cooperate with God and in the doing of it transform the world. Where naked branches rattled yesterday, today a canopy of gracious leaves spread their shade and coolness. The miracle of the tree and of the man is woven in the sunshine of each today. The leaf makes chlorophyll, and the man makes character, each by the same divine alchemy. Living in the sun, taking from the sun, they both expose their souls to the rays of that light that lightens every man coming into the world. Trees cannot live in the dark, neither can men. Both are born of the light and live and thrive only in the light. Observe the efforts of every leaf to stretch itself out and so dispose itself as to catch the most sunlight possible. Note the arrangement of maple and beech leaves, of pine needles and spruce needles, all formed by different patternings of the leaves seeking for more light.

"If we live in the light as He is in the light," says John, "we have fellowship with one another and the blood of Jesus Christ is cleansing us from all sin" (1 John 1:7, preacher's translation). The trees learned that secret long ago, and in every characteristic spread of bough and patterning of twig we see its quiet dim persistence to live in the light as He is in the light. Yet humans often forget this primary lesson of spiritual and physical health, and struggle into shadows as if they belonged there, cherishing their griefs, wrapping themselves in their sorrows, refusing the comforts of God's warm sunshine. They lead defeated, and thwarted, and selfish lives. But . . . not righteous men—they are like trees planted. They rejoice in God [even from] prisons [of] disease, poverty and death. They clap their hands as do the trees and rejoice in God forever more.

Then trees bring forth their fruit also in their season. So do men. There is nothing so wonderful as the fruitage of great character. Its season of dropping fruit is perpetual. You find the fruit of its life springing up in the most unlikely and distant places, like palm nuts in a coral reef. The heart of a tree is to give, and so is the heart of a good man. In the apples, the peaches, the cherries, the oranges, the mangoes, the guavas, the tree expresses its deepest self. It gives itself to mankind. So, too, the saints bear fruit for God; in Christ abiding they bear much fruit, for this they were born, in this is hid the secret of their lives—it is the joy and beauty of the world. Servants of all like him, "the serving man"; they pour out the riches, and fragrance, and flavor of their goodness in abiding fruit.

5. Live Wire—Beware!

A Divine Healing Sermon

Aimee Semple McPherson
(1890–1944)

Aimee Elizabeth Kennedy was born near Ingersoll, Ontario. Her mother, Mildred Pearce Kennedy, took her daughter—at six weeks of age—to a Salvation Army mission where Aimee was dedicated to God's work. Aimee was reared in the Salvation Army tradition, but she experienced a dramatic conversion at a Pentecostal revival when she was seventeen years old. From all indications, she knew from this moment on that a part of her service to God would be preaching.

The evangelist in that service was Robert James Semple whom, within a year, Aimee would marry. She joined him in his travel and in his conduct of revivals. Her own preaching career began to take shape. In 1909, in Chicago, Aimee Semple was approved as a preacher of the Full Gospel Assembly; she never sought further ministerial credentials or formal ordination.

In early 1910, Robert felt the call of God to preach in China. Arrangements were made for him and his wife to go. Both of them became ill soon after they arrived; they went to Hong Kong for medical attention. Tragically he died in August of that year. About a month later, their daughter—Roberta Star Semple—was born.

Penniless and still not well, Mrs. Semple and Roberta returned to the United States—to New York—in January of 1911 where, among other responsibilities, Aimee began giving missionary lectures. She also joined her mother in a daily routine of trying to raise money for Salvation Army causes. There was not yet sufficient money for Aimee to support herself and her daughter.

On February 28, 1912, Aimee Semple married Harold Stewart Mc-Pherson who said he wanted to take care of her and her baby. In March of 1913, their son—Rolf Kennedy McPherson—was born. Soon after the birth, Mrs. McPherson became ill again, and she came to believe that the illness was God's way of punishing her for forsaking her calling to do evangelistic work. In 1915, she took her children and returned to her father's farm intent on resuming her preaching. Separated from Mr. McPherson most of the time for the next several years, they divorced in 1921.

A woman from a small Pentecostal mission in Mount Forest, Ontario, invited her to serve as evangelist at a series of revival services. No doubt, her hearers were moved by what they heard and experienced, but this was an important event for Mrs. McPherson too. Her call to ministry was further clarified. She believed that God wanted her to preach the simple gospel message Robert Semple had preached. She was further convinced that she should emphasize the importance of glossolalia* as the sign of being baptized with the Holy Spirit. In this Pentecostal revival, Aimee Semple McPherson first demonstrated faith healing that, for her, included the laying of her hands upon the ill and anointing them with oil.

In June of 1916, Aimee began her career as a traveling evangelist. Her mother came to help her with the children and with the financial and administrative affairs of her ministry.

Mrs. "Minnie" Kennedy's keen, practical executive ability combined with Mrs. McPherson's personal charm, handsome appearance, and extraordinary preaching talent to make an effective revival team. At this time, Aimee McPherson adopted the white dress, white shoes, and flowing blue cape which became her hallmark.[1]

Aimee Semple McPherson preached all across the United States, and in many other countries such as Australia, England, France, and Mexico. In 1922, while conducting a revival in San Francisco, she preached via radio broadcast, and she claimed that this was the first time a woman had done so.

Her work became focused in Los Angeles where, in April of 1921, she began construction of the Angelus Temple. On January 1, 1923, it

---

* A formal designation for the spiritually ecstatic experience of speaking in tongues.

was dedicated as the Church of the Foursquare Gospel; it was incorporated in 1927 as the International Church of the Foursquare Gospel. A new Pentecostal denomination was born. She revealed that the name for her church had been given to her by divine revelation and was based on an interpretation of the prophet Ezekiel's vision in which he saw the beings with four faces; she said these pointed to the fourfold ministry of Jesus Christ: Jesus the Savior, Jesus the Baptizer with the Holy Ghost, Jesus the Healer, Jesus the Coming King. As she explained it:

In the face of the lion, we behold that of the mighty baptizer with the Holy Ghost and fire. The face of the ox typifies the great burden-bearer, who himself took our infirmities and carried our sicknesses, who in his boundless love and divine provision has met our every need. In the face of the eagle, we see reflected soul-enrapturing visions of the coming King, whose pinions soon will cleave the shining heavens, whose voice will vibrate through the universe in thrilling cadences of resurrection power as he comes to catch his waiting bride away. And in the face of the man we behold the Savior, the man of sorrows, acquainted with grief, dying upon the tree for our sins. Here is a perfect gospel, a complete gospel, for body, for soul, for spirit, and for eternity, a gospel facing squarely in every direction.[2]

Her devoted followers called her "Sister Aimee," and they loved her. From 1923 to 1926, they came to hear her preach in her dramatic and flamboyant style every night and three times on Sunday. She had particular skill in encouraging persons who were defeated and hopeless.

In affiliation with the Church, Aimee Semple McPherson founded LIFE Bible College (Lighthouse of International Foursquare Evangelism), KFSG radio station (Kall Four Square Gospel), and a monthly magazine that was entitled *Bridal Call*. At the time of her death in 1944, the college had graduated more than three thousand students who became missionaries, pastors, and evangelists; many of these were women.

In response to the frequent criticism by Fundamentalists outside the Pentecostal tradition that women were forbidden to preach by the Bible itself, she once gave a direct and thorough response:

Woman brought sin into the world, didn't she? Then surely she should have the right to undo the wrong and lead the world to Eden above. Woman's personality, her tender sympathies, her simple, direct message—the women, motherheart, working over the world, yearning to help its wayward sons and daughters—these are all qualities in favor of her right to tell the story of God's love.

Women were co-laborers with Peter and Paul in their work. But did not the apostle say, "Let your women keep silence in the churches?" Yes, but he did not refer to a Godly woman's right to preach the eternal Gospel, for he also gives specific instructions as to how a woman should conduct herself when preaching or praying in public.

The best reason in favor of a woman's right to preach the gospel is that God's favor has attended it and blessed results follow. Called into the work at seventeen, I have been in active service practically ever since. I have seen thousands come to the altar laden with iniquity, then rising to their feet changed men and women.[3]

LIVE WIRE—BEWARE! The great question is: How shall we draw nigh unto God? Can we come with impure hearts and unclean hands? Can we expect a pure and holy God to countenance sin and heal us if sin is in our hearts?

"Who shall ascend into the hill of the Lord, or who shall stand in his holy place? He that hath clean hands, and a pure heart; who hath not lifted up his soul unto vanity, nor sworn deceitfully" (Psalm 24:3,4).

Before you come for healing, be sure your heart is right with God, then come boldly, claiming the promise, and God's fire will fall upon you, burning out every vestige of disease. You can not tamper with a live wire, neither can you be careless in approaching God. There is a way to contact a live wire, and to approach it in the wrong way is bound to bring disastrous results. The same is true in the spiritual realm.

Electrical equipments are such a blessing to mankind. I have always been subject to bronchitis, and, perspiring after a service, it is very easy to chill so one of my precious members bought me a costly electric blanket. My, how I did appreciate it, as I came in one night after a strenuous day of preaching. I had stopped to speak with various ones after the meeting, and I was thoroughly chilled. The bed looked so inviting, and I said: "I shall have a wonderful rest tucked in between that blanket." I fell asleep almost immediately in its warmth and slept soundly until almost two-thirty o'clock when I awoke with a start. I could not, at first, conceive what had happened, but there was a short-circuit; and my body became contorted and twisted and thrown in all directions. It seemed as though two Bengal tigers were clawing me to death. My heels were drawn up tightly against my head. I tried to cry for help, but my chest was, seemingly, crushed in against my lungs; and I could barely gasp. I managed to pray, and God heard my cry though I could not speak. But, finally, the power was shut off, and I was thrown across the room and "banged" against the clothes-press door. My secretary came running into the room exclaiming: "O Sister, dear, what in the world is the matter?" And there I lay, pointing to the bed and could just manage to say, "That . . . that . . . that. . . . ." Although there were no visible burns upon my body at the time, one week later they appeared, and for an entire year the effects of that burn could be seen.

Electricity is beneficial, but a live wire can produce disastrous results. For instance, those who live in the vicinity of Echo Park Lake remember how, a few weeks ago, one of the pelicans from the lake decided to "take off" into the air for an adventure. He was aiming to soar high, evidently, when BANG! he came into contact with the power line with the result that every street-car in this part of the town was thrown out of commission, and cars were stalled. And so it is with the power of God. When you come for healing and have the anointing oil applied it is symbolic of the fact that you are asking the motivating force of the universe to lay His hand upon you. The oil, in itself, has no meaning, only as a symbol.

O Man, O Man of Galilee,
Draw nigh and lay Thy hand on me,
In all this world I want but Thee,
O wondrous Man of Galilee!

Think of it! When you come for healing you are asking the great God of the universe, you are asking Almighty God who sent the sun, the moon, the stars and planets whirling into space, the great *hand* that controls the tides and the winds— you are asking Him to lay His hand upon you.

Oh then, the *connection should be right*. This is a very wise question and an intelligent one: "Who shall ascend into the hill of the Lord, or who shall stand in His holy place? He that hath clean hands, and a pure heart; who hath not lifted up his soul unto vanity, nor sworn deceitfully. He shall receive the blessing from the Lord, and righteousness from the God of his salvation."

Again, Psalm 15:1–3: "Lord, who shall abide in thy tabernacle? Who shall dwell in thy holy hill? He that walketh uprightly, and worketh righteousness, and speaketh the truth in his heart. He that backbiteth not with his tongue, nor doeth evil to his neighbor, nor taketh up a reproach against his neighbor."

Now you can be healed in a flash of that cancer; that tumor can go down like a punctured balloon. But whom does the Word of God say the blessing is for? "*He that walketh uprightly . . . and worketh righteousness . . . and speaketh the truth.*" Who shall be healed? "*He that backbiteth not with his tongue.*" WHO? He that "taketh not up a reproach against his neighbor." Should you come up for healing if you backbite with your tongue? If you do not make things right as far as in you lies with that neighbor, should you come? The Word says: "Thou shalt love thy neighbor as thyself."

Remember when you come to God, the great God of the universe, you are coming into contact with POWER. Do not come with unclean hands and impure heart. GOD IS ALL-POWERFUL.

Electricity is a wonderful thing. It furnishes power for the ice-box, the radio, the electric-iron, washer, and fan. Oh, there are so many uses! There is the electric-toaster and the electric-heater by which we can warm ourselves, but if we approach these in the wrong way and get hold of a live wire, dire things can happen.

CAIN touched "a live wire" that day when he did not approach the altar according to God's directions. Abel, his brother, approached the altar upright in heart; and God had respect unto his offering, and Abel *contacted the Most High* Who sent down the fire in answer and consumed his offering. Cain, who did not walk uprightly "touched a live wire," and God marked him from that hour. Even today we hear of "the brand of Cain." There is a right way to approach God and a wrong way. Cain did not receive the blessing for the fire did not fall when he prayed so this man, whose heart was not right with God, slew his brother.

In Numbers 16:31, we read of a man whose name was Korah, and his company of men began to *murmur* and *back-bite* against Moses. You are surely taking hold of a "live wire" when you do that! This man did. You know if you back-bite God's anointed preachers and God's anointed children, it is a rather serious thing. Moses called all the back-biters together and stood them at a distance and spoke to them, and when Moses finished speaking, *the ground clave asunder and* the earth swallowed them up. We read, "the earth opened her mouth, and swallowed them up, and their houses, and all the men that appertained unto Korah, and all their goods." The earth closed upon them, and "they went down alive into the pit."

LIVE WIRE—BEWARE! In Exodus 19:12–13, God spoke to Moses that he say to the people: "Take heed to yourselves. Whosoever toucheth the mount shall be surely put to death." And we read that even a beast dare not touch the mountain. Why? That mountain was "charged with the power of God." What would have happened to them had they touched it? They would have been "electrocuted"; they would have taken hold of a "live wire" so to speak to have touched that mount of God's power.

If the Church ever gets back to the old-time power it will be "LIVE WIRE—BEWARE!" It is a dangerous thing to tamper with holy things. The sons of Aaron came one time and offered "strange fire." They came with hypocrisy in their hearts. (You can tell when people testify, and it is not really what happened to them.) LISTEN: "And there went out fire from the Lord, and devoured them, and they died before the Lord." Why? They "offered strange fire before the Lord, which He commanded them not" (Leviticus 10:1,2). What happened to these sons of Aaron that offered "strange fire"? They were electrocuted. The fire from the altar of the Lord reached out and devoured them.

"Our God is a consuming fire." Approach with clean heart, and He will burn out that disease for only with the BLOOD upon your heart can you approach the holy God. The only prayer of the sinner God hears is: "God be merciful to me, a sinner!" So take that first step before coming for healing. Let Him apply the BLOOD and forgive your sins.

LIVE WIRE—BEWARE! Uzziah(2 Samuel 6:3) was a man who tried to steady the "ark of the Lord," a symbol of the Holy Ghost's power, as the ark was coming up the road. The ark was shaking, and Uzziah put out his hand to steady it. Where the Pentecostal "ark" is, somebody is bound to be shaking.

A lot of people may sit there like ice-bergs or old dead sticks. I wish you could see yourself; some of you are so cold. Why, some of you have not said an "Amen" or a "Hallelujah" in years!

Well, old Uzziah did not have the power himself, and he didn't want anybody else to have it; and when he saw the ark shaking he said: "This isn't right to have this ark shaking this way. I'll steady it!" AND HE TOUCHED A LIVE WIRE, FOR UZZIAH FELL DOWN DEAD!

If you are praying for power, friends, and God sends the power, let it fall, and do not try to steady the "ark" or stop the shaking. Let the fire fall.

LIVE WIRE—BEWARE! Speaking of the three Hebrew children, they were on fire for God, and when they were thrown into the fiery furnace, nothing hurt them. They were in their own *element*—their "God, a consuming fire," and they could walk in the fire. But as for the men who threw the three Hebrew children into the fire, they did not escape. That same fire had a different effect upon them. They were surely not "fire-proof."

Daniel, as we read in Daniel 6:20, was cast into the lion's den, but he was not eaten because Daniel was "on fire for God," and the lions knew he was *"too hot to handle"* so they left him alone until he would cool off. But Daniel did not "cool off." He remained steadfast, on fire for God, and they dare not come near him. When the king saw Daniel alive in the den, he ordered his men to bring him forth, and those who had thrown Daniel in were cast to the lions. Every bone of their bodies was broken before they reached the floor of the den. When you come into contact with God, you are coming into contact with infinite Power.

ANANIAS AND SAPPHIRA were hypocrites and pretended to be real Christians who gave largely of their tithes and offerings unto the Lord. So they decided to sell a piece of land and give the proceeds to the early Church. They received a good price for the land for the Lord had blessed them, but, though they had made a vow to God that they would give the money to the Church, "they kept back part of the price." Now, they did not, in the first place, *have to give* that money to God, but they had promised Him they would before they had sold [the land]. And Ananias said, "Sapphira, old girl, what do you say we hold back part of that money? We will walk down the aisle, and they will say: 'Look what they have given to God!' And they will sing, 'My all is on the altar!'" The Word says: "Peter said: Ananias, why hath Satan filled thine heart to lie to the Holy Ghost. . . . Thou hast not lied unto men, but unto God." And Ananias and his wife, Sapphira came into contact with "a live wire," for that very moment God struck them dead—Ananias first, and his wife who came after.

THE point of my sermon is this—we have not come to a dead God of stone or clay, but to a God Who is back of His promises, the God Who can save and heal, the God Who is alive and Who loves us; and He has made a way we can approach Him. It is through JESUS CHRIST and His BLOOD. If we approach with sincere and clean heart, we shall be blest.

PAUL, who was called Saul, as he rode to Damascus to persecute the Christians was sincere, but he did not know Jesus and was pretty nearly electrocuted. That is all that saved him; he thought he was doing the right thing. God knew his heart. God's power touched him, and he fell to the ground. He saw a great light and heard Jesus speaking. "Why persecutest thou Me? I AM JESUS WHOM THOU PERSECUTEST."

In Acts 19:13, we read that "certain of the vagabond Jews, exorcists, took upon them to call over them which had evil spirits the name of the Lord Jesus, saying, 'We adjure you by Jesus whom Paul preacheth.'" And (vs. 15) "the evil spirit answered and said, 'Jesus I know, and Paul I know; but who are ye?'"

"And the man in whom the evil spirit was leaped on them, and overcame them, and tore all their clothes from them so that they fled 'naked.'" Up the road went these exorcists, lickety-cut, screaming at the top of their voice. Say, they touched a "live wire" when they attempted to do what Paul in the power of the Holy Ghost did. *There is a power of God, and a power of the devil.* These exorcist Jews could not use that holy name for their hearts were not clean. They found out that even the demons must obey a cleansed and Holy Ghost-filled man as was Paul.

In 2 Kings 20:3–5, Hezekiah had been given up to die, and Isaiah, the preacher, had come to say good-bye. The preacher had gone, and Hezekiah was alone; and he turned his face to the wall and prayed and wept bitterly. And the Lord said: "I have heard thy prayer, I have seen thy tears; behold, I will heal thee; and on the third day thou shalt go up into the house of the Lord." God added fifteen years to his life that he might serve Him. I do not believe in the saying, "Well, when my time comes, I will go." God can lengthen that life if you really mean to serve Him.

ENOCH contacted God. He got hold of a "live wire" and up, up he went, for Enoch's head was always above the clouds. He walked and talked with God always, and we read: "Enoch was not, for God took him."

The man at the Gate Beautiful who had never walked took hold of a "live wire" that day when Peter reached forth his hand in the name of Jesus.

When the son of the widow of Nain was being carried for burial, Jesus touched him and said, "I say unto you, arise!" He came into contact with POWER.

Who shall ascend to the holy hill? He that walketh uprightly. He that backbiteth not with his tongue.

Do you have something you are holding back from God? Are you asking that you might consume it upon lusts? Do not fail to pay your vows unto God. Approach Him with clean hands. Many times, "we ask and receive not because we ask amiss." It is a terrible thing to fall into the hands of an angry God. Let us have no obstacles in the way of God's power that He may send the fire and consume the offering. "A contrite and a broken heart the Lord will not despise." He resisteth the proud. Draw nigh with clean hands and pure heart, and He will answer.

6. God Is Love

Evangeline C. Booth
(1865–1950)

William Booth left the Methodist ministry in 1865 to begin an evangelistic organization that would become the Salvation Army. Herbert A. Wisbey, Jr., describes the Salvation Army as a ministry that emphasizes "personal religious commitment, strict moral principles, and unlimited compassion for the less fortunate."[1] This consuming work of Booth's also affected the lives of Mrs. Booth (Catherine) and their eight children, seven of whom would become prominent leaders in the Salvation Army. The seventh of these children was Evangeline—born on Christmas day, 1865, in London. Catherine Booth, known as the Mother of the Salvation Army, was—like her husband—an effective and inspiring preacher, and she was Evangeline's role model. Mrs. Booth was suspicious of secular education so her children were taught by tutors and governesses in the home.

When Evangeline—called Eva until she began her work in the United States—was fifteen she put on a Salvation Army sergeant's uniform and sold copies of the group's newspaper, War Cry.

At an age when girls of equal years were thrilling to the dawn of adolescence, she was mounting chairs in the open street and preaching her first sermons, and, while still in her teens, was championing the cause of religious liberty, lending the grace and verve of her youth to battles against prejudice and persecution and winning for the then despised Salvationists the right to carry the gospel to the streets.[2]

By seventeen, she had been given official responsibilities in the Salvation Army.

Dynamic in personality, she preached in rundown halls, sang in public houses, accompanying herself on the guitar, faced hostile magistrates on charges of "disturbing the peace," and melted hardened roughs.[3]

Early on, she spent a great deal of her time in the slums of London—often in the disguise of a ragged flower seller or a match girl. Her appearance and her compassion caused her to be called "White Angel of the Slums."

She was called Miss Eva when she was principal of the International Training College at Clapton which trained young women and men for missionary work all over the world. From this position she became field commissioner, for four years, of all London and was known especially for her ability to solve internal as well as legal problems. In 1896, she became the national commander of the Salvation Army in Canada where she served until 1904.

On November 9, 1904, her father—General Booth—commissioned Evangeline as commander and gave her responsibility for all the work of the Salvation Army in the United States. She served in this capacity for thirty years.

Evangeline Booth proved to be an exceptionally complicated woman. Raised as a kind of junior princess in her father's hectic household court, she was allowed—even encouraged—to abandon herself to her strong, inherited dramatic impulses. The young woman was placed in authority over thousands, in which she was responsible to no one save God and her father (who usually left her to the Former). Thus it is natural that at age thirty-nine Evangeline was imperious and condescending. . . . She was at the same time a compassionate soul, thoughtful, full of little kindnesses, genuinely sympathetic with the poor and lonely in their sufferings, and a dedicated, fearless evangelical. . . . Above all else, Evangeline was an exceptionally good public speaker, who could hold large audiences spellbound for hours.[4]

She had the ability to attract to her meetings and her cause, the wealthy, the professional, and the common folk. She was in almost overwhelming demand as a speaker and preacher. She traveled all over North America as well as in Great Britain, in the Scandinavian countries, in Europe, Japan, India, and the Far East. She was accustomed to crowds that overflowed the rooms in which she proclaimed her message of salvation for all and the need to give to the less fortunate. She received numerous honorary degrees as well as the Distinguished Service Medal awarded by President Woodrow Wilson, the Vasa Gold Medal presented by the king of Sweden, and the gold medal given by the National Institute of Social Science.

Music was her avocation, and she especially enjoyed playing the harp, which she had begun playing as a young girl. She actually composed a number of songs that became Salvation Army songs. Some were published in 1927 as a collection entitled "Songs of the Evangel."

In 1934, Evangeline Booth left the United States to return to London where she became the general of the Salvation Army, its fourth. She served in this capacity for five years—responsible for the international ministries of the organization. She continued her travel, her preaching, and her skilled administration. She retired in 1939, the last member of the Booth family to head the Salvation Army. After her retirement, corporate leadership took over.

General Booth returned to the United States, to her home in Hartsdale, New York. She died at the age of eighty-five and was buried near White Plains, New York, in the Salvation Army's plot in the Kensico Cemetery.

GOD IS LOVE

And we have known and believed the love that God hath to us. God is love; and he that dwelleth in love, dwelleth in God, and God in him.

—1 JOHN 4:16

T o speak to this audience tonight upon the text—GOD IS LOVE—is, I realize, the most formidable task I have ever attempted, and I stand before you trembling with the consciousness of my utter inability to touch even the fringe of so colossal a subject.*

The text itself is a short one. But three words—each a monosyllable. Yet short and apparently simple as it is, it covers the whole realm of Divine teaching.

It reaches the highest heights. It fathoms the deepest depths. It sweeps the circumference of the eternities. GOD IS LOVE!

In God, the highest heights—for His throne is high above all other thrones.

In love, the lowest depths of human distress.

In the IS—GOD IS—that little word reaches back into a measureless past without beginning, and on into an interminable future without end—ETERNITY.

So these three words are the Alpha and the Omega of the Bible.

Every judgment that has thundered across its pages;

Every promise that has rainbowed the storms of the saints;

Every solace that has soothed the dying pillow;

Every warning that has arrested an endangered course;

Every efficacy that has blotted out sin;

Every refuge that has harbored a wrecked soul, has been by virtue of this indestructible truth of the ages—GOD IS LOVE!

First, permit me to try and impress you with the GREATNESS OF GOD.

GOD IS GREAT!

We cannot live and have our being without this fact being pressed upon us from every side.

THE MIRACULOUS EVIDENCES OF NATURE IMPRESS US WITH IT.

This is a great, grand old world of ours. It is a world full of miracles—the miraculous handiwork of God.

Some people find it difficult to believe the story of the miracles wrought when God was upon earth. This I cannot under-

---

* Editor's Note: This sermon is from the unpublished sermons of Evangeline Booth. Used by permission of the Salvation Army, New York.

stand. For while we have eyes with which to see, ears with which to hear, mental capacity with which to perceive, we surely must be cognizant of the miracles daily wrought all round us.

The new, fresh, upturned face of every spring daisy is a miracle.

Old Father Autumn, making the forest blaze with his Autumnal flame, and the red sparks to fly from its foliage with the hammer of his anvil, is a miracle.

Every shower from the heavens which satiates the thirst of the earth, and every sunbeam-cup that refills the chalices of the sky is a miracle.

We talk much of our advanced age. We cannot say too generous things about it. But there is no sense in which Nature has ever been or ever will be old-fashioned.

No trees to surpass the cedars of Lebanon, with their girth of forty feet, and their height of two hundred feet, and their age of two thousand years.

The almond tree, which bursts into lavishness of bloom in the middle of January the—fruit of which bore down the dromedaries of the desert, and made the ships of [Tarshish] to battle with the seas.

IT IS A GREAT WORLD
Its valleys of bloom, its silver lakes and flowing rivers,

ITS VETERAN MOUNTAINS
heroes of ten thousand storms, scarred by the battle-axe of the elements, standing with their sun-crowned heads, and snow-armored shoulders, imperishable monuments to the glories of nature.

THESE GREAT HILLS
with the treasures of light and heat hidden in their bosom!

THESE GREAT SEAS
the highways of commerce, with their pearls and their gems hoarded in their deeps!

THESE HEAVENS
with their burning firmament, and their army of countless mil-

lion stars on guard as sentinels of light, fighting back the enemies of the night.

THAT FLAMING HERALD OF THE MORNING, THE SUN! A master-work of God! It is by its attraction that our world is held to her proper path as she swings around it.

If the sun's influence were withheld for but one moment this world, and all the worlds upon which it shines, would perish. A GREAT SUN!

You say, "Well, I am not a man of the hills or the forests, and I have never gotten very near the heavens as yet. I am a man of the city, and the city is man-made."

My friend you are wrong!

The city is not man-made!

When I see the forests unloading their burden of cedar, and elm, and oak, and maple, and ash, I say the forests made the cities.

When I see the elements marshaling down their forces to drive our railways, to lighten our darkness, to flash our messages, to tug at the straps, and spin the wheels and shuttles of all the mammoth machinery which makes our cities thunder with enterprise, I say that from the exhaustless storehouses of His creation GOD MADE THE CITIES, and GOD IS GREAT!

But neither the earth nor the Heavens show how great God is as does MAN.

The Christian anatomist gazing upon the human body exclaims—"fearfully and wonderfully made."

These bodies of ours—this castle of life—no piece of mechanism so intricate—so elaborate—so divine.

HERE IS THE HAND

It is difficult to describe the full power of the human hand, after the brain, rendering the greatest service to man.

THE EYE

catching earth, sky and sea in one glance, giving the distant object and those things close by our side their correct proportions without any conscious readjustment of the lens or change of focus.

THE PERPETUAL TELEGRAPH OF THE NERVES—THESE JOINTS—
the only hinges that do not rust;
THESE MUSCLES and BONES,
with their fourteen thousand different adaptations.
THIS HEART,
the most wonderful of all engines, contracting four thousand times every hour, and pumping through its channels two hundred and fifty pounds of blood every sixty minutes.
THIS CHEMICAL PROCESS OF DIGESTION—
But above all,
THE INTELLECT,
which stamps us above the beast—the candle which lights the path of life; the scales into which men lift life's ever arising questions and adjust their legitimate proportions by the balances of thought.

And God made this castle of life! I look upon it and I say, GOD IS GREAT!

Yet men live their lives independent of this great God.

They leave Him out of all their reckonings, out of their homes, out of their business, out of their families.

Some men defy God—

Some even deny God.

You say your heart is hard—suppose it were ten times as hard;

Your sin is long-continued—suppose it were ten times as long-continued;

Your evil habits are strong—suppose they were ten times as strong.

Is there any lion this Samson cannot slay?

Is there any fortress this Conqueror cannot take?

Any foe this God cannot overcome?

GOD IS JUST.

I have walked through the long corridors of the large prisons of this and other countries.

I have made my home in the midst of the most poor, the

most desolate of the shadowed, melancholy slums of the underworld.

I have been the honored guest in the luxurious homes of the high and wealthy.

I have sat in the places of legislation.

I have stood in the witness-box, and pleaded the cause of the wronged in the court-rooms, and I stand before you here tonight and solemnly declare that my heart has derived almost as much consolation from the conviction that GOD IS JUST as from the conviction that GOD IS LOVE.

First, let me say that God's justice is evidenced by His impartiality in His dealings with men.

In our present day it would seem that justice is at a premium! Influence can do so much.

Money can do so much.

Name can do so much.

Politics can do so much.

Skill can do so much.

Often these powerful agencies enter with the plaintiff and take up their place in the Court, and justice is perverted; the real offender escapes, and punishment is inflicted upon the innocent.

But not so with this ALL-JUST GOD!

The Bible says, "Shall not the Judge of all the earth do right?"

What difference do looks, our official or social standing, learning, or clothes make to this great, just God?

The Bible says: "The candle of the wicked shall be put out," irrespective of who he is, where he lives, what his possessions, or with what success his wickedness has met—"his candle shall be put out."

Many candles God puts out that friends and relatives and associates know nothing about!

Sometimes while their faces smile, hearts are a load of ashes. The light of joy is out—the light of peace is out.

Oh, the miseries men suffer because of their sins. Oh, the fears they battle with—the regrets they carry about! The world thinks we have got off Scot-free, but we know that God is just.

Sometimes no one knows until the words of anguish flung from dying lips tell the story.

GOD'S JUSTICE IS SHOWN IN THE UNALTERABLE, IN-EVITABLE LAW OF RETRIBUTION.

No human ingenuity can change the decree that is written in God's own Word that "whatsoever a man soweth that shall He also reap."

The reaping is not always of the character or at the time we would think. Sometimes it is much delayed, as in the case of Nebuchadnezzar—when it came late in life, when God touched him on that vital point, the intellect, and made him as the oxen to eat grass.

Sometimes early, as with Belshazzar, when in his prime he was weighed and found wanting.

But it comes! It is sure. "Whatsoever a man soweth that shall he also reap."

I saw my father sow righteousness!

Mercy toward the erring and the faulty;

Uprightness, integrity, honor and truth and love.

He sowed with toil and tears, with privation and sacrifice, and the seed spread to the uttermost ends of the earth.

There shall be an handful of corn in the earth, upon the top of the mountains; the fruit thereof shall shake like Lebanon.

And with my own eyes I looked upon him at the age of eighty-three, erect of stature, prophetic of countenance, his head silver-crowned with the honor of old age, and I heard him with my own ears, in a voice that reached the furthest corner of the building, with its human burden of thirteen thousand people, declare that God's Word is true, that whatsoever a man soweth that shall he also reap.

My friends, it is true—

What are you sowing?

No picture thrown upon the canvas of time is more emphatic of this statement than MORDECAI AND HAMAN.

Haman the all-powerful, Haman the all-skillful, Haman the arch-conspirator, Haman, who laid his diabolical plans for the extermination of a whole race, to get one man, and with such fiendish cunning and human perfection that he could not conceive of any possible power that could thwart his design—

Haman dipping his hands deeper and deeper into blood.

Every preparation complete, the signature of the king attached, the decree gone forth, the date fixed when the innocent must die—the innocent for the guilty.

The stupendous gallows are erected. All is ready, when clad in the black mantle of retribution, in walks that great figure, the figure of Justice!

And the boomerang returns straight to the throat of him who threw it; the bird of evil design spreads its black wings and flies straight to the nest wherein it was fledged; and we see swinging from the gallows, not the form of Mordecai the innocent, but swinging—swinging—the withered form of Haman the guilty. God is just!

But high above all else—

beyond God's greatness—

beyond God's justice—

GOD IS LOVE!

Some of us think we understand that word "Love." And perhaps we do when it is related to the human heart.

For sweep of influence, for magnitude of power, it rivals every other sentiment known in the human family.

It is the oil to the grinding wheels of life.

It is the daybreak of every earthly night.

It is the star in every human sky.

What is money, or beauty, or fame when compared to love?

And this love still remains in the world, and as long as the solar system swings round upon its axle, it will be with us.

THERE IS THE LOVE OF COUNTRY.

What evidence we have had of the power of this love!

We have seen the long lines of the fairest and best of our land leave friends and comforts, and father and mother, and wife and sweetheart, and turn their faces toward privation, and stress, and wounds, and death—FOR THE LOVE OF COUNTRY.

THERE IS THE LOVE OF CHILDREN FOR PARENTS.

This is a wonderful love.

This summer when I asked a young lady—a remarkably gifted musician—why she did not go to the great city and make money and fame, as she could so easily do, she said she could not leave the old folks.

The other day in Chicago a gentleman asked a ragged little newsboy for a certain paper. In running to get it the boy was run over by an automobile. His dying words were—"The fifty cents is for my mother."

A MOTHER'S LOVE

Is a wonderful thing. How can we describe a mother's love?

Into what depths of sorrow and suffering will it not plunge for her child?

What hardships will it not suffer—what toils of the hands, what toils of the feet, and what toils of the head will it not embrace!

What long, hard roads will it not travel? Oh, mother's love!

AND FATHER'S LOVE

There is nothing more beautiful than a Christian father's love.

Yet human love, in comparison to God's love, is as a candle to the sun. No, even this does not compare with it.

THERE IS NO COMPARISON!

Can I compare it to the oceans? No, God can gather these in the hollow of His hand.

Can I compare it to the Heavens? No, as a scroll the heavens will roll away, but GOD'S LOVE WILL NEVER PASS AWAY.

Can I compare it to the space which envelops worlds? No, because worlds will burn, and Divine Love can never burn. Its power is omnipotent; its breath infinite; its life eternal.

IT IS LOVE THAT COMES DOWN.

The whole plan of Redemption was worked on the coming-down principle from the beginning to the end.

Christ did not come to this poor world of ours through palatial arch, but through a barn door.

He began in a horse's trough in a stable, and ended ON THE CROSS! None so poor but he was poorer. Starved in the wilderness, a stone for his pillow. Oh, what a coming down!

Coming down from heaven for a home, angels for attendants, fruit of the tree of life for the table, the arches of light for the banqueting hall,

To talk with fishermen, associate with publicans and sinners, to wait on table at the great free feast, or to eat his bread on the rigging at the back of Peter's boat. All the way along to the end—coming down! coming down! coming down! condescension divine! coming down!

Oh the depth into which He plunged that He might lift us up!

How deep is your sorrow?

Is it as deep as the grave of a little child?

Did all the music of the house stop when the undertaker carried a little white box with white handles out through your door?

How deep is your sin?

Is it five years—ten years—forty years—fifty or sixty years deep? Is it as deep as a wasted life? Is it as deep as massacred opportunities? Is it as deep as a lost hope?

The bed of the Atlantic running out from the Coast of Spain is called the Continental Slope.

For two thousand miles it goes gradually deeper until it reaches the depth of five thousand fathoms—over five miles.

At that depth the blackest night we have ever seen is broad daylight compared to the darkness of the ocean-bed.

Yet there are fish with eyes so regulated that they can see their way about—while others are totally blind.

The pressure just under the surface of the water is fifteen pounds per square inch.

At the depth I have just mentioned the pressure is three tons per square inch.

So men go down into the depths of sin—lower—lower—darker—darker—deeper—deeper—heavier—heavier. Oh, that we could grasp the awfulness of sin!

"I learn the depth to which I have sunk, from the length of the chain let down to updraw me."

"I ascertain the awfulness of my ruin by examining the machinery for my restoration."

THE LOVE OF GOD HAS BROUGHT US MANY THINGS.

IT HAS BROUGHT US REST.

Has anyone come in with this crowd tonight who is weary?

Are you tired of life?

Are you tired of your own vain struggle after better things? "Come unto Me all ye that labor and are heavy laden and I will give you rest."

IT HAS BROUGHT US PEACE.

Are you weary of battling with the conflicting evils that beset your path?

You know you are not right.

You know you are all wrong.

As someone said to me the other day, "I am a defeated soul; I go down before the enemies of truth and righteousness every time; every good impulse I have ever had has failed, and I am too disheartened to make one more effort."

Oh, listen to His word of LOVE:

"O that thou hadst hearkened to my commandments! then had thy peace been as a river, and thy righteousness as the waves of the sea" (Isaiah 48:18).

IT HAS BROUGHT US COMFORT.

Are you bereaved?

Are you here with a broken heart tonight, desolate and lonely? Is your home empty?

Oh listen!

"As one whom his mother comforteth, so will I comfort you, and ye shall be comforted" (Isaiah 66:13).

Are you an ORPHAN?

Or a WIDOW?

Are you ALONE in the world?

Do you feel that you can easily be IMPOSED UPON AND OPPRESSED?

Listen to His words:

"A father of the fatherless, and a Judge of the widows, is God."

Oh, if I am sure of anything, I am sure—I am sure—that God takes care of His children.

You may ask me a hundred questions I cannot answer, about this theory and that theory, but I shall believe until the day of my death that I am overarched by unerring care, and that though the heavens may fall, and the earth may burn, and the judgment may thunder, and eternity may roll, IF I AM A CHILD OF GOD NOT SO MUCH AS A HAIR SHALL FALL FROM MY HEAD, or a shadow drop on my path that shall not be known to my HEAVENLY FATHER and be under His watchfulness.

He bottles our tears, he catches our sighs, he is our Shelter.

To the orphan He will be a Father; to the widow a husband; to the outcast a Home, and to the worst, loathsome wretch who today crawls out of the ditch of his abominations crying to Him for mercy, He will be AN ALL-PARDONING REDEEMER.

We could do without rest—peace—comfort—and care, but how could we ever do without PARDON?

What other escape is there from our sins?

What abundance of measures men have tried to flee them?

Give me the swift feet of the hind, can I outrun them?

Give me the passage of the whirlwind, can I outstrip them?

Give me the waters of the oceans, can I o'erflow them?

Add sea to sea, river to river, lake to lake, and in one great, measureless, fathomless volume of water, can I drown them?

O poor sinner! What thought have you?

What is your idea?

What arrangement have you made?

What plans designed?

What power looked to—to escape your sins?

Every day we learn of desperate attempts men make to rid their consciences, their memories, their souls of sins.

They leap from the parapet of the bridge.

They level a revolver at their aching forehead.

They drink to the dregs of the cup of poison.

They leave home and country.

They change name and appearance.

They deny their guilt by every word and means and measure they can marshal to their dilemma—all to escape their sins.

But do they succeed? Do they discover a power that can help them?

Oh, I ask ye sinners here tonight to call out loud to the hills, "O hills, will ye cover our sins?"

The voices of the winds come down from the brow of the hill and answer: "No—no! We cannot cover your sins."

Call out to the oceans: "O ye seas, can ye cover our sins?"

Waves billow upon billow, and lash back across the sweeps: "No—no! We cannot cover your sins!"

"O ye accumulated wealth, and hoarded gold, can ye cover our sins?"

"No, no!" clinks back the gold and rattles back the paper— "we cannot cover your sins."

"O ye sweet silver streams, pure and deep and tender—my mother's tears. O ye, surely, will cover my sins!"

"No, no!" sob back those crystal drops—"Even we cannot cover your sins."

Oh, you say, is there naught to cover sin?

Is there no power to save my soul from going down into the pit?

Is there no ransom?

Polluted—sin-torn—crushed and broken—must I die?

Your sins rise up and answer, "Thy ways and thy doings have procured these things unto thee." Ye must die.

Those whom you have harmed, and hurt, and wronged cry out: "His own iniquities shall take the wicked, and he shall be holden with the cords of his own sin." Ye must die.

Justice cries out: "Whatsoever a man soweth, that shall he also reap." Ye must die.

Judgment thunders: "The wages of sin is death." Ye must die.

But breaking through the ranks of heaven and hell there comes one with garments died crimson-red.

His brow drops blood,

His side is torn,

His hands have nail prints,

His feet are bruised,

His heart is bleeding,

and He throws his emaciated body across the gaping chasm twixt justice and mercy, and cries, "Stand back, ye lawful accusers.

I die a ransom!"

I turn aside the blood-soaked mantle and I see, "Five bleeding wounds He bears,"

And I say, "Behold the Lamb of God, who taketh away the sins of the world."

My friends, the rocks will turn grey with age, the forests will be unmoored in the hurricane, the sun will shut its fiery eyelid, the stars will drop like burnt-out coals, the sea will heave its last groan and lash itself into expiring agony, the continents will drop like anchors in the deep, the world will wrap itself in a sheet of flame.

But God's love will never die!

It shall kindle new suns after all other lights have gone out.

It will be an overbillowing sea after all other oceans have swept themselves away.

It will sing while the Archangel's trumpet peals amid the crash of toppling sepulchres and the rush of the wings of the rising dead.

7. The Imperishable Jewel

Georgia Elma Harkness
(1891–1974)

Probably the first American woman to gain wide recognition as a theologian and certainly the first woman ever to hold a professorship at a theological seminary as well as the first woman member of the American Theological Society, Georgia Harkness was born into a decidedly Methodist home. She grew up in this home in the village that was named after her grandfather: Harkness, New York. Stirred and influenced by the evangelists in the annual revival meetings, Georgia formally joined the local Methodist church when she was fourteen years old. She continued as a member of this congregation throughout her life.

When she graduated from high school, Georgia Harkness won a scholarship to Cornell University where she continued her studies. Having been accustomed to small town life and having never traveled very far from home, she was lonely in her early days as a university student. Through becoming part of the Student Christian Association and the Student Volunteer Movement, she found friends. As a student, she volunteered for foreign mission service though family considerations would prevent her from following through with this desire.

She completed her studies at Cornell in 1912 where she earned the A.B. degree with a major in history and political science. In order to be near her parents, she spent the next six years teaching Latin and French in high schools. She then learned of a church-related vocation that was newly opened to women; churches had begun to hire women directors of Christian education. Therefore, in 1918, she entered Boston University School of Religious Education, earning her M.R.E. degree in 1920. However, the dabbling she had done in the field of theological study served to draw her interests more strongly in that direction. Though there was some concern on the part of the faculty about having a woman involved in the doctoral program, Miss Harkness was admitted; and she earned a Ph.D. in philosophy from Boston University in 1923.

During the last year of her doctoral work, she taught religious education at Elmira College in Elmira, New York. Upon the completion of her prestigious degree, Georgia Harkness began teaching philosophy in 1923; she continued until 1937. She toured Europe in 1924, finding the effects of war overwhelmingly dramatic. After what she saw there, she called herself a pacifist, wrote widely on the subject, and participated in numerous groups involved with peace and justice to help make her point. There were academic leaves at Harvard and Yale Universities and at Union Theological Seminary in New York. The time at Union, however, was pivotal for her personally and professionally. During a year and a half of study (which occurred from 1935 to 1937), Harkness shifted her focus from philosophy to theology.

With her new emphasis in view, Dr. Harkness took a new position as well. She began teaching religion at Mount Holyoke College in 1937. In 1940, she began teaching at the Garrett Bible Institute in Evanston, Illinois; her field was applied theology or ethics. As she looked back on the decade, 1929 through 1939, she wrote:

I have become more of a theologian, probably less of a philosopher. My religion is more Christ-centered. I have rediscovered the Bible. Mysticism and worship have taken on added richness. I seem in a small way to have become a perpatetic evangelist, speaking often on personal religious living. . . . I am more church-minded.

Ten years ago, I was a liberal in theology. I am still a liberal, unrepentant and unashamed. This does not mean that I have seen nothing in liberalism that needed correction. We were in danger of selling out to science as the only approach to truth, of trusting too hopefully in man's power to remake his world, of forgetting the profound fact of sin and the redeeming power of divine grace, of finding our chief evidence of God in cosmology, art, or human personality, to the clouding of the clearer light of the incarnation. Liberalism needed to see in the Bible something more than a collection of moral adages and a compendium of great literature. It needed to see in Christ something more than a great figure living sacrificially and dying for his convictions. It needed to be recalled to the meaning of the cross and the power of the resurrection.[1]

She always remained an active part of her church. She said, "Apart from worship, faith lacks resonance and power."[2] In 1926, she was ordained as a local deacon, and in 1938, she was ordained as a local elder. She accepted many of the frequent invitations she received to preach, and over time Dr. Harkness preached not only in Methodist churches, but also in the churches of most every Protestant denomination.

The years 1939 to 1945 marked a very difficult time in the life of Georgia Harkness. She was physically ill; she suffered from insomnia; and she was depressed. Finally, she sought psychiatric help. In 1945, when there had begun to be rays of light and hope, Harkness wrote *The Dark Night of the Soul*, which dealt with the religious meaning of suffering, and—further—it was a most practical book. In it she suggested:

A word may be in order here for the person who must counsel the person in depression. There are few things we do more poorly—not so much because of culpable insensitiveness as from a baffled sense of helplessness. Yet there are few things more necessary. Everybody needs someone—whether professional counselor, member of the family, pastor, or friend—on whom to cast part of his burden if he is to cast it fully upon God. . . . One ought neither to coddle nor to condemn the sufferer, for he needs to rid himself of both self-pity and self-condemnation. . . . Often the best thing a wise counselor can do is by sympathetic understanding to show in himself something of the love of a God who always understands—who knows our frame and remembers that we are dust.[3]

In February of 1949 she gave the E. T. Earl Lectures at the Pacific School of Religion in Berkeley, California, as a part of an interdenominational pastors' conference; the lectures were published under the title *The Gospel and Our World*. Her point was that

the churches in America, though far from decadent, are doing much less effective work than they might be doing with their resources, and . . . the major cause of the difficulty lies in failure to present the meaning and claims of the Christian faith in terms that seem vital to the common man. In short, there is need of a much closer connection than we have had thus far between theology and evangelism.[4]

Soon thereafter, she was offered a position on the faculty of the Pacific School of Religion, and began in 1950, continuing instruction in the field of ethics.

While not a radical feminist, Harkness often spoke out for the cause of women's rights. Her full treatise on the subject was her book, *Women in Church and Society: A Historical and Theological Inquiry,* which was published in 1972. She was not bitter about her role in the Church, and it had been a most active one; but she was still concerned about the general oppression that women suffered. She pointed out that the Church was the last societal institution actively to oppress women by limiting their role in much ecclesiastical decision making and, in particular, by a general refusal to ordain women to professional ministry. Her own proposed responses had originally appeared in the journal, *The Women's Pulpit;* and she reiterated them in her 1972 book.[5]

1. We must maintain our feminity, never forgetting that we are women.
2. Be cooperative in spirit, working with men on all suitable occasions.
3. Trust our men friends (there are times when they can better speak for us than we can for ourselves).
4. Keep up with the times. Do not forget the lessons of history, but look to the future.
5. We must choose our priorities. The gospel is more important than women's rights.
6. Be faithful to your calling.

Harkness was a prolific writer. What follows is an extensive listing of some of her books by year of publication.

The Church and the Immigrant (1922)
    (her first book published while still a student)
Conflicts in Religious Thought (1929)
    (a philosophy of religion)
John Calvin: The Man and His Ethics (1931)
Holy Flame (1935)
    (her first book of poems)
The Resources of Religion (1936)
The Recovery of Ideals (1937)
Religious Living (1937)
The Faith by Which the Church Lives (1940)
The Glory of God (1943)

The Dark Night of the Soul (1945)
Understanding the Christian Faith (1947)
Prayer and the Common Life (1948)
The Gospel and Our World (1949)
Through Christ Our Lord (1950)
The Modern Rival of Christian Faith (1952)
Toward Understanding the Bible (1952)
Be Still and Know (1953)
The Sources of Western Morality (1954)
Foundations of Christian Knowledge (1955)
Christian Ethics (1957)
The Bible Speaks to Daily Needs (1959)
The Providence of God (1960)
Beliefs That Count (1961)
The Church and the Laity (1962)
Our Christian Hope (1964)
What Christians Believe (1965)
The Fellowship of the Holy Spirit (1966)
Disciplines of the Christian Life (1967)
The Ministry of Reconciliation (1971)
Women in Church and Society (1972)
Mysticism: Its Meaning and Message (1973)
Understanding the Kingdom of God (1974)

She loved her writing. In fact, she worked until the day before her death, completing the proofreading of the galleys for *Understanding the Kingdom of God.*

Recently I came across some words in the Bible that I did not know were there.* Of course the words had been there all the time, but it took the freshness of the Revised Standard

* Editor's Note: This sermon was preached by Dr. Georgia Harkness for radio

Version of the New Testament to bring out their power. The words are in First Peter, the third chapter and the fourth verse, "the imperishable jewel of a gentle and quiet spirit." In fact, the whole passage is interesting, for in some advice addressed especially to women the author counsels them not to give too much attention to their hair-dos and robes and ornaments of gold, but says of their real adornment, "Let it be the hidden person of the heart with the imperishable jewel of a gentle and quiet spirit, which in God's sight is very precious."

As I read these words, my thoughts turned to a number of persons whose lives have blessed mine because they had this imperishable jewel of a gentle and quiet spirit. There was that neighbor in the little country community where I grew up—full of good works and deeds of kindness to all the countryside— who when any personal calamities befell her (and plenty did) met every turn of fortune with the simple philosophy, "There's always a way provided."

There is that other neighbor of today, who for years has kept what others might call a rooming-house but which to her and those who lived in it has always been a *home*, for by the alchemy of her gentle and quiet spirit she took the most diverse group of people and welded them together into a happy and cooperative community. The sequel is that when in her eighties she herself was about to be evicted, she had done so much for others that the prayers of her steadfast faith were answered and she still has her home.

Then I thought of a gentle-spirited Christian woman I met in Germany last summer, calmly, unpretentiously, lovingly making a home for disabled prisoners of war whose legs and arms had been shot away, and helping them back to self-support. I

broadcast on the "Faith in Our Time" hour on March 4, 1949, in observance of the World Day of Prayer under the auspices of the United Council of Church Women. She was professor of applied theology at Garrett Biblical Institute at this time.

met with her scarcely more than an hour, but the fragrance of her quiet spirit has lingered with me through the months since.

And my mind turned to a Chinese friend, beautifully Christian and highly trained, who might have stayed in this country in comfort but who chose to go back to help her people in war-torn, inflation-ridden China. Working in an unheated building and without enough for her own physical necessities she nevertheless could write: "Christ is our hope. We are so thankful for His rich blessings and sufficient grace."

What is it that makes such persons able to take what Shakespeare called "the slings and arrows of outrageous fortune" and turn them into a blessing? There is but one answer. They are persons of faith and prayer, who because the inner life is nourished by the perennial springs of God's Spirit are able to refresh those about them by kindly words and gracious deeds. Their adornment is not in the externals to which both the men and women of our time give so much attention and money, but as the verse quoted has it, in "the hidden person of the heart with the imperishable jewel of a gentle and quiet spirit, which in God's sight is very precious." Because it is so precious in God's sight it costs much, and this cost is in earnest prayer and faithful effort to live according to the leading God gives us.

In 145 countries today, Christian women are observing the World Day of Prayer. The observance began last evening in the Fiji Islands, and as the earth turns, will swing around the globe to close on Lawrence Island off the coast of Alaska. Nobody knows how many persons will be assembled today in churches, thatched-roofed chapels, mud-walled structures, under the open sky to pray together, or how many others will be praying in their own homes or places of business—but we do know that it will be a mighty company. Some will be praying who have spent years in concentration camps, some who even now are in hunger, cold, and want; some will be praying in lands that lie under the shadow of dictatorship or of war; some will be praying from beds of sickness; others will be praying in health, comfort, and relative security. In this praying company there will be black, brown, yellow, and white-skinned Christians, and the prayers will be uttered in the more-than-a-thousand languages and dialects into which the Bible has been translated. All will unite with a common mind in thinking upon the theme chosen for today's observance, "Take courage. The Lord is thy keeper." And all will be praying to the one God who is the Father of us all, and "who made of one blood all nations of men for to dwell on all the face of the earth."

What then might happen from this day of prayer together if we entered into it with enough seriousness? Clearly our prejudices would melt away, and with a gentle and quiet spirit we could be led to see those of races and groups other than our own—to see the Germans, the Japanese, the Russians—all as children of God and brothers of ourselves. Instead of talking *against* any of these groups we should be praying *for* them, and when we pray for anybody it is hard to keep hating or fearing them.

If this should happen to enough people—even to a determined and earnest minority—the peace of the world would be enormously advanced. War is not inevitable, and if hysteria and suspicion can be kept down and good will and understanding built up, it can be averted. Praying Christians, whether men or women, have had placed in their hands by God resources for reconciliation which are more powerful than atomic bombs. One of the most vivid pictures in the Bible is that in which Jesus, weeping over the folly and strife of Jerusalem, says, "If thou hadst known in this day, even thou, the things which belong unto peace." Jesus has taught us the things which belong unto peace, and by the steadfast effort born of prayer and a gentle and quiet spirit, these things can be made to work.

But what if war, depression or public disaster come, as in our private lives suffering is bound to be our lot? Even so, God will not be defeated, and our spirits need not be. The Lord is our keeper. Earthly calamity can rob us of much, but not of what is imperishable. It is in the resources of God to give strength, and courage, and beauty to the inner life that our true treasure lies. This we must guard in sacred trust. If we would have "faith in our time," we must make every day a day of prayer for ourselves and for our brothers and sisters around the world, and we must do what we can to help God answer our prayers. So shall we find our best jewel, not in the things that the world praises, but as this third chapter of First Peter puts it, in "the hidden person of the heart with the imperishable jewel of a gentle and quiet spirit, which in God's sight is very precious."

II. CONTEMPORARY WOMEN PREACHERS

Introduction

Edwina Hunter

In this second section of the book we listen to the voices of fifteen women preachers in the present to catch something of the theological and homiletical visions that inform their work. It is our belief that the presence of women preachers in pulpits and preaching classes around the country is contributing to a new movement in preaching—perhaps even to what may well be called a revival in preaching.

Recent Historical Signposts

What has happened in recent years that has made it possible for the voices of women preachers to be heard in new ways? Why have their visions begun to matter? Certainly, there are a number of events that are now a part of the history of the Church.

One of the most significant signposts for mainline congregations was the 1974 ordination of eleven women as Episcopal priests. On July 29, 1974, at the Church of the Advocate in Philadelphia, Pennsylvania, these eleven and the bishops who dared to ordain them took action that can now be seen to have changed the course of church history. Carter Heyward, one of the contributors to this volume, was among the "Philadelphia Eleven" as was the Reverend Jeannette Piccard, who was seventy-nine years of age when she was ordained. She died on May 17, 1981, but lives in the memory of all those who continue to celebrate her courage and share her vision.

Those first eleven were known as "irregularly ordained." However, the Episcopal church ordained the first "official" woman priest in 1977. How many more years would the Church have waited had not the Philadelphia Eleven taken the step they did? There are now more than five hundred women priests and, just this past year, one who was present for the ordination of those original eleven, the Reverend Barbara Harris, was elected the first woman bishop of the Episcopal church.

Congregationalists (United Church of Christ), Disciples (Christian Church), and American Baptists have ordained women for almost one hundred years; however, real progress in full acceptance of women in parish ministry has come only recently. There are still those in all these denominations who object to the presence of women in the pulpit.

Presbyterians and Methodists approved the ordination of women in roughly the same time period. As was indicated in the introduction to the first part of the book, northern Presbyterians ordained the first woman in 1956, and southern Presbyterians in 1964. The number of women students in Presbyterian-affiliated seminaries has grown tremendously in the last fifteen years. The Methodist Episcopal church granted full ordination standing to women in 1956. By 1970, these privileges were also offered to women in the Lutheran Church in America and the American Lutheran Church.

Southern Baptists ordained a woman in 1964, but have taken a noticeable step backward in recent years. Due to what has been described as a "fundamentalist takeover," the majority of delegates present at the Southern Baptist Convention in June, 1984, voted a resolution against the ordination of women. Moderates from among Southern Baptists are opposed to this resolution and some women continue to be ordained, even called by individual churches as pastors. This is legal in that denomination because of the basic Baptist concept of the autonomy of the local church.

Roman Catholic women are preaching and speaking publicly, in spite of papal edicts against this. In most cases, they cannot refer to their activities as "preaching"; however, that is exactly what they are doing and most effectively. They and their sisters from other denominations are continuing their commitment to the gospel as they interpret it: a gospel of true liberation for all persons.

Unfortunately, the reality pointed out in the opening introduction of this book—that women experience difficulty in being fully accepted in the pulpits of most churches—is still widespread. Many report a relatively easy first parish single pastor appointment; however, it is unusual for a woman minister to be called to second or third senior or single pastor appointments. Percentages from a number of mainline denominations indicate that ordained women fill 30 to 40 percent of denominational posts and less than 10 percent of parish pastor positions. Many ordained women choose to return to graduate school and pursue doctoral degrees in biblical studies, theology, Christian ethics, pastoral theology, or homiletics. It is hoped that their increased presence and visibility on theological faculties will help open more doors for women in parish ministry in the future.

Women in Preaching Classes

The very presence of an increasing number of women on theological school campuses and in preaching classrooms is making a difference in how the act of preaching is perceived and the study of preaching is approached. While this claim cannot be substantiated by quantitative study, it is nevertheless considered an accurate observation by many who are engaged in teaching in seminaries around the country.

In the summer of 1984, on a grant from the Association of Theological Schools, I interviewed thirteen professors at ten selected seminaries. One of the questions asked had to do with the overall quality of women's preaching, that is, what kind of grades they were making in preaching. The second had to do with whether or not the professors observed any gender differences in preaching. Over and over the answer was given that women were making the highest percentage of "A" grades in preaching and, at Fuller Theological Seminary, a woman had received the top award in preaching and a grant to continue her study of preaching abroad.

Little consistency was found regarding assessment of gender differences; however, it was significant that fewer gender differences were noted by a professor in a school where there were no women faculty members, and women students were still imitating male role models. In addition, few gender differences were noted in schools where there were women faculty members and where women students had been present for over ten years in sufficient numbers to make an impact on each other and on the seminary community at large.

Generally, professors of preaching at such institutions agreed that when women first entered Master of Divinity programs in greater numbers, they tended to imitate the same male role models as did their male counterparts. After they had become more comfortable in the theological school environment, however, they began to explore their own gifts for preaching and to discover what Carol Gilligan has called their "different voice."[1]

Once women student preachers began to find their own voices and to risk more creative forms of preaching, their own hermeneutics, and their own way of telling stories, it appears that men students became freer to take similar risks. The result has been that, at those seminaries where there is an almost equal ratio of men and women students, there seem to be few marked gender differences as such because each woman and each man feels released to search for their own best form in light of particular Scripture passages and his or her own theological and hermeneutical stance.[2] In other words, it appears that fewer persons of either gender are seriously attempting to imitate older, more established, or well-known preachers.

The pedagogical assumptions and approaches in preaching classes are also undergoing changes. A number of factors may contribute to this, for example, more second- and third-career students, and the emerging theologies of liberation; however, it seems almost certain that the increasing presence of women students is also having an impact. Women are far more comfortable in settings where community, collaboration, and relationship are emphasized rather than competition. And preaching classes are moving toward what some have begun to call the "ecclesiology of the preaching class" with an emphasis on seeing the class as a microcosm of the church and a place where persons support and help each other in sermon preparation.[3]

Women students are drawn to preaching and liturgy as a discipline of study. Both at the Graduate Theological Union in Berkeley and at Princeton Theological Seminary, women graduate students are pursuing the Ph.D. in this field. There are now several women teaching preaching in theological schools and one, Joan Delaplane, has served as the first woman president of the Academy of Homiletics—the professional academy for those who teach preaching in theological schools. In addition, several women have published books on preaching.

The hypothesis, then, is that with women impacting what actually takes place in preaching classes, approaches to preaching in the parish will gradually change. Some evidence can already be seen that this is happening. Many women are much more comfortable preaching at floor level rather than from the pulpit "power position." Women enjoy sharing the process of sermon preparation and often invite members of their congregation or other clergy to a time of exchanging exegesis, ideas, and imaginative responses to a text. Certainly, most women are not at all comfortable with a competitive model of preaching evaluation and, from the classroom to the parish, are encouraging a model that allows for greater sharing and support among clergy colleagues and from groups of laypersons in the churches where they preach.

Contemporary Women Preachers

The women preachers whose sermons appear in this section were not chosen because of their outstanding ability in the pulpit, although some are certainly outstanding preachers. They were not chosen to illustrate a feminist mode of preaching, although some preach almost exclusively from a feminist perspective. They were not chosen to demonstrate characteristics of preaching that many or even most women hold in common, although some of these will be highlighted.

These preachers and their sermons were chosen to illustrate the variety of voices that are being raised during this period in homiletical history. These are women preachers from many different denominations and many different ethnic backgrounds. They are pastors, college teachers, seminary teachers, theological school administrators, and denominational administrators. They come from all parts of the country and even from other parts of the world. Some are more comfortable with conventional theological perspectives and others embrace radically feminist perspectives. The age range among them is considerable. Some preach in what is considered a more traditional, rationalistic mode while others assume a more overtly creative stance. And, on different occasions, each one may choose a different approach to preparation and to the sermon itself.

Among these contributors are a number of "firsts": Leontine Kelly, the first woman bishop in the United Methodist Church; Joan Delaplane, the first woman president of the Academy of Homiletics; Barbara Brown Zikmund, the first woman president of the Association of Theological Schools; Christine Smith, the first woman teacher of preaching on the regular faculty at Princeton; Toinette Eugene, Black woman Roman Catholic, first woman provost of Colgate Rochester Divinity School/Bexley Hall/Crozer (primarily American Baptist and Episcopal); Carter Heyward, one of the Philadelphia Eleven, the first women priests ordained ("irregularly") in the Episcopal church.

The sermons themselves have been preached in many different settings: the local parish, large conventions, preaching convocations, special occasion celebrations in churches, a liturgy conference, a Bible college chapel, and in a television studio. The settings are crucial to the ways in which these women prepare to preach and the content, language, and form of the sermons they ultimately choose to preach.

How Women Preach

We asked each contemporary woman preacher to write an essay that included the following: personal autobiography, particularly as she sees, on reflection, that some of her own story has informed the sermon; the context in which the sermon was preached; and theological and/or homiletical concerns, particularly as reflected in the published sermon. The value of asking these questions has been pointed out by students in preaching classes who are asked to read and evaluate sermons as they analyze them in response to class assignments. Answers to such questions help us understand more about how these particular women go about the preaching task.

One of the first things that becomes evident is that all women do not preach alike. They are, in reality, finding their own individual voices. There are, however, similarities in how they go about preparing to preach. Many women preachers in this section have spoken of wanting to "talk over" the sermon ahead of time with others either imaginatively or in person. Rita Nakashima Brock speaks of sharing her sermon ideas with her roommates, Margaret Ann Cowden tells how she prefers to consult with other conference speakers, Joan Delaplane tells of inviting eight others to pray over the text with her and join her in conversation, Kim Mammedaty reflects on how the text can come to life for her people, and Nancy Hastings Sehested leads Bible studies on texts from which she will preach.

Almost all continue to recognize the importance of adequate scholarly exegesis as a part of sermon preparation. Certainly, as one reads the essay by Elizabeth Achtemeier, this is evident. Many find considerable excitement in discovering what biblical scholars have to say about particular texts. A good example of this is found in the sermon and essay by Jana Childers.

At the same time, some women consistently approach both the biblical text and commentaries with what is known as "hermeneutical suspicion." Too many of the biblical texts are seen as overtly patriarchal. We read with the eyes of those who are inclined to ask what is left out of the text and why, where the women are, and how they are treated. This comes across particularly well in the essays and sermons of Christine Smith, Carter Heyward, Joan Delaplane, Nancy Hastings Sehested, and Rita Nakashima Brock.

The Reverend Myrna Tuttle, who is presently working toward her Doctor of Ministry at Pacific School of Religion, made this observation in a recent paper: "Even though there are more women preaching than ever before, even though some of us are being taught by women, even though our sermons are collected and circulated in book form, a feminist perspective on preaching is not a common occurrence."[4] The sermons in this collection would seem to corroborate Tuttle's observation. However, it is possible we need to examine the question of what elements constitute a feminist perspective.

Feminist writers seem generally agreed on certain principles. A concern for justice is primary. This goes back a long way in women's struggle for equality, not only for themselves but for all oppressed persons. Sarah Grimke, an early leader in the women's rights movement, once said:

If in calling us thus publicly to advocate the cause of the downtrodden slave, God has unexpectedly placed us in the forefront of the battle which is to be waged against the rights and responsibilities of woman, it would ill become us to shrink from such a contest.[5]

Other elements that constitute a feminist perspective are these: (1) the use of gender-inclusive or mutual language for humans and for God; (2) the modification of theological, especially Christological assumptions; (3) the use of a feminist or liberation hermeneutic for interpretation of the biblical text; (4) the manner in which imagery is used, particularly images of

God (according to Toinette Eugene, "feminist theology isn't simply a matter of moving the images from 'masculine to feminine' or of women doing theology for the benefit of women, but rather that we're talking about a whole new way of thinking, a fresh way of living and breathing");[6] (5) the evidence of a relational or communal approach to authority; (6) the use of personal story—either as told within the sermon or as drawn on to help the preacher "own" the text and, therefore, give a greater sense of ethos to the message. This is emphasized by the Mudflower Collective when they write, "Human stories are rich with lived experience, laden with passion and struggle for meaning. Our own God-stories are filled with theological implications that might be developed at length."[7]

For the most part, these perspectives are embraced by white Anglo-Saxon women and men feminists; however, as is evidenced by some of the sermons in this volume, not all white women preachers identify themselves as feminists. In addition, these perspectives may be modified by women of color to one degree or another. Afro-American, Asian American, or Latin American women may be even more vocal than white feminists in their call for justice. See the sermons in this volume by Leontine Kelly, Daisy Machado, and Rita Nakashima Brock. Some women of color are not nearly so concerned about gender-inclusive language as are white feminists. At the same time, Afro-American women, tapping into their cultural heritage, often have exceptional skill in the use of imagery and metaphor, and are particularly adept at drawing on their own personal story and their heritage in developing sermons. An excellent example of the creative use of this dimension of the personal is Ella Mitchell's sermon "The Stumbling Enemy."

Christine Smith has explored the metaphor of weaving to illustrate how women (and men) preach, making use of feminist theology and methodology. She cites women's use of story and the manner in which they weave their concern for justice out of the stuff of their own lives. She says:

Justice and human wholeness are embodied in our proclamations both in content and style. The spirit of our creator moves us to make deeper and broader connections with all creation. Preaching must help us make these connections. It must empower us to sustain the work and intentionality which those webs of connection demand, and strengthen us to develop increasing clarity about the systems, forces, and structures in our world that must be dismantled if we are to weave the new. Preaching as an act of weaving demands that preachers be prophetic in their confrontations, hopeful in their voices of vision.[8]

Smith has made an excellent case for the metaphor of weaving in feminist preaching. It appears, however, that most women may well lay a claim to the metaphor whether they identify themselves as feminists or not. A reading of the sermons and essays in this book illustrates the degree to which all these women have spun sermons out of the very stuff of their own lives and experiences to connect them with the lives and experiences of those among whom they preach. Their own experience of injustice connects them with the Sarah Grimkes of the early women's rights movement in their concern for justice for all people. Women preachers take very seriously the context, the occasion, and the pastoral needs of the people with whom they are preaching. One of the clearer examples of this can be traced through the accompanying essay of Kim Mammedaty as she writes about the people of her parish in Hobart, Oklahoma. Also, examine the essay by Nancy Hastings Sehested and read her sermon "Let Pharaoh Go." The same awareness of and attention to context is evidenced in every sermon in this volume.

With the exception of only three or four of the contributors, justice is an expressed theological and homiletical concern. Even though justice may not be the explicit theme, it is almost always implicit whatever the stated theme. Notice, for example, in Margaret Cowden's convention sermon and essay how she consciously struggles with the prophetic and pastoral role and how to communicate both perspectives. In the same vein, LaTaunya Bynum, preaching in a local church as a guest denominational leader, lifts up justice concerns but focuses on the theme for the occasion. Or, look carefully at the sermon by Toinette Eugene in which her concern for ethical and justice mandates is evident, but where she is also attempting to lead her listeners in a Black Roman Catholic parish to remember, celebrate, and renew their own commitment to the ideals of leaders who had gone before.

The sermon and essay by Barbara Brown Zikmund, who is a strong and committed feminist, illustrate yet another dimension of this. She knew her home congregation well and her primary sermon purpose was to invite them to be more tolerant of those of other religious faiths even to the point of willingness to engage in dialogue. She draws heavily on her own personal experiences but the overall form of the sermon is more logical and instructive and not primarily feminist or justice-oriented. Therefore, it seems apparent that awareness of context, occasion, and listeners may modify how and whether feminist and justice concerns are presented either implicitly or explicitly.

Summary Remarks

Perhaps the clearest statement we can make, then, is that this is a presentation of how fifteen different women preached one sermon each. Each preacher almost surely prepares and preaches differently given different contexts and occasions.

These sermons may be analyzed by a student for the presence or absence of feminist theology or methodology; however, such in-depth analysis is not the purpose of this volume. The purpose, first, is to illustrate the fact that women are indeed finding their own different voices for preaching and, second, to let readers know something of how these particular women preachers are going about the task of preaching and something of the theological and homiletical visions that inform them on their way.

8. What's Left Behind?

Elizabeth Achtemeier

"What's Left Behind?" was written for an ecumenical service of the Stuart Circle Parish in Richmond, Virginia. Five different denominations make up the parish. The occasion was the celebration of Ascension Day, on a Thursday evening.

This sermon attempts to review the sacred history with which the congregation has identified and lived through during the course of the church year, bringing them to the climax in the life of Christ on Ascension Day, and then asking about the significance for us of Christ's departure, in the flesh, from us.

Text: Luke 24:44–53; Acts 1:1–11

And so we reach the end of the story on this Ascension Day. Jesus takes leave of his disciples and ascends into heaven. We have come a long way since we began this church year, back there in December at the beginning of Advent. We heard Mary sing her Magnificat. We followed the shepherds and the wise men to Bethlehem's stable. We listened while an aged Simeon blessed the child, and while John the Baptist breathed out his fire. We saw Jesus' ministry begin, that day he stood up in Nazareth's synagogue and read those words, "The Spirit of the Lord is upon me, because he has anointed me to preach good news to the poor." We climbed the Mount of Transfiguration with Peter, and we waved our palm branches to hail the entrance of our Savior into Jerusalem. We sat at table in an upper room with the twelve, and we wept with shame when the cock crowed on Good Friday morn. But we too walked a road to Emmaus and learned that the crucified One was risen. We heard his question, "Do you love me, Peter? Enough to feed my sheep?" And we answered the question, "Lord, you know that we love you." And now, here we are at the end of the trail; our Lord has taken leave of us. He came into our lives as the infinite love of God, bent down to find all us lost children. But now he returns to the Father whence he came, and we have reached the end of his earthly story.

And I suppose the question that must be answered on an Ascension Day is, Just what is it now that Jesus leaves behind? According to the account in the first chapter of Acts, there's not much left, at least not much that amounts to anything—a little group of eleven men, left standing on the Mount of Olives outside the holy city, gazing up into a sky that suddenly has become empty: four fishermen, two tax collectors who once collaborated with the Roman occupation, a former zealot terrorist, and four others we know little about—really rather an ordinary bunch, a ragtag group of eleven followers of Jesus.

Oh, of course there were others. Luke, the author of Acts, tells us later on that the eleven regularly met together in prayer with Jesus' mother and his four brothers, and that all told, Christians in Jerusalem numbered about 120 people.

But 120 ordinary people are all that Jesus leaves behind as he returns to be with his Father—120 quite simple souls, occasionally forming a prayer group. It seems something of a come down from that angel choir we heard in the beginning, that sang "Glory to God in the highest. Peace on earth, good will towards men." Surely 120 people are a disappointing result of gold and frankincense and myrrh. And in a way, we can't help wondering if they are worth all that Jesus went through—the whip, the nails, the crown of thorns, the three days in the dark of death. One hundred and twenty ordinary people hardly seem worth all the suffering and dying.

What has Jesus left behind? Well, how many are we here tonight? Do we make up 120 people also met together for prayer? Certainly we're just as ordinary as that group was in Jerusalem: housewives, businessmen, secretaries, and clerks, maybe a sprinkling of professional people. And in Stuart Circle parish, we are all there are to show right now for Jesus' twenty-eight or thirty years. A little group left behind is the outcome of his life. And one can't help asking if we too are worth all his passion. We do not seem to be much to show for all he had to go through.

To be sure, we do things differently now because Jesus has been among us. Luke tells us that ragtag bunch in Jerusalem formed a little community. They quickly elected another person to fill Judas Iscariot's empty place among the twelve who led them. And then they went every day to the temple together and broke bread in their homes at a common table. They even shared all their material possessions and sold their things to support one another's need.

And we do things differently now because Jesus has been among us. We share a cup together and break a common loaf and remember things that Jesus said and did. We meet once a week, sometimes more often, and sing and pray and listen to words from the Bible. And what a strange ritual that is that draws us all together. But I wonder, is it worth all the suffering our Lord had to go through?

What's left behind, friends, now that Jesus has taken his leave of us? And is the result worth that life of his, and his death and resurrection? Has the story ended now, or is there more to tell of, than just this little ordinary group of people gathered together here on a Thursday evening?

Well, for one thing, there is a strange and awesome power at work among us and in our midst. According to our Scripture lesson, Jesus told that little group in Jerusalem to stay in the city until they were clothed with his power from on high. They were very ordinary people, you see, and they could not do much on their own. But that power did indeed descend on them from the Lord, like the rush of a mighty wind. They had been given a promise: "I will not leave you desolate. I will be with you; I will come to you in the Holy Spirit." And Jesus did come, and he has come to us also in the Holy Spirit in our baptisms. He has poured out his power upon us also. And because of that, you and I are not so ordinary anymore.

For example, we now have the power to forgive those who have wronged us. Do you remember how Jesus forgave his executioners when they reared his cross up against the sky, when they played that crap game for possession of his robe and circled round his dying form in mockery? "If you are the King of the Jews," they railed at him, "then save yourself and come down!" But his answer was that prayer gasped out in compassion: "Father, forgive them for they know not what they do." And that power—that power of Christ in the Holy Spirit—has now been poured out on every one of us, and we have been given his ability now to forgive one another.

The English preacher, John Huxtable, told a story once about his pastorate: "One of the hardest things I ever had to do," he wrote, "was to persuade a young wife to forgive her husband. It was asking a tremendous lot. He was in the navy. After a long and dangerous voyage, his ship put into port; and when he and the lads got ashore, they had at least one too many; and then, when he scarcely knew what he was doing, he went off with one of the women who haunts the ports. He wasn't that sort of boy at all; but still it happened, and his wife heard about it. You can imagine how she felt. She came to me to say she was going to divorce him. I tried to persuade her to forgive him; and I told her that would be the one thing that would bring him back to being the sort of man he had always been. If she didn't forgive him, he would probably just go all to pieces. As I tried to persuade her, I knew I was asking more than most people would do; and I was afraid she was feeling too bitter even to try. After a bit, I called at their home to see how things were going. He answered the door, and his face told me that she had done the big thing; and her forgiveness had done what I knew it would do. It had given him a new beginning. I don't think anything else on earth could have done it; but that did."

Christ has poured out on us the power to forgive like that. And because he has given us the ability to forgive as he forgave, maybe we are not so ordinary anymore.

Or do you remember the love of Jesus? How full of it is the Gospel of Luke! Some of it is put in the form of those familiar parables all of you know: the Good Samaritan taking time to bind up the wounds of a battered and helpless traveler; the Prodigal Son met by a father running down the road to greet him; the lost sheep for whom the shepherd leaves the ninety-nine and goes out and searches. But there are Jesus' actions in the gospel story, too: that woman bent over and crippled for eighteen years, and Jesus defying the ruler of the synagogue to heal her on the sabbath day and to release her from her bondage; those little children received and touched by the Master, when the disciples would have shooed them off; the dinner eaten, despite all criticism, at despised little Zacchaeus' house; the unimportant and meek little widow dropping her mite into the temple offering and having it forever acclaimed by her Lord as an example for faith. Yes, we do remember the love of Jesus.

And that is the love poured out now in our midst by Christ in his Spirit, and it keeps us from ever being ordinary again. That love has fed the poor in every city in our modern times. It has built hospitals and schools and homes for the aged. It sent Schweitzer to reverence life in the midst of Africa's jungles, and it prompted a Father Damien to bind up the bleeding stumps on the arms of lepers. And yes, it works in every kind deed and every comfort in sorrow you show a neighbor. And because that love has been lent us by our Lord, maybe we are not so ordinary anymore.

Indeed, maybe it is that love that really makes us human. The anthropologist Dr. Richard Leakey tells us that it is not our brains that first separated us in the course of evolution from the other animals. No, "what truly separated them from the relatives, the chimps and baboons," wrote Leakey, "was not their intelligence but their generosity. Sharing, not hunting or gathering as such is what made us human. We are human because our ancestors learned to share their food and their skills in an honored network of obligation." We were made in the image of God, you see, restored to us in the love of Christ. And because that love is poured out on us now, we are not ordinary creatures.

But of course we must not forget the last battle, either—the battle against death. Do you remember that story too—how Mary Magdalene, and Joanna, and Mary the mother of James, and the other women went to the tomb to anoint Jesus' body, and how they found two men in dazzling apparel instead, and heard the joyful words, "Why do you seek the living among the dead? He is not here, he is risen"? That power—that power over death, the might to defy it, to be raised victorious from it—that power has been poured out on this little company assembled here tonight. And because that is true we surely can never be ordinary again.

> The heir of heaven, henceforth I fear not death;
> In Christ I live! In Christ I draw the breath
> Of the true life! . . .
> Is that a deathbed where a Christian lies?
> Yes, but not his—'Tis Death itself there dies.*

---

* S. T. Coleridge, "On His Baptismal Birthday," lines 7–14. *Masterpieces of Religious Verse*, ed. James Dalton Morrison. New York: Harper & Brothers, 1948.

The Spirit of the risen Christ has been poured out on you and me. Death has lost its sting for us, the grave its victory. And that fact makes us very extraordinary creatures in the universe.

Besides all that, for a final mention, we have an unquenchable hope. It is not as if our Lord has ascended once and for all. Our Scripture lesson tells us he is coming again to bring in his kingdom on earth. He talked about it, according to Acts, with his disciples before he left them there in Jerusalem. The Kingdom is coming, when God will finally rule over all his earth. Evil will be put down once and for all. The injustice we know out there on the streets and in the marketplaces of Richmond, the pain we suffer, the anxieties we feel, the fears we carry inside of us, the turmoil within our hearts and on the battlefields of our world—those will all be done away, and God will be everything to all. You and I know how it is all going to turn out! As Christians, we have been shown God's plan for his universe. And surely people who know the goal of human history are not so ordinary anymore!

John Cheever, the writer who won a Pulitzer Prize for his short stories, was scoffed once by a friend for his regular habit of churchgoing. Replied Cheever, "I don't think it unreasonable to go to church once a week to thank God for the coming glory and wonder of life." The coming glory and wonder of life! Cheever knows, Cheever the Christian knows, how it is all going to turn out. God will establish his kingdom on earth, even as it is in heaven. In Jesus Christ, we have been given that unshakable knowledge, and surely people who live with that certainty and who can therefore radiate it to all those about them, are no longer ordinary people, in any sense of the term.

So let us return, then, to our original question. Just what was it that Jesus left behind him when he ascended into heaven? Was it just a little ragtag group of several dozen ordinary people? Oh no. He left behind him his church, empowered by his Holy Spirit to forgive and to love one another, as he had forgiven and loved even them; recipients of his resurrected life, against which the forces of death and sin have lost all their power; sustained by the certain hope that Christ comes again to bring his good kingdom on earth.

Christ left behind him you and me—this little group gathered here this evening. He lived and suffered and died and rose again that we may be his extraordinary people. We are his witnesses; we are his proof; we are the evidence of his work. By being here and by being his church, we show forth his life and death and the power of his resurrection. And because that is true, good followers of Christ, we can never be content—O let us never ever be content—to be ordinary people again! Amen.

THE PREACHER REFLECTS

There is a marvelous grace that guides and follows the life of any ordinary Christian. I was born in 1926 into a Christian home and raised in the First Presbyterian Church of Bartlesville, Oklahoma. Three influences led me into the Christian ministry: one, a Christian mother, who nurtured me in the basics of the Christian faith, who prayed for me every day, and who literally lived and moved and had her being in her Lord; second, a succession of fine Christian preachers and teachers, who guided my youthful growth in the church; and third and perhaps surprisingly, a marvelous church choir, with a superb lead soprano named Myrtle Ringo, who could sing the greatest music of the Christian Church as it was meant to be sung. God, quite truthfully, sang his call to me through Bach and Handel and Brahms.

I took undergraduate work at Stanford University, and then, advised by the university chaplain, went on to Union Theological Seminary in New York, to study under Niebuhr, Muilenburg, Tillich, Scherer, Buttrick, Richardson, Bennett, Van Deusen, and Terrien. I married Paul J. Achtemeier in 1952, and the two of us were granted fellowships to study abroad under Von Rad, Barth, Eichrodt, and Cullmann. I received my Ph.D. in Old Testament and the literature of religion from

Columbia University in 1959, the same year in which our second child was born.

Determining always to seek first a job for my husband, the doors nevertheless have never been closed to me. I have taught Old Testament or homiletics at Union in New York, and at Lancaster, Pittsburgh, Gettysburg, and Duke theological seminaries. At the present time, I am visiting professor of Bible and homiletics at Union Theological Seminary in Richmond, Virginia, where my husband is professor of New Testament. Our son Mark is a Presbyterian minister, our daughter Marie is an attorney.

With such a background, I think that faithfulness in my ministry surely must have the primary form of gratitude—gratitude for the Christian faith and hope handed on to me, gratitude for the path on which I have constantly been led, gratitude for the training to pass on that which I have received from such a cloud of faithful witnesses. When one is given the gift of the Christian faith, one receives, very literally, abundant life. There is no way in which one can keep that all for oneself.

I have some firm convictions about the responsibilities of my call, however. First, I have always been convinced that part of my call has been to be a wife to my husband and a mother to my children. As my wise teacher, James Muilenburg, once told me, "Betty, if you don't do a good job with your children, you haven't done anything." No call to preach or teach has ever allowed me to forget that I am also equally called to care for those entrusted to me in my family.

Theological and Homiletical Concerns

I was educated theologically at a time when there were giants on the earth—Barth and Reinhold Niebuhr at the head. We are now in a time when there are no giants, when theology is all in transition and confusion, and when the church sometimes seems adrift, blown about by all the winds of transitory fads and ideologies. In the midst of it all, one sure foundation remains—the word of God in Jesus Christ, mediated to us through the Holy Scriptures. "The word of God will stand forever." In that word I find my sure guide in the midst of every confusion, the one true authority for all faith and practice. Therefore, faithfulness in my ministry must always be based upon it. Indeed, everything I preach and teach must try to live up to the glory of it.

And everything I do and say stands under the judgment of it. Though I have often failed that word in Jesus Christ, he has never failed me. And like Jacob of old, I am quite convinced that he will never leave me, until he has done all that of which he has spoken to me.

9. The Courage to Choose/ The Commitment to Being Chosen

Rita Nakashima Brock

"The Courage to Choose/The Commitment to Being Chosen" was preached in October of 1987. When I walked into St. Luke's United Church of Christ in Jeffersonville, Indiana, I looked immediately into about two hundred friendly faces in a warm, intimate sanctuary. I had volunteered to be a visiting preacher during the biennial General Assembly of the Christian Church (Disciples of Christ) taking place across the river in Louisville. I was a guest preacher, but I felt immediately at home. About twenty of the faces were those of friends who were attending our national assembly. These friends from all over the country had come to hear me preach, some for the first time. I began this sermon by introducing my friends to the host congregation. At one point halfway through, as I mentioned Japanese Americans interned during World War II, I spoke directly to two friends present who had been in the camps. The atmosphere of friendly intimacy in that sanctuary made such gestures of including people in my sermon easy.

Text: Ruth 1:1–19; Matthew 22:15–22; I Thess. 1:1–10 (Inclusive Language Lectionary)

There was once an ordinary woman who lived in a small town near Modesto, California. She was not famous, powerful, or influential. I do not recall her name. I was told this true story about her. She was the kind of person we'd call a good neighbor. She was friendly, liked by her neighbors, and was good to her family. When the United States entered the Second World War, she supported our government—until California Supreme Court Justice Earl Warren signed an order requiring all U.S. citizens of Japanese ancestry to be interned in relocation camps.

Many of this woman's neighbors were Japanese Americans. She knew them and loved them as her friends. She went to Sacramento and lobbied the legislators. She wrote to the president to try to stop the camps and the government confiscation of Japanese property. She could not move the powerful and famous. She was a lone nobody. Few others protested. The Disciples of Christ was the only official church body to protest the order to intern Japanese American citizens. So this lone woman did what she could. She bought all the Japanese farms and homes in her town for a dollar each and watched her friends be taken away. When the camps were closed, when the Japanese who survived had no homes left, when their lands were stolen by our government, this woman's neighbors were lucky. She gave her friends and neighbors back their homes and land so that they might live.

There is a group of other ordinary women. A dozen years ago they lived in Argentina under one of the most brutal military dictatorships in Latin America. That government was taking its citizens and torturing and killing them. Many died without a trace. The dead were called the "Disappeared Ones."

Anyone who was critical of the government, who chose to work with the nation's poor and suffering masses, or who was associated with someone in those categories was in danger. These ordinary women watched their daughters, sons, husbands, sisters, brothers, and grandchildren disappear without a trace. Finally a small handful decided that their pain and loss were too great to keep silent. They went to government offices demanding word of their loved ones. Nothing. They were seen as crazy, stupid old women. So they organized other women. For a long time, no one would give them a place to meet. Finally, a local Catholic church gave them space—the only church or synagogue to risk reprisals from the government. No one else would help them.

When many attempts to get information about their lost families failed, they decided to take to the streets. Wearing white kerchiefs in mourning and pictures of the lost ones in their families around their necks, on a Thursday afternoon at five o'clock, fifteen women walked a silent hour vigil around the Plaza de Mayo in front of the government buildings. No official protests against the government were allowed. These women risked becoming Disappeared Ones themselves. One later did disappear. But on this day the government left these crazy old women alone. Within months their numbers had swelled into hundreds until on some Thursdays there were several thousand. By then they were too visible for the government simply to kill them. These crazy women of Argentina felt they had nothing to lose once those they loved were taken. They began to be called the Mothers of the Plaza de Mayo, the conscience of Argentina. The international press had noticed their weekly vigil. Their active lobbying for information began to call international attention to the massive slaughter, the enormous human rights violations in Argentina.

Women in France, New Zealand, and Sweden began to put pressure on their own govenments to censure Argentina. A delegation from Holland came to march with them around the plaza. The women sent them money to buy a house. The money helped the mothers to provide clothes and food for the children of the Disappeared. It also helped them to continue lobbying the government.

Many believe the Mothers of the Plaza de Mayo were an important, visible witness that helped bring the downfall of that government and the return of democracy to Argentina. Their witness also spawned an international movement. There are mothers in Lebanon, Peru, El Salvador, Guatemala, and Chile where killings are taking place. Especially poignant is the massacre still taking place in Chile, for the Pinochet government is one the CIA helped put in place, and it is supported by the U.S. government.

Ruth and Naomi were ordinary women. The two had nothing except each other and a bleak future together. When Ruth is offered an opportunity by Naomi to look after her own self-interest, she refuses in one of the most impassioned statements of commitment in the entire biblical text:

Where you go, I will go, and where you stay, I will stay. Your people shall be my people and your God my God. Where you die, I will die, and there I will be buried. I swear a solemn oath before the Sovereign One, your God: nothing but death shall divide us.

Two ordinary women who love each other. In the midst of pain and loss they cling to each other and take their lives into their own hands. These two poor and crazy women set out for Bethlehem.

Ruth's action comes with no guarantees. She has no promises from God about what she will find in this strange and dangerous land to which she is traveling. And she has no animals, land, or money by which to live. Her society of male-dominance makes her its victim. She has only her wits and her love for Naomi, a bitter widow who has nothing to offer her except her continued kindness. Ruth's act is the most radical commitment of love to another anyone can make. And we all know what her leap of faith into the unknown future produced—hope for all Israel. Her child became the grandparent of David, and David became a messianic symbol of a just and peaceful society.

Out of her love, Ruth acts, out of the passion of her heart. Her courage, just as the courage of the woman in California and the Mothers of the Plaza de Mayo, comes from her heart, from her capacity to love in the face of fear and hopelessness. The courage to choose, to be a redemptive, liberating, whole-making presence in a world gone mad with greed, fear, and violence—that courage rests in our passions, our ability to love, not authority and power, but each other and those who suffer under structures that hurt them. For we must go where our hearts lead us. We must choose our people and our God on the basis of what we love, not on what we fear.

Where you go, I will go, and where you stay, I will stay. Your people shall be my people and your God my God. Where you die, I will die, and there I will be buried. I swear a solemn oath before the Sovereign One, your God: nothing but death shall divide us.

Matthew in his story about Jesus entreats us to make choices, too. We are asked to choose where our hearts belong. Render unto Caesar what belongs to Caesar and to God what is God's. But what does render to Caesar mean? Matthew is not telling this story about Jesus to tell us something simple about money and paying taxes. Caesar's image is on the coin because he symbolizes for the community of Jesus the most destructive power on earth. Just as the governments of South Africa and Chile, Rome killed people who stood in its way. They even killed Jesus and others such as he.

The courage to choose between Caesar and God means to render to Caesar nothing, for our whole heart belongs to the God of love.

Caesar is the power that seeks to control, dominate, and kill—power that enslaves human beings under legal, social, and economic systems, grinding down the poor, hungry, outcast, and weak. And those committed to the God of love have no business paying allegiance to power such as that.

When his enemies seek to entrap him in an overt statement of treason, the choice that Jesus gives us is clear. Jesus is smart enough not to get trapped, and he has enough faith in his community to know that they knew the right answer. Give to Caesar what is his due and to God what is due to God. If your heart truly belongs to God, you will know where to pay your dues. And the early Christians who were noted for their refusal to serve in the Roman army and for their refusal to worship Caesar knew to whom they paid dues.

Where you go, I will go, and where you stay, I will stay. Your people shall be my people and your God my God. Where you die, I will die, and there I will be buried. I swear a solemn oath before the Sovereign One, your God: nothing but death shall divide us.

But the courage to choose what is right is not all there is to the courage to choose. For we are also chosen. Long before we come to a conscious awareness of our existence, we are loved by God, and the spirit of that gracious, wholehearted love is what Paul celebrates as the life-giving power of the Thessalonian church, a church living under difficulty but thriving nonetheless. "You received the word in much affliction, with joy and inspired by the Holy Spirit."

We are loved—chosen—before we know it, and we are born hungry to know it. Not all of us are born into loving families. About 1.7 million children annually between the ages of three and seventeen are abused. Much of our population, one in five children, is born into poverty. One in every four daughters and one in every ten sons is molested. The visible incarnation of God's love in our lives may not be obvious. But the commitment to being chosen, of knowing somehow that we deserve to be loved because God already loves us empowers us to search for those people who will love us back, love us into wholeness and well-being and who will work with us to defeat Caesar in all his oppressive forms.

At its best this is what the church means, the place where we can find the love of God when our families or societies hurt us. As visible manifestations of the loving grace of God, our commitment to being chosen involves our responsibility and commitment to be God's loving hearts and hands in the world. This loving activity of the church, this incarnate love empowers us to love passionately and to protest against all that hurts others. Knowing we are chosen, that we are loved by others, and being committed to that chosenness is what gives us the courage to choose to live by our hearts and not by our fears.

Our ability to love and be loved, passionately, not sentimentally or nicely but with our whole being, empowers us to stand against Caesar and render to God what is due. For in living by passionate commitment we come to know that we have nothing to lose when we love with a whole heart, and much to gain.

But, you say, our government is not Caesar. We are citizens in a democracy. And I tell you our government is just as capable of hurting people as any other government. My friends Ayako Grace Kim, Phil Shigekuni, Maureen and James Osuga, and the late David Kagiwada are evidence of the hurt our government can cause because they were in those internment camps where people died. They are a host of witnesses. Today the Hopi and Navaho are being relocated unwillingly from their homelands, and the relocation is killing many of them. Our government helped create the government still slaughtering its citizens in Chile. And right now in 1987, on this very day, our government is trying to stop the Central American Peace Plan by insisting on more money to the contras while, since 1981, it has cut or eliminated every school lunch program in this country, even as poverty has increased 25 percent.

We may not be able to change the governments of Nicaragua, Russia, China, Iran, or Cuba. They are not ours. But we are our government, and it will not change if we do not. We are the city, county, state, and federal governments. Our courage to choose to love those who suffer, rather than loving power and authority, comes from our commitment to being chosen. All of us, in our own context and our own way, are called to pay our dues where they belong in ways we can find, and the ways are countless.

We have to see what is going on. Our lifestyle and our government's covert activities make it hard to see. All traces of our government's weaknesses are erased from what we are told it has done. I went all the way up to my senior year in high school without knowing about the Japanese internment camps. In fact, I don't know when I would have found out if I hadn't discovered the information by accident while doing a research paper on the Supreme Court. Because I am Japanese myself, I was struck by the name of a court decision called Korematsu vs. the U.S. Government. I couldn't imagine why a Japanese American might be suing the U.S. Government. So I read the case and, at seventeen years of age, found out what our government is capable of.

I have driven many times up the Owens Valley in California. It leads to my favorite place to ski in the Sierra Mountains. I had traveled that road many times before I found out that Manzinar is on that road. It's the site of one of the internment camps, but the marker is so small you have to know it is there to see it.

But seeing what is happening, really opening our eyes to the suffering around us can seem overwhelming. And how can we, ordinary individuals that we are, do anything? The God of love asks us to see, but the God of love also gives us courage. In seeing, we must never doubt, as Margaret Mead says, "that a small group of committed, concerned people can change the world. Indeed, it is all that ever has."

At the 1987 General Assembly of the Christian Church (Disciples of Christ), I had the privilege of hearing an ordinary woman named Barbara Wiedner speak. She is the mother of ten and the grandmother of twenty-three. Barbara is a friendly looking woman with sparkling eyes that blaze enthusiasm when she speaks. She was a keynoter for the Disciples Peace Fellowship Pre-Assembly Conference, "Make the Connections: Justice, Wholeness, and Peace." Until 1981, she claims to have been so busy with her personal life that she barely even knew who was president. But one day she suddenly saw. She saw that if she didn't get involved in stopping the nuclear arms race, her wonderful grandchildren would never reach adulthood.

Barbara called a group of a dozen or so other grandmothers she knew to a meeting in her living room and asked them to help her do something. They founded Grandmothers for Peace, which now has hundreds of international members including Raisa Gorbachev who is a grandmother. Barbara now travels all over the world to talk about peace. And she is wonderful to hear. She begins by saying she has no credentials. She is not a minister, professor, or expert, only a grandma who cares about peace for her children and her grandchildren. She has grandmas all over the world working for peace. Oh, in case some of you are feeling a little left out, Grandmothers for Peace has a large and active men's auxiliary. So, here we have another ordinary woman who has chosen to act in love with the courage of her convictions. Just as Barbara, the Mothers, Ruth, and the anonymous woman in California, we are called to the courage to choose because we have been chosen by the love of God.

Where you go, I will go, and where you stay, I will stay. Your people shall be my people and your God my God. Where you die, I will die, and there I will be buried. I swear a solemn oath before the Sovereign One, your God: nothing but death shall divide us.

THE PREACHER REFLECTS

I am a feminist theologian and director of the Women's Studies Program at Stephen's College. My Ph.D. is in philosophy of religion and theology from the Claremont Graduate School. I have published a book, *Journeys By Heart: A Christology of Erotic Power* (Crossroads Press, 1988). Feminist theology and Christian thought are the definitive intellectual shaping forces in my life, and both feminism and Christianity are my communities. The two are often in tension. A third, no less important aspect of my life, creates a third ambiguity as I struggle to be a feminist and Christian. I am a woman of color.

I come from Fukuoka, Japan, and am biracial. Japan is my country of origin. Japanese is my mother tongue. My birth father is Puerto Rican. My mother, Ayako Nakashima, married a white American soldier, Roy Brock, and we emigrated from Okinawa when I was six. At that point, Protestant Christianity became my religious upbringing. My being raised in east Kansas in the virtual absence of Japanese American peers was an upbringing similar to many Nissei and Sansei (first- and second-generation U.S.-born Japanese Americans) who were relocated after the internment camps. We have grown up learning to adapt to an almost entirely white church and environment.

During my seventh-grade year in 1963, our family lived in rural Mississippi with my stepfather's family, and I experienced firsthand Southern Baptist revivals and preaching. Ever since, I have been allergic to the guilt and fear such ideologies evoke, and to speakers who exploit people's fear or hate to manipulate their listeners to change. I think I felt such tactics as a violation of the gentleness and compassion I experienced in my Buddhist family in Japan. My Japanese grandfather had been a lay Pure Land Buddhist preacher. That year in Mississippi I especially missed the atmosphere of my original Asian home. I had no access to an Asian American community until my family, after three years in Germany, moved to California when I was sixteen.

Theological and Homiletical Concerns

I am far too Americanized now to feel totally at home in Japan, but certain theological issues, reflected in this sermon, affirm my Asian roots, in addition to my feminist convictions and Christian commitments.

Four aspects of my life lead me, whenever possible, to choose stories and images for sermons that are about ordinary people and things, about the textures of life lived by the majority of the world's people, especially those oppressed and excluded by the powerful and wealthy: (1) In Japanese aesthetics, the common and the ordinary, the irregular and imperfect, such as bamboo, wind-swept trees, water, stones, rough-hewn pottery—even humble peasants—reveal spiritual truths. (2) In feminist reversals of patriarchal power, we look not to the famous and powerful for truth, but to the marginal, to the invisible and unheroic courage we find in the lives of ordinary women and men. (3)

In the United States, the struggle for justice by people of color has emerged from the grassroots, not from the powerful. (4) The power of the gospel is revealed all through the New Testament in stories and parables about broken, imperfect, ordinary people, including an unwed pregnant teenager whose son became a carpenter.

I believe the gospel is a call to embrace the largest world possible— to include people and to invite them to be active participants in a community of God that liberates, heals, and empowers those it touches. When I preach, I try to be inclusive in several ways. I use the past traditions, the texts, theology, and stories to open a way to an authentic encounter with the divine spirit. I try to evoke positive commitments and empowering transformations that emerge from the human heart, from the root of our connective capacity to love life passionately. Whenever possible, I speak of people I know, of experiences I have had. Nothing is more important than personal witness. When I can, I use myself as a bad example, as many good preachers I have observed do. I believe making myself vulnerable is empowering to hearers and demystifies the authority of the pulpit. Finally, I include multiethnic and multicultural elements in virtually all of my sermons. I have lived my life on three continents and six states and find it hard not to think of myself as a global citizen.

I seek in preaching to create encounters within the community of God, with our tradition and past, with the canon, with transformative images, with stories, with our deepest selves, and with the power of the divine spirit. For me preaching is a powerful creative art that weaves the reality of our lives into a vision of what we love and what we hope will come to pass. I consider carefully my use of language, images and metaphors, and style and form of delivery.

10. The Church: The Family of God

LaTaunya M. Bynum

"The Church: The Family of God" was delivered in Sunday morning worship in a Black congregation of approximately 150 people. On the Sunday the sermon was preached, the Fifth Christian Church of Cleveland, Ohio, was celebrating its twenty-fourth anniversary. Its anniversary theme was "The Church . . . The Family of God."

Text: II Corinthians 6:14–7:1

Several years ago a historian named Barbara Tuchman wrote a book about life in fourteenth-century Europe called *A Distant Mirror.* She gave that title to her book because the fourteenth century with its many wars, killings, diseases, shifting political allegiances, and people who sought security in weapons and kingdoms instead of God, reminded her of the twentieth century.

Just as Tuchman held up a mirror to the fourteenth century and found the late twentieth century looking back at her, so we have that same experience when we hold up the books of the Bible to our lives as a church and to us as individuals. The Bible functions as a mirror because it lets us see ourselves reflected with our bad and good features absolutely exposed. It's all there. The grace and the degradation. Our sin and the source of our salvation. It also helps us reflect on a pattern that is as old as Adam and Eve and continues to this day. God *blesses* us, we *prosper*, we *forget* who gave us the gift of prosperity (health, employment, a loving spouse or partner, deep friendship, children, wealth). We fall into *sinfulness* often with people who care very little about us, but who, nevertheless, try to make us feel good. Remember Jesus, Satan, and the wilderness temptations—which of *us* wouldn't go for *food* (stone to bread), *power* (I'll give you authority over the whole world), and *fame* (throw yourself down, the angels will bear you up), everyone will know who you are. After the sinfulness comes the *judgment* of God, then *contrition, forgiveness* by God, *restoration,* and *blessing,* then the whole cycle starts again.

Instead of weapons such as catapults and swords, we fight with nuclear weapons and high-powered ships and airplanes and horrible, unspeakable terror. No longer do we worry about the bubonic plague, which was the so-called black plague in its day; now we worry about AIDS. And with both the plague and AIDS, unreasonable fear is as much a factor in the diseases' destructive spread as the viruses that bring such misery. We can name other issues that are not so much new to us as they are *newly devastating* because they create fear and tear down systems and supports that are important to us. The Church is the family of God, and we have some family business to attend to.

We know that teenage pregnancy is at an *alarmingly high rate.* And we know that young men and young women are becoming parents when they haven't yet learned how to be teenagers, and some are even younger. Babies suffer and whole families suffer because we don't always have the tools to help us cope in good ways. (Neglect, abuse, and abandonment are the signs that we cope in bad ways.) That's family business.

We know that throughout every neighborhood—rich and poor; Black/white/Hispanic/Asian; urban and rural—drug and alcohol abuse cause havoc and insecurity in our families and in our lives and all of us are affected. That's family business.

We know that in every neighborhood there are people who have not learned that the way to be in a family relationship is to hold and not hit. So husbands and wives beat up each other, parents beat up on children, some adult children beat up on their elderly parents, and some folks in the street beat up on strangers just because they feel like it. That's family business.

We know that the leading cause of death for Black men between the ages of fifteen and thirty-five is murder and that the murderer is likely to be another Black male in the same age group. That's family business.

We know that even as the *Black middle class rises, a Black underclass sinks deeper into poverty* and hopelessness. That's family business.

We know all this and more, so it ought to mean something when we say that we are the Church, we are part of the family of God. We need to see each other in order to most fully be the kind of people God wants us to be. We are family.

Paul's letters to Corinth give us some clues about family life. Corinth was a city at a crossroad. People from everywhere came to Corinth. It was the big city for its part of the world. It had Christians, Jews, and various cult worshipers in its midst. They struggled with issues that aren't solved yet:

- How to care for the poor and needy among us (homeless, ill, the poor ones without resources).

- How to best use spiritual gifts (Are they to be celebrated, or do they become the test by which I determine if you are as good a Christian as I or vice versa?).

- How to understand the role of women in the Church (Should women be silent and if we were, what would the

Church be; or should women's gifts be freely offered and accepted?).

* Where to get authority for leadership—from age? From maleness, or femaleness? From being the loudest? Or from having demonstrated care for congregation and community?

* What the proper behavior is during the Lord's Supper (Some were getting filled fully by food and drunk off the wine; while others were going hungry at what was to be a feast for all.).

* How to understand family and marriage.

The problem of the Church in a city like Corinth or a city like this is the same as that of churches everywhere. Whatever is going on outside inevitably gets brought inside. At Corinth there were three major problems that needed attention.

The first was that Christians with different ideas about the gospel were entering the Church and causing upheaval. People had come into the community who sounded good, who were very impressive and outwardly pious, but inwardly were very egotistical. How many of us know of congregations split down the middle when one group of Christians begins to say to another,"Unless you sing, pray, worship, dress, think, or act as I do, you are not really Christian." It is a *presumptuous, sinful* attitude and it is dangerous to make determinations that only God is able to make.

The second problem in Corinth was that the Church was facing persecution. The Romans demanded every citizen declare "Caesar is Lord." The Christians had another proclamation, "Jesus is Lord," and that was not a safe proclamation to make. The price men and women paid for saying Jesus is Lord was imprisonment, torture, and sometimes death. I have heard, and believe it to be true, that we are not neutral in a crisis. We become our best selves or our worst selves when we are in trouble. We *either* rise to the occasion *or* sink under the weight of trouble and despair. Some of both was happening in Corinth. The faith got stronger for some; others abandoned Christ to save their lives.

A third problem for the Corinthians as they tried to carry on their day to day functions as church was that some members of the Church were still practicing aspects of their pre-Christian faith. They had not completely given up pre-Christian behavior. They held on to some of their pagan practices. They were still *in* and *of* the world. They were spiritually mismated; they were unequally yoked.

To help them understand the issue of being mismated—not just in intimate relationships but in business partnerships and in any life situation that jeopardizes one's own walk with God— Paul asks a series of questions using several words that help us understand that our Christian journey is not ours alone but it is as a family with God as father and mother that we journey with our brothers and sisters. In order for the journey not to be *unusually* difficult (we will face normal difficulty—that is part of what it means to be human), we need to be as balanced on this family stroll as possible or we will fall and fail. Everyone has to carry their part of the weight, or we will not move with balance.

So Paul asks: What PARTNERSHIP has *righteousness* with *iniquity?* What FELLOWSHIP has *light* with *darkness?* What AC-CORD has *Christ* with *Belial?* What has a believer in COMMON with an unbeliever? What AGREEMENT has the temple of *God* with *idols?*

Partnership, fellowship, accord, common, and agreement are all words that speak to right, just, and fair relationships. None of the pairs Paul mentions are in right relationship to each other.

Righteousness is the opposite of sin and iniquity.

Light and dark are as different as they can be from each other; one *hides,* the other *exposes. Believers* have a *foundation* on which to stand while *unbelievers grab* hold to every *handle* they can.

The temple of God is *hallowed*, sacred ground—God is there. We cannot *easily say who lives in statues made for idols*.

God calls us to be in right relation with each other, to be healthy family members and to remember that the covenant given to Moses and renewed in Jesus is still alive and well and in effect for us. We are the temple of the living God, we are God's dwelling place, in our minds, our hearts, and our souls, using every ounce of our strength, we are the household of God.

"I will live in them and move among them." The Word became flesh and dwelt among us. (Raymond Brown, at Union Theological Seminary in New York, says that most properly and accurately the phrase reads, "The word pitched a tent and dwelt among us.") God through Jesus Christ has cast the divine lot with us. Wherever we are, God is there, moving among us. And there is more. If we ascend to heaven or make our bed in hell, God is there. "I will be their God, and they shall be my people." We have this divinely yoked balanced relationship with God; for what possible reason would we want to be unevenly yoked with anyone?

We are called again to be clean and balanced rather than unclean (polluted by things that separate us from God—clean up the hate, bigotry, idolatry, self-serving, gossip, back biting sabotage—we don't need it) and to be welcomed into the family as the righteous daughters and sons of a righteous, loving, forgiving, welcoming God.

What does it mean to be the Church, the family of God? It means that we have come into this place the way we enter our own families—we are either *born into it*, we *marry into it*, or we *are adopted into it*. We are now in the family, heirs to all that God has to bestow on us, eligible for every blessing.

To be the Church, the family of God, is to be part of a divine household. We are part of a *living community* that through *study*, *worship*, and *prayer*, through *opportunities for care and nurture* strengthens itself day by day.

To be the Church, the family of God, is to know who else is in the house and to know what the house looks like and that the household has value as a dwelling place of God.

So our part of the family is worthy whether it has two parents or one or if it is an extended family with brothers, sisters, grandparents, aunts, uncles, and cousins. It is part of our experience as Black Americans, that what kept the church family and the blood family strong was the network of support that having relatives close by has provided.

The family has worth (as does the Church) when it is made up of single persons who unite with loving bonds to the Church and declare themselves a family.

The household and the church house is valuable whether it is large or small, whether the space is cramped or has lots of room. It has value as a faith community whether it is in a good neighborhood or a not-so-good neighborhood—suburb, city, rural area. A family is there.

Whether the household of God has every luxurious convenience we can imagine—plenty of classroom space, a well-lit comfortable sanctuary, office space, and workrooms or whether it is enough to meet, teach, worship, and work in an urban storefront—the household of God has value. A family is there.

What we are called to remember is that we are the dwelling place of God. The Church is God's household, not ours. We are servants in it, we are the deacons, the table servers in the divine household, keeping things in order till the Master returns.

It is not our prerogative to decide who is in and who is out of the family. God has already decided. All of us were at one time out of the family of faith—we were adopted into it by our baptism. The Letter to the Ephesians has it right, all of us who used to be far away have been brought near in the blood of Christ . . . no longer are we mere travelers, now we are fellow citizens with the saints, and members of the household of God . . . Christ Jesus himself being the cornerstone . . . in whom we are a dwelling place of God in the spirit.

We are already in the family; we are already part of the extended family of God that moves from this place to other churches in Cleveland, throughout Ohio, the United States, Canada, Latin America, Africa, Asia, Europe. The whole earth is God's, we are God's sons and daughters and brothers and sisters in this house.

"Since we have these promises, beloved, let us cleanse ourselves from every defilement of our body and spirit and make holiness perfect in the fear of God."

We are family together, and each of us is called to take honest inventory of our contribution to the household. What is our role? Do we contribute to the household's health or sickness? Do we contribute to its upkeep or add to its shoddiness? Do we keep the family active or do we encourage it in a do-nothing passivity? Do we help build it up or do we help tear it down?

Are we a healthy loving family that knows God is here and do we support, challenge (but not harm), rejoice, mourn, together?

The Church as the household of God is called to be safe and loving, to say a loving yes to our souls when others say a harsh harmful no. It is the temple of God. How is your's doing? Is it all right? Is it what God wants it to be? Is it a family of a collection of casual acquaintances? Are you balanced in your walk?

You all know the answers.

The grace and peace of God cause you to be strong and keep you strong.

THE PREACHER REFLECTS

I am a native of Los Angeles, California, and have been an active member of the United Christian Church in Los Angeles and in the

Pacific Southwest Region. I was ordained by the Disciples' Pacific Southwest Region in September, 1980. After serving as interim pastor of First Christian Church in Lynwood, California, I completed two units of clinical pastoral education at St. Elizabeth's Hospital in Washington, D.C.

Except for the Clinical Pastoral Education (C.P.E.) work in Washington, D.C., all of my academic education was in California. My bachelor's degree in religion is from Chapman College in Orange, my Master of Divinity from the School of Theology at Claremont, and the Doctor of Ministry is also from the School of Theology at Claremont.

In 1982, I moved to Indianapolis to begin my work as director of Women in Ministry on the staff of the Division of Homeland Ministries, Department of Ministry, in the Christian Church (Disciples of Christ). In this position I am responsible for the nurture, advocacy, and support of Disciple clergywomen and ministerial candidates. I maintain the network of clergywomen and help all manifestations of the Christian Church (Disciples of Christ) to take advantage of the opportunity to develop and maintain healthy, supportive attitudes about the gifts and abilities of ordained women and women seminarians.

My responsibilities also include administration of continuing education and career assessment scholarship funds for all ordained ministers in the Christian Church (Disciples of Christ).

Theological and Homiletical Concerns

My ongoing theological concern has to do with the ways we interpret the gospel as a living entity for all people. I believe that when Jesus says he has come that we may "have life and life abundant," and when Paul writes to the Galatians that "For freedom Christ has set us free, do not submit again to a life of slavery," Christians are being called to a life of liberation for themselves and for others. We, therefore, have an obligation to preach good news to the spiritual and economic poor. We have a word of judgment, redemption, and grace for oppressors and for those whom they oppress. And, we are called to be honest enough to recognize times when we benefit from oppression and to call upon God to be present with us as we seek freedom from oppressive situations. I believe in the presence of the Holy Spirit and I believe and try to incorporate into my sermons the promise of God, where God says, "I will be with you."

11. One Stone Upon Another

Jana Childers

"One Stone Upon Another" has never been preached on a Palm Sunday. It was written for a "Liturgy as Art" conference held at San Francisco Theological Seminary as part of the school's continuing education program. The event focused on several liturgical festival days and featured "sample" worship services for each day studied. Palm Sunday was one such day.

Hence, "One Stone Upon Another" was preached on a Wednesday afternoon in January at San Francisco Theological Seminary's Stewart Chapel to clergy, lay readers, and professional church musicians who were experimenting with various seasonal liturgies. They were an unusual "audience." Unusually innovative, unusually knowledgeable, and unusually able to transform a rainy weekday clinical experience into a meaningful Palm Sunday worship service.

Text: Habakkuk 2:9–11; Luke 19:28–44

T here are no palm branches in Luke's Palm Sunday. Did you notice? No crowd-lined curb. No Hosanna's. No palm branches. Just the disciples, a few stray Pharisees, a colt. Oh, and some by-standing stones.

It's a little disappointing. You can hardly help thinking that Luke could have done a little better by us in terms of pageantry. After all, following for the most part Mark's account, as he was—it looks like it would have been *easier* to leave in that line about the palms—and forget all that mumbo-jumbo about stones crying out. (Who knows what that's all about anyway?)

A palm-less Palm Sunday is kind of a sad thought. Just imagine if Luke's version had been the only account to survive— without palms. What would we do for the children's sermon? If it were up to Luke, we'd be left struggling to explain to those wiggling five-year-olds what Jesus meant when he said stones might be able to talk! On second thought, I can think of years when I'd have been more willing to struggle with the question of talking rocks than with the reality of dueling-palms. . . .

Anyway, in the (somewhat unlikely) event that you are looking around this year for a children's sermon that accurately reflects the lectionary text—for instance, sans palms—I have a suggestion for you. It's a story born of another religious tradition. And it's a little unorthodox. Actually, I myself wouldn't face the Palm Sunday crowd of five-year-olds armed only with this story. But you can decide for yourself if it would be worth the risks. I tell it to you because I think it says something of what Luke is trying to say.

Sheldon Kopp tells the tale from *The Gospel of Sri RamaKrishna* of an Indian holy man who taught his disciples to see God in all things. One day while the disciples were deep in the forest gathering wood for a sacrificial fire, they heard a voice shouting, "Out of the way! Out of the way! A mad elephant is coming!" The disciples scattered as the crashing and shouting became louder, running through the woods for their lives. Through the trees and over bushes they dove . . . all except one young disciple who, kneeling dead in the path of the charging beast, began to sing its praises.

The Mahout who was driving the elephant yelled frantically to the young disciple. However the boy remained in place. Closer and closer the animal bore down on the singing disciple, trunk swinging, saliva flying, pounding up clouds of road-dust. The Mahout yelled. The boy sang on. Finally the elephant reached the kneeling boy, seized him with its trunk, tossed him aside and charged on. Soon thereafter the boy was carried home, limp and unconscious—but still breathing—by the other disciples. Some time later, when the injured young man opened his eyes his teacher asked why he had not run from the elephant. The boy protested, "You taught us that *all creatures* are manifestations of God. Why should I have made way for that elephant? I am God. The elephant is God. Should God be afraid of God?"

The holy man smiled, "Yes, my child, it is true that you are God and that the elephant is also God. But why did you not listen when God's voice called out from the Mahout telling you to run away?"

Sri RamaKrishna's whimsical story is trying to tell us something, I think, something about the importance of recognizing God when God comes to us. It strikes me that that is more or less what Luke is up to—that it was to make that very point that Luke left out the palm-crazy crowd and put in the talking stones.

The arrival of Jesus in Jerusalem is not portrayed by Luke the way it was by the other evangelists. For Luke it is neither an eschatological event (as it is for Mark who has the crowds blessing the coming Kingdom) or a political one (suggested in the other three accounts by the nationalistic overtones of the palm-waving). It is instead a picture of the God of peace calling on humankind. Luke wants to emphasize that, in Jesus, God had "come calling" (as Charles Talbert says) on Jerusalem—bringing the peace announced by the herald angels seventeen chapters earlier. In Jesus, God came calling, on Jerusalem. And, Luke wants it to be clear, *it's a visit that requires recognition* and response.

Now, at first blush, this makes Luke's good news not *sound* so *good* to me! I mean it's not as if many of us aren't already anxious—*overanxious*—about recognizing God's comings. In fact it's probably not stretching it too much to say that many of us here are downright preoccupied with the past, present, (and some of us even with) *future* comings of God. Especially preoccupied, I think, with those daily comings—the seasonal ones— the "hour-of-need" comings.

Fred Craddock says it's this kind of yearning that makes people come to church week after week. Preachers, he says, shouldn't think that people's attendance is a tribute to their preaching. People come to church every week because of their hunger. "Maybe there will be a word from the Lord today," they say.

I like, too, Annie Dillard's observation about just how anxious human beings are to discern God's comings. She reminds us that we human beings are the ones who, in the days of our wandering in the wilderness, begged God through Moses not to speak to us from the mountain anymore, because, we said, "The thunderings and the lightnings and the noise of the trumpet and the mountain smoking" scared us witless. *And*, she says, "What have we been doing all these centuries [since] but trying to call God back to the mountain, or, failing that, raise a peep out of anything that isn't us? What is the difference between a cathedral and a physics lab? Are not they both saying: Hello? We spy on whales and on interstellar radio objects; we starve ourselves and pray 'til we're blue."

A lot of us are looking, watching, praying, invoking—peering out—Hello? Hello out there?

How is it then that we who try so hard often end up standing around on the corner of Main and Vine in downtown Jerusalem while the disciples are stripping off their jackets and Jesus is weeping? How is it that we who are so well-intentioned, who have searched the nooks and interstellar radio objects of the universe for God, wind up mingling our mutterings with the Pharisees? Can it be—*how* can it be—that *we* are ever among those who "do not know what makes for peace," who have "shut their eyes" to God's coming and who "do not know the timing of their visitation"—among those who inspire our Lord's tears?

What is it that gets in the way of our knowing and seeing? What is it that (to switch to the lighter metaphor)—what is it that leaves us bruised, crumpled, and covered with the elephant spit on the embankment?

Where do we go wrong in recognizing God? What gets in our way? Let's look at Jesus' cryptic remarks about stones for a clue. The first one, "If these [disciples] fall silent, the very stones will cry out" has always gone by me as a way of saying that songs of praise could be raised from stone if God wanted to do that. Sort of like Jesus saying elsewhere that God could raise up sons and daughters to Abraham "out of these stones here." So, if *people* refuse to recognize God's coming, embrace the things that make for peace, and render appropriate praise, then inorganic *nature* will render it! "So there!" I always suspected Jesus really wanted to say.

But a wider look at biblical usage points us in a different direction. For the Bible often speaks of the *accusing cry* of lifeless objects . . . objects that turn, as it were, against their human owners, invoking divine retribution. The blood of murdered Abel cries out, for example, in Genesis 4:10. So does the plundered field of Job 31 and the withheld reward of the workers in James 5.

AND—SO DO THE STONES—THE STONES—AS INVOLUNTARY WITNESSES OF VIOLENCE AND IDOLATRY—cry out in Habakkuk 2.

Woe to the one who gets evil gain for his or her house—
For the stone will cry out from the wall—
Woe to the one who says to a wooden (idol): Awake—
To a dumb stone: Arise!

So, construed along these lines Jesus' cryptic remark can be read to imply that if the disciples withheld their acclaim the stones would cry out, not in praise, *but in accusation!* And the second reference to stones—Jesus prophesying the destruction of Jerusalem, saying, "One stone will not be left upon another"—strengthens this imagery, adding another possible layer of meaning. Jesus is saying (between the lines and for those who have ears to hear) to us as well as to Jerusalem, that the stones—those very stones you raise in violence and idolatry—those stones that you so carefully pile up in self-tribute—those stones in which you trust—by which you oppress and exploit laborers—with which you wall each other out—those very stones you pile up—one upon another—in the building of your "city"—in the foolhardy pursuit of "peace"-apart-from-God—those stones . . . will in the end cry out against you *and* share your destruction.

You are idolatrous. Seeking God's voice in creations of your own hands; your dumb-stone idols will cry out against you.

You are violent. Building memorials to yourself at others' expense; violence will explode your monuments.

"One stone will not be left upon another," Jesus says.

Could it be that our lives are full of such stones? Even the lives (especially the lives) of those of us who listen diligently for God's footfall?

Stones . . . to fill some gap within, to wall someone out, to memorialize our own egos? Stones so carefully piled up—one stone upon another?

Witnesses to our ability to use others . . . one stone upon another.

Monuments to our efforts to bring God to finger-tip control . . . one stone upon another.

Could it be that these very stones, the ones we so carefully pile up thinking to build peace in our lives, are the very ones that get in the way of our recognizing peace when it rides into our lives on the back of an unbroken colt?

"Would that you knew the things that make for peace," Jesus said, "but now they are hid from your eyes."

How about the names of your stones? What stones do you pile up only to have them hide peace from your eyes?

"Hello? Hello?" we say—peering around our carefully constructed piles.

"Hello? Hello?" we say—pressing our yearning ear to a stone mouth.

Hello?

And the good news according to Luke is that the peaceable King who, trailing shirtless disciples, quietly entered Jerusalem on that palm-less Sunday—was God's answer.

In Jesus Christ, the peace of God came calling. In Jesus Christ, God calls still. Let us make a path through the stones of our lives—for the entry of peace.

THE PREACHER REFLECTS

I could boast of being a native Californian but, actually, I have lived in nine different communities across the United States. In addition to living in quite a number of places with my family, and after graduating from college with a major in speech, I worked as director of public affairs and public relations at a New York radio station.

Then came my increasing interest in and commitment to professional ministry. I completed a Master of Divinity degree at Princeton Theological Seminary and, along the way, served in assistant pastor positions at two churches. In 1982, I was ordained to the Ministry of Word and Sacrament by the United Presbyterian Church U.S.A. From 1982 to 1985, I served as assistant pastor in a Presbyterian church in New Jersey and as instructor in speech at Princeton Theological Seminary.

Through all this time, my primary foci were theater and church. I acted in and directed plays even as I grew in my love for preaching and the sacraments.

In 1986, I was appointed to the faculty of San Francisco Theological Seminary where I now serve as assistant professor of speech communication and homiletics. This has also afforded me the opportunity to pursue the Ph.D. in religion and the arts at the Graduate Theological Union. My emphases in this degree program are preaching and theater. I have recently done a number of presentations of a one-woman show, "Berries Red" by Pat Schneider.

I was not always Presbyterian. In fact, I was born and raised in the Pentecostal church where self-abnegation was the ideal and material success a sign of God's blessing. Stumbling blocks (obstacles in the path of the Christ who would enter our lives) were more apt to be identified as pride, self-will, and lust, rather than greed, xenophobia, and fear. To a certain extent in "One Stone Upon Another," you see a former Fundamentalist (in process) struggling with the nature of "material blessings" and trying not to fall head-long into Pelagianism (we can move those rocks by ourselves!) or self-flagellation (why haven't I cleared this path already?). How to evoke repentance in God's people without leaving the impression that God's grace depends on their feeling bad enough? How to facilitate self-examination yet stop short of encouraging inappropriate self-denial (if I can just get myself out of Christ's way . . . if I can just lose myself . . . turn it all over to Jesus).

Theological and Homiletical Concerns

Surely, it is because of my reaction against that early influence that "One Stone Upon Another" tries to call people to repentance without inflicting inappropriate guilt. Their yearnings are affirmed. The irony of the text is treated as something that comes as a genuine surprise to us; we are let off the hook a little because there is a surprise, a trick, a reversal being played on us. Multiple, open-ended images are offered as suggestions of what the stones might represent in our lives. Finally, a warm, even triumphant, tone is meant at the sermon's end to convey the inevitability and the grace-full-ness of Christ's coming. But then, maybe the sermon, even as its preacher, has a few stones left to move.

I wrestled throughout the sermon development process with the text's ironies. It was a struggle, first, to stay clear myself about what the stones represented, and then to find a graceful way to evoke that recognition in the minds of the hearers. I often envied Professor Marvin Chaney his clarity and eloquence and think that, if I were to preach this sermon again, I would quote and credit him, and do a little explaining about the "large stone tradition" before the last section of the sermon. From Professor Chaney I learned about the "small stone tra-

dition" and the "large stone tradition." The former concerns the significance of Scripture's references to field stones and, the latter, the
significance of Scripture's references to monumental architecture: am-
phitheaters, palaces, water systems, temples and tombs, for example.

Marv's comment, "The large stone tradition is problematic. . . . For
the very concentrations of wealth, power and control that are its pre-
requisites tend to seduce mere mortals into blasphemous attempts to
immortalize themselves in stone" was the pivotal insight in this sermon's development. Connecting Chaney's understanding of the large
stone tradition to Jesus' second comment, concerning Jerusalem's
stones, resulted in the sermon's theme. However, I sacrificed some
specificity about just what those stones represented in my attempt not
to explain away the text's rhetorical punch. In the end, amid the rib-
bons and banner fragments, I felt a little torn myself. Had I made it
obvious enough? Did the people see the connection between what the
text said and what the sermon said? Had I drawn it tight and clear
enough?

Some preachers worry about leaving room for the Holy Spirit to
work. I worry about driving the point, pressing the image, about nailing things down—counting all the time, of course, on the Holy Spirit
to be the one placing the nails. The nailing-down impulse doubtless
has something to do with personal idiosyncracy. But it also has to do
with a desire to be fair to the text. What I worried most about in
working on "One Stone Upon Another" was establishing a clear connection between the sermon's kerygma and the text's. I always worry
about that. The poignant refrain from the preaching of Dr. J. Alfred
Smith, Sr., one of the great contemporary preachers in the Afro-American tradition, plays through my mind over and over when I am com-
posing a sermon. Says Dr. Smith, even as he is "nailing" home a
particularly compelling point, "I wish I knew how to make it plain."

12. Growing Pains: Learning to Relinquish in Order to Receive

Margaret Ann Cowden

The occasion of "Growing Pains: Learning to Relinquish in Order to Receive" was the biennial meeting of the American Baptist Churches in Pittsburgh, Pennsylvania, in June 1987. The theme of this denominational gathering was "Partners in Mission: Alive and Growing." The planners intended for each of the plenary sessions, which drew between three and four thousand participants, to focus on a particular word from the theme. My sermon was to address the issue of growth, and I preached it on the last morning of the four-day event.

Text: Deut. 30:19; Isaiah 43:18–19; Jeremiah 22:13–16; John 12:24 (RSV)

A friend who knew I was working on this message, asked what I was preaching on. I realized that she had not been to many denominational conventions, and instead of giving a single response to her questions, I went into a long-winded explanation of the convention theme—Partners in Mission: Alive and Growing." I explained that beginning with "partners" and ending with "growing," different sessions would try to focus on a particular word. She was silent for a moment, and then said, "gosh, I'd hate to be the person who had to preach on 'in!'" She was relieved to hear that I had a more substantial word.

At first glance the theme "growing" seems simple enough, if not somewhat innocuous for a sermon topic. My mind ran through a collage of images related to growing. Perhaps due to the time of year, my thoughts turned to nature, where growth seems to be a given, unless you happen to be a plant in my apartment. I was reminded of the times I have been accused of running a plant mortuary at home, thereby proving that growth is a more complicated process than first meets the eye.

Then my thoughts turned to how unpredictable and unruly the growing process can be. I once went to the pound, where I found an *adorable* puppy, that looked like she might be part Saint Bernard. She turned out to be a mixed breed, with the emphasis on *mixed*, and what began as an adorable puppy grew into the ugliest dog I have ever *seen*, much less owned!

As I continued to recall these kinds of experiences, before long, growth seemed less easy to approach in this sermon. My musings made it seem unruly, unpredictable, even painful at times. It is hard to spot in a moment, and often goes unnoticed, as I evidenced by a church work party where I pulled up all of the freeway daisies that someone else had carefully planted during the last work party—they looked like weeds to me.

Growth—it's not to be trusted; it happens when you least expect or want it; it can't be neatly controlled; you often don't even recognize it when it happens; and sometimes you get in the way of it, or stunt it by lack of notice or nurture. Perhaps it is not as easy to understand as it seemed at first glance. And we haven't yet looked at how the biblical texts will further complicate matters.

Listen to three passages from Scripture, looking for the messages on growth woven into them:

From Deuteronomy 30:19—"I call heaven and earth to witness against you this day, that I have set before you life and death, blessing and curse; therefore choose life, that you and your descendants may live."

From Isaiah 43:18–19—"Remember not the former things, nor consider the things of old. Behold, I am doing a new thing; now it springs forth, do you not perceive it?"

From John 12:24—"Truly, truly I say to you, unless a grain of wheat falls into the earth and dies, it remains alone; but if it dies, it bears much fruit."

These passages were selected because they point out a paradox in growing that is found throughout the Scriptures. It is the paradox of learning to relinquish in order to receive, a paradox shown in each of these passages, but also woven throughout the story of God's people. Walter Brueggemann, in his book *Hopeful Imagination*, sees the twin aspects of relinquishment and receiving as pivotal to an understanding of the message of the prophets. Let me briefly describe how this enlightens our understanding of the messages of Jeremiah and Isaiah, and then turn to how it might inform our life as American Baptists in the twentieth century.

In the first passage read from Deuteronomy, we are reminded of God's covenant with the Israelites, in which God sets before them life and death, that is, sets before them a way of ordering their life within the community and in the world around them in life-giving ways, as opposed to death-dealing ways.

Centuries later the prophet Jeremiah declares that they have ignored that call to choose life, and have, by their repeated unfaithfulness in fact chosen death. He goes to great lengths to point out to them the ways in which the current reign of injustice has weakened them unto death. Jeremiah 22:13–16 is one example, in which says the Lord:

Woe to him who builds his house by
unrighteousness,
and his upper rooms by injustice;
who makes his neighbor serve him for nothing,
and does not give him his wages;

who says, 'I will build myself a great
house
with spacious upper rooms,'
and cuts out windows for it,
paneling it with cedar,
and painting it with vermillion.

Do you think you are a king
because you compete in cedar?
Did not your father eat and drink
and do justice and righteousness?
Then it was well with him.

He judged the cause of the poor and
needy;
then it was well.
Is not this to know me?

Critical to Brueggemann's understanding of Jeremiah is the prophet's call to Judah to grieve over its impending death: to grieve, even as God grieves, over this people who have forgotten they were formed out of God's love, shaped for God's obedience, and entrusted with God's vision for the future. Only if they relinquish their current view of reality and see, with God's eyes, their need for grieving—only then can they open themselves up to receive the newness God can bring them even in the exile that is about to befall them. But if the grief is silent, the newness cannot come.

Nearly fifty years later, word comes again to the Israelites now in exile, that God is doing a new thing. This time the prophet Isaiah tries once again to open their eyes to the new thing God is doing. Once again, the people of God have difficulty relinquishing their own view of reality in order to live into God's reality for them and for the world.

Over the years their reading of reality has changed. For some, perhaps exile seems not so bad. Some have settled in, accommodated, made themselves at home. Isaiah would have to stir them with a powerful memory of whose people they are in order to move them. Homecoming would mean nothing to a people who have forgotten where home is. Once again, it would require them to relinquish *their* hold on reality to receive the new reality of God's movement in the world.

Two things must be noted in this *very* brief account of a critical period in the history of God's people. First is the need to learn to relinquish in order to receive. The second is what it is that the prophets are calling God's people to relinquish. What they must relinquish is reality as it is defined by the dominant culture. Before the exile it took the shape of trust in military power and political alliances to fend off destruction, when what was destroying them was injustice and corruption from within. After the exile, it took the shape of assimilation into the dominant culture so that the values and dreams of God's people were forgotten. Home itself became that which was familiar and secure, not the home that God intended as a reign of justice, in a community of faith shaped by God's will for shalom.

The voice of the prophets railed against the voice of the empire, whose messages of "might makes right, bigger is better, have it your way" require the voice of prophets even today. If we accept exile as more than a historical, social fact, but rather as a lens through which we view social reality, are we not exiles today, who choose to live by the message of the gospel? Exiles often accept the views of the dominant culture because they have no alternative. Is not our greatest call to ministry in this time, the call to preach alternative ways of seeing reality, ways that defy the values and power structures of the dominant culture? Is not our greatest challenge to create and strengthen alternative communities with the imagination, the courage, and the determination to see and participate in the new thing God is doing among us?

I believe that this call to minister in ways that present to people an alternative reality is exactly what Jesus was doing in his use of parables, which constantly challenged the reality of the dominant culture of *his* day. His teaching continues to challenge: calling his followers to leave the flock in search of the one lost sheep; suggesting that those who came last to work in the vineyard be paid as those who had worked *all* day; calling for those who were without sin to cast the first stone; telling those who would be leaders that they must become the servant of all; she who would be first must be last, he who would be greatest must become the least; and all who would save their lives, must be willing to lose their lives, even as a grain of wheat falls to the ground and dies in order to bear much fruit.

In every word he taught Jesus countered the reality of the Roman empire; but worse, he challenged reality as it was presented by the religious leaders of the people of God—for they, too, had fallen prey to the empire's perception of reality. And the empire's message is communicated with such certainty that the dominant system appears to be normative and beyond criticism, ordained and enduring, beyond question and certainly beyond change—so much so that we cannot remember a time when it was not so, nor imagine a time when it will be different. If we live in a system long enough, learn how to play its games, enjoy enough of its benefits, we come to accept it as a given and it becomes too risky to participate in its transformation.

That, my friends, is what it means to live life as an exile. I have used the word *we* to emphasize that that is a constant temptation to the people of God—to live by the reality of the empire, meaning whatever power dictates the reality of the dominant culture. And if the Scriptures constantly present us with this theme of relinquishing in order to receive, perhaps it is because of the ever-present temptation to live as exiles who have no alternative reality.

In the midst of exile, comes the word of God—"Behold, I do a new thing—now it springs forth—now it grows within you and around you—do you not perceive it?" Perhaps we cannot see it because the lens through which we look is prescribed by the reality of our culture rather than by the vision of our God. And if that is so, what can we do about it? Well, one thing we can do is to search out what growth might mean for us according to these insights from Scripture.

First, in order to grow, we must learn to relinquish in order to receive. Now, as is the case in much of the truth of Scripture, this truth addresses us at many levels. Personally, it calls us to be more open to change, to be more willing to tolerate the insecurity of newness, trusting that God is *in* that newness. A poem by Marilyn Zdenek catches some of our ambivalence about that as she writes:

> It is this that I crave:
> a place to be
> to grow
> season to season
> tomorrow rooted in today
> tendrils reaching through the past
> growing deeper into time
> stretching higher into space
> a world of order
> a sense of place
>
> A woman who fears the tremor
> shouldn't settle on the fault
> or plant herself where soil's been known to shift.
> my life it seems is always set in change
> and growth must come within the midst of this.
>
> With an angry cry protesting—
> then accepting—
> the severing from all that's been,
> with roots in pocket
> I move on,
> again.

Relinquishing old habits and patterns, particularly those we know to be death-dealing as opposed to life-giving, is an inevitable part of choosing a life that is growth-oriented. Now, in a gathering of this size, I will not presume to name what those patterns might be, but I would challenge you to examine your own life to see what new thing God might be doing in *you* that might call you to relinquish older, more familiar patterns.

If as individuals, we learn how to relinquish, it will surely affect our life as community. What would be the effect on your congregation if as a community of faith you relinquished your hold on old patterns, ways of doing things, or leadership styles that are familiar but not always life-giving, or past images of who you are as a congregation and to whom and with whom you minister? What new thing might God be doing in your midst if you only could see the seedlings of growth?

Congregations open to such newness would certainly awaken us as a denomination to the new thing God is doing in our larger life together. As American Baptists we must explore how much our reality is shaped by images of success as the world sees it, growth as the dominant culture measures it. In relinquishing our old vision of reality we would discover that those we once saw as objects of mission are indeed now our partners in mission, and the new thing God is doing among us calls us to new patterns in our leadership and the manner in which we work. I fear that much of what God is doing in our midst goes unrecognized, and growth that is bursting forth within us is perceived as a threat to what we once were, rather than a celebration of who we now *are*. It is unsettling to relinquish that which is familiar in order to receive that which is new, but if we are to choose life in the newness in which God offers it, we must at times let go of the old.

Now, if in order to grow, we first must learn to relinquish in order to receive, then *second, we must learn at times to grieve*. As I understand the prophetic call for the people of God to grieve, it took several forms—sometimes it was a call to grieve over the wrongs they had perpetrated, over their unfaithfulness as a covenant people, over their stubborn refusal to see and live out God's vision for the world and sometimes it was simply a kind of permission to go ahead and admit the pain of letting go. It was an indication that God knew their pain at leaving the familiar and the comfortable. But in either case, God could not begin a process of healing, until the grief was recognized and experienced—only then could newness come.

In the very early stages of shaping my thoughts for this sermon, I had a rather silly experience that drove home some important insights about relinquishing and grieving. I'd like to share it with you. I was at a meeting, and after a rather long day, I returned to my hotel room, feeling good about the day, about the people I was working with, about what we had accomplished, and feeling pretty good about myself. As I entered I saw across the room on a table a little box of Godiva chocolates, delivered by the hotel at someone's request. I love Godiva chocolate and I was struck by what a nice gesture it was for someone to send me candy. So, as I walked across the room I was thinking, "Now who would have done such a thing—what did I do during the day that would merit such a thoughtful response?" And, like a little child surprised by a gift, I began to reflect on all the nice things I had done that day that might have resulted in someone sending me candy. I thought of a report I had made that I thought was pretty good, but that didn't seem to fit. I thought of a breakfast conversation when I had encouraged someone in their work, but that didn't seem so profound. I thought of a colleague who seemed a little down on one of our breaks, and I had tried to cheer him up, but surely *that* wasn't such a big deal. I even thought of friends elsewhere who cared for me, but none of them would have known where to find me.

In short, I slowly walked across the room going through this list of little acts that might merit Godiva chocolates, and just about the time I thought I knew who they were from, I looked at the name on the box, and read "Sam Watson, Room 322." I was in Room 222.

I can't tell you the transformation I underwent. This person who had just gone through a list of all the good deeds she had done throughout the day was tempted *just for a moment* to eat the chocolates anyway. Sam would never know—they were in my room—it wasn't *my* mistake!

Let me hasten to assure you however, justice did prevail. I called the hotel desk, told them of their mistake, and a few minutes later turned over the chocolates to a bellhop who came to retrieve them and deliver them to their rightful owner. And this woman who had entered the room feeling good about herself, who revelled for a few brief moments in what a good person she was, suddenly felt very unappreciated and more than a little embarrassed by her little exercise in self-flattery. I won't go into great detail about how I moped around the rest of the evening, but later, as I pondered the experience, I learned something very important about relinquishing and about grief.

I had to relinquish something that was never mine to begin with, and the result for an evening, was a period of self-pity and a feeling of worthlessness. How interesting that in losing something that was never intended for me in the first place, I came to feel so bad about myself.

What does that mean for us as a people of privilege? What does that mean for us as a *nation* of privilege? What do we learn from this regarding a loss of power and privilege, and what it does to those who must do the relinquishing? What would it mean for us in the United States if we could no longer perceive ourselves as the economic and political center of the world? What would it do to those in leadership in *this* empire?

Or to risk bringing it closer to home, what does the changing face of the American Baptist Churches mean to those who have grown used to positions of power and influence? If we are to become in our leadership what we *are* as a people, it will involve some relinquishing and some grief. The faces of our general board, our regional boards, our pastoral and denominational staffs would change, and many who perceive themselves as *deserving* of a place of power and influence, will find themselves without it.

If the words of the prophets apply to us today, then perhaps we must develop a new sensitivity to the role that grief plays in welcoming the new thing God is doing. Perhaps we must learn to support and love each other through a process of change, trusting that God is in that newness, and will bless us with new hope, new growth, and a new sense of aliveness as a people; trusting that the grief will only last for a time, but that in our relinquishing, we open ourselves to receive the new thing God is doing in us, around us, and through us.

If we are first to move faithfully through a process of relinquishing in order to receive, and second, through a period of grief involved in that, then we must *learn to develop communities with an alternative view of reality.* Often people who are discouraged or without hope are people who see their lives as having no alternatives. Perhaps as a denomination, our greatest gift in ministry would be a revival of preaching that declares to people a *new* reality, a *new* vision of ordering our life together, modeling *new* styles of partnership where people who are different than us are not merely tolerated, but loved and celebrated as true partners in mission and ministry, as persons whose *very differentness* can inform and enrich our life together.

It's a different world in which we live—one in which power and privilege are being restructured. God is doing a new thing—we must not stunt or impede that growth, for *it will surely* come to fruit out of the power of God's vision for the world. Let us be part of it. Let us take leadership in it. Let us thrive on the power of God's newness within us, and nurture the growth that is of God. Let our longing for security and our dread of change be transformed by the power of a God who is forever faithful, who is forever inviting us to choose life—and forever ready to give us life abundant.

THE PREACHER REFLECTS

I began my ministry as a local church pastor. After five years in pastoral ministry in two congregations, I joined the national staff of the American Baptist Churches (ABC). For three years I worked for educational ministries as program associate in the Department of Ministry with Adults. From 1982 through 1985 I was the director of the Women in Ministry Project of the ABC, on the staff of the Ministers and Missionaries Benefit Board. Since 1986 I have been associate executive director of that board.

Theological and Homiletical Concerns

The nine years that I have been a denominational staff person have been years of significant growth and change for the American Baptist Churches. We are a denomination of great theological, racial, and cultural diversity. Nearly 40 percent of our membership is people of color. Over 60 percent of our members are women. At the beginning of this decade, there was little evidence of that diversity in our denominational staff or elected leadership. But as we approach the 1990s, the times, they are a 'changin'.

As I try to be a responsible participant in that change, there are at least two themes that stand out for me. The first has to do with an understanding of what it means to be the people of God. I believe strongly that the people of God are called to be not only a people of privilege, but also a people of responsibility. We are a people of privilege because we are invited to participate as co-creators with God in bringing about God's reign in this world. We are a people of responsibility because we are called to understand and to implement God's vision of justice and partnership in the world. Our use of power, then, must always be tempered by this call to be a responsible people. Anytime power is exercised more in the service of privilege than in the service of responsibility, it is following a vision other than God's. Old Testament scholar Walter Brueggemann eloquently speaks of this "other" vision as reality defined by the dominant culture, or by "the empire," and calls the church to be true to an "alternative reality." His books *The Prophetic Imagination* and *Hopeful Imagination** have greatly enriched my understanding of the church's struggle to be true to God's vision for the world.

I also believe, though, that in calling people to give voice and allegiance to this alternative reality, we must distinguish between those times when we speak a pastoral word, and those times when we speak a prophetic word. Both are necessary if we are to move people to participate in creating a more just world.

At the risk of oversimplifying, I believe that the time and place for a more prophetic word is on those occasions in which we address ourselves to institutions, organizations, and other structures of society that perpetuate the evils of corporate sin. On those occasions, we need to impress upon people the degree to which corporate sin overwhelms the good intentions of individuals and seduces us into compliance in ways that we can scarcely identify for ourselves. We need to call people to accountability for decisions that perpetuate institutional racism, sexism, classism, and other forms of injustice, while seemingly benefiting the organization itself.

At the same time, though, we must realize the insidious nature of corporate sin, and recognize what a painful reality one is faced with when one first recognizes one's compliance with it. We must also take seriously the high cost of changing an institutional or organizational system by challenging its rules and its reward structures. To call for a redistribution of power inevitably means that some who have been led to expect positions of prominence and power must redirect their expectations. Some will experience a loss of power in that redistribution.

It is precisely in those moments of *perceived* loss that we more appropriately speak a pastoral word. Whether the perceived loss is real or imaginary is somewhat beside the point. What is called for is a pastoral response that addresses one's sense of loss, one's sense of disenfranchisement. And who is more able to address that pain than those who have repeatedly experienced disenfranchisement themselves?

---

* Walter Brueggemann, *The Prophetic Imagination.* Philadelphia: Fortress Press, 1978; and Walter Brueggemann, *The Hopeful Imagination.* Philadelphia: Fortress Press, 1986.

What I am suggesting here is not intended to confuse the roles of prophetic and pastoral preaching, nor to oversimplify the occasions in which one preaches in one way or another. Rather, I am suggesting that frequently both voices are needed within the same message. I judged the occasion of this sermon to be one of those times. In addressing a denominational convention in which people would repeatedly be encouraged to celebrate the diversity of who we are as a people, I thought it appropriate to suggest that some could not enter into that celebration without some acknowledgment of grief, if those changes within our corporate life meant changes within their personal aspirations and expectations. I found Brueggemann's perspective on the role of grief in the prophetic voice to be enormously helpful—and appropriately pastoral for this message. I sincerely hoped that the call for some pastoral awareness would in no way be perceived as a weakening of the prophetic call to be the inclusive people we are intended to be.

13. Draw Near

Joan Delaplane

"Draw Near," a sermon from the point-of-view of the Canaanite woman, was preached at the Third Harry Emerson Fosdick Convocation on Preaching and Liturgy on the occasion of Union Theological Seminary's 150th Anniversary, October 6 through 8, 1986, in New York City. The theme of the Convocation addressed the question, "Which Gospel Shall We Preach?"

Each morning the more than twelve hundred convocation participants were given eight options for worship. This sermon and its worship context were offered as one of the eight options for three straight mornings in the Interfaith Center Chapel at 475 Riverside Drive in New York. Approximately two hundred people were in attendance at each service. They were men and women, young and old, students, professors, and pastors, from many different denominations and many different ethnic backgrounds.

Text: Matt. 15:21–28

Here I am, a grandmother now, and, I must say, in some ways I'm amazed that this story about my mother's encounter with this Jesus is still being told. I know that the incident was initially a kind of embarrassment for his disciples, but I guess that it made an impact on more than just my mother and me. But I'm getting ahead of myself.

You would have liked my mother. Those who never knew her—only this story about her—picture her as a real gutsy lady, maybe even "pushy," but they didn't really know her. My mother was much more retiring, almost shy. She shunned the limelight, in fact. But as a single parent, raising a daughter, many a time she had to take initiative that cost her a lot.

Then, when I got sick, well, life got complicated indeed. I remember crying often because children made fun of me. Mother used to hold me, and rock me, and try to explain that they thought suffering was a punishment from the gods for doing wrong. Somehow, though, I knew that my mother never really believed that. I knew that she hurt when I hurt.

I did have to fight feeling bad about myself though; and, most of all, I felt bad that I was such a burden to my mother. We were so poor. The few shekels we did have were quickly used up in medicine, and I wasn't getting any better. Yes, we were poor; but now looking back, I realize more and more how rich I really was in an experience of being loved.

I realize that it was that love that drove her to do what she did that day. It wasn't for herself, or she may have never found the courage; but she ached so for my health and happiness, nothing could hold her back from what she had to do.

Have you ever known that kind of love? The kind of love that enabled you to do something you would never have thought yourself capable of doing? I learned so much from that woman that day.

Just the week before, however, I had overheard my mother telling a neighbor lady about a conversation that she had heard at the marketplace that morning. They were all talking about this Nazarene who was preaching and teaching and healing. Apparently, a blind man had drawn near to him and called out:

"Son of David, have pity on me," and this Jesus cured him. The man could see.

I heard my mother say in a soft voice: "I wish I could bring my little girl to see him, but I'm not sure she's strong enough. And, besides, I just couldn't risk her getting hurt one more time. I know that it's part of their Jewish tradition," she said, "for them to have nothing to do with us 'goyim.' Because we're not Jews, they say that we're pagans and unbelievers."

The neighbor lady chimed in to say that she had heard that this Jesus was in real trouble with some of his own religious leaders because he was attacking some of their other traditions—like touching lepers, not obeying some of the laws and regulations regarding eating, talking with women. He angered them by insisting that the only real impurity was evil in one's heart. "He even said, 'Why do you transgress the command of God for the sake of your tradition?' You can be sure that he is headed for big trouble taking like that," said the neighbor.

"You've got to give the man credit for saying what he believes, however," said my mother. "I admire a person like that. Strange, isn't it, how we from afar seem to be able to appreciate him even more than those who are close to him?"

It was just about a week later then that I took a turn for the worse. I awoke that morning with a lot of pain; then, I had a seizure. I screamed with panic. Mother was beside herself. I tried to hold back because I could see the fear in her eyes. She ran out and got the neighbor lady to stay with me. She grabbed her shawl and darted out of the house. I wasn't sure where she was going; she had never left me like this before.

It was a matter of hours. All of a sudden, my tormented body relaxed. A sense of well-being encompassed my whole person. I couldn't remember when, if ever, I had felt like this. I jumped up. The neighbor thought that I had lost my mind. "No, I'm healed!" I shouted. "I must find my mother."

I dashed down the hilly road. In the distance I could see someone coming toward me. I recognized her walk; I'd recognize it anywhere. I ran! She stopped for a moment as though she couldn't believe what she saw. All of sudden she picked up her skirts and we almost flew into each other's arms. We laughed and we cried and we hugged all the way down the road.

We got back to our little one-room and sat on the edge of the bed. She laughed as she told me how "brazen" and bold she had been. She could hardly believe it herself. She couldn't get near to Jesus at first, she said. There was quite a crowd, and his friends tried to guard him; but she would not be intimidated. She kept pleading. Finally, they turned to the Master and begged him, "Give her what she wants!" They knew she would not go away, and she was a bother and an embarrassment.

When the disciples turned to speak to Jesus mother saw her moment—a crack now in the hostile barrier between them—and she slipped right through and skidded to the feet of Jesus. Her knee got skinned in the process, but she didn't even care.

Mother heard him say to the disciples—for her to overhear, she was sure—"I was sent only to the lost sheep of the House of Israel." Mother knew that he really believed that; she also believed that he would set aside that tradition in his compassion for a human need. As long as she had come this far, she thought to herself, there was no turning back. She remembered the words of the blind man that expressed faith in him and in his power, and she cried out: "Son of David, have pity on me." He answered not a word—but mother saw the expression on his face, almost a questioning going on within him.

"When he referred to me as a dog," mother said, "I just wanted to say 'Forget it!'" but the memory of my cry of pain and panic drowned out the name-calling—and she held her own. Then he spoke of bread only for the Israelites, but another story that the people in the marketplace had told flashed before her mind. "This man had fed five thousand people," they said, "to say nothing of women and children, with baskets of food left over." It's time, she thought, to say something of women and children. And she was so proud of herself as she argued right back: "Even dogs eat the crumbs that fall from their master's table."

She said that even she was surprised when Jesus threw back his head and laughed. He seemed almost to enjoy that he had finally been outdone in an argument—and with a woman—and with a pagan woman at that. He was never one, others had said, who was much impressed by people's classy titles or prestige or even clever arguments; but he was moved by this kind of faith in him, and by such obvious deep, deep love for him by another.

It was as though his horizons had been broadened; such powerful love expression had shattered a last barrier. Anyone who drew near in faith and love would be welcomed to eat as friends at this man's table.

The look of disbelief—almost scandal—on the faces of the disciples, to say nothing of the Scribes and Pharisees looking on, was clearly evident. Jesus must have taken those twelve aside that night, reflected on his experience, and told of his insight, and why he did what he did.

They must have been deeply touched by this event—just the fact that this story is still being told years after this Jesus was crucified. One of his followers, I understand, wrote a letter to the Corinthians saying: "Face plain facts. Anybody who is convinced that they belong to Christ must go on to reflect that we all belong to Christ no less than they do" (2 Cor. 10:7–8). Some, of course, are still finding that hard to accept. I hear that there are still many arguments and discussions regarding who and what is impure and not acceptable at the table or at their worship service. But the decision has been made: Nothing that God has made is unclean—not lepers, not sinners, not Canaanites—and you can add to your own list. Nothing that God has made is unclean!

All I know is that I learned something about the power of love that day from my mother, and—know what? I believe that Jesus did too!

THE PREACHER REFLECTS

Born in Chicago, I grew up Roman Catholic and entered the Dominican Order, the Order of Preachers, in Adrian, Michigan, at a young age. I earned a Master's of Arts in English and a Master's of Arts in religious studies from the University of Detroit. Later, I did graduate study in guidance and counseling at Michigan State University. In addition, I was the first woman to receive the Master of Divinity degree from Saints Cyril and Methodius Seminary.

I have been associate professor of homiletics at Aquinas Institute in St. Louis since 1977. One of my greatest joys has been in leading workshops in preaching and preaching retreats around the country, and in preaching for special occasions. In 1988, my colleagues in the Academy of Homiletics honored me by electing me as the first woman president of the academy, after I had served the year before as vice-president.

My background as a Roman Catholic sister, who has completed seminary studies and teaches homiletics, but is denied the right to preach within our eucharistic liturgy, impacted my choice of and approach to Matthew 15:21–28, the story of the Canaanite woman. I could resonate with a woman who must have experienced herself as alienated and an "outsider."

Theological and Homiletical Concerns

The scriptural form can suggest a sermon form. The Word taking shape within me found story format a natural overflow from my meditation, prayer, study, and listening to this biblical story.

From whose point of view would the story be told? I had initially considered first person Canaanite woman, but I realized that the daughter could present a little more objective portrayal of the mother's personality, and, therefore, address the issue that caught me where I live: Love impels us to persevere in mediation for the suffering and for those in need.

Also, to enable my congregation to resonate with the community of Matthew's time, I decided to tell the story from hindsight. The young girl would be a grandmother now. The struggle of who is welcomed at the table, both then and now, is addressed in the preaching. The Canaanite woman's perseverance and endurance because of love, and Jesus' own openness to truth wherever he found it, continues to challenge us today in our narrow, self-righteous, and self-centered world.

14. Liberating Love: Pass It On

Toinette M. Eugene

"Liberating Love: Pass It On" was preached in the month of February. February is particularly significant for people of Afro-American heritage, since it is the time when Black History Month is traditionally celebrated in Black churches, in schools with a significant Black enrollment, and by the Black civic community when it gathers to remember our survival and to recount our successes.

At the time this sermon was delivered, one Sunday in February, I was a member and a minister in a middle-sized, middle-class Black Catholic church in Rochester, New York. This particular Christian community had developed a reputation for excellence in the way it commemorated the religious and social history of our Afro-American heroes and sheroes. This Christian community, located across the street from the place in which the abolitionist Frederick Douglass first published his paper, the *North Star,* had not forgotten its own special circumstances and origins. This Catholic church, formerly a bastion of well-established white families, had harbored fugitives in its basement and in the attic of the rectory while former slaves made their way along the Underground Railroad on a journey to freedom. In the past and in the present, those hoping for liberation and willing to risk new discoveries in faith met here, and found ways to share knowledge and experience for life.

This particular sermon was therefore preached to a congregation who had a rich heritage of liberating love, which they had not lost or forgotten although families and pastoral leadership had changed greatly with the course of time and events. This now Black Catholic community had established a style of worship that was widely known for the enthusiasm and jubilation exhibited by its youth choir and for the exquisitely crafted vestments of its liturgical leaders, once an image of bouillon consisting of white, ordained, celibate males, now resembling a spicy gumbo made up of white and black, male and female, lay and ordained persons, dedicated to continuing a mission and a ministry of liberation and reconciliation.

By intentionally offering an Afro-American style of worship that was countercultural to the style of mainstream Catholic homiletics, music, religious icons, and sacred symbols, the Parish of the Immaculate Conception established itself as a place where personal and social transformation were stressed and professed and proffered without apology or patronizing explanation for not choosing a more "status quo way to go." In this context, "Liberating Love" was not a sermon for an irregular or out of the ordinary eucharistic celebration. The sermon was not preached as a means of taking care of an obligation to honor Black folks during Black History Month, so that the greater saints of God might eventually receive the bulk of attention that is due them during the rest of the year. The homily, focused on responding to the prophetic Word of God, was not significantly distinctive from the kind or quality of sermons that would regularly be offered on any ordinary and regular service during the year.

However, during Black History Month, the content and method of preaching intentionally shifted to address the quite specific educational needs of the community and its visitors. The use of Martin Luther King as a familiar teaching reference within this sermon was employed primarily as a means of making welcome the multitudes of visitors who swelled the ranks of this congregation during the season of Black History Month in order to be inspired and informed at the same sacred event. We had discovered, as a community of faith and over time, that especially during Black History Month the community expected to be taught something new about themselves and their past heritage as well as to be challenged by the Scripture to think and to act in new ways in the present and for the future. For this month, at least, the dimensions of preaching and teaching were expected to be more evenly combined. This request and shared expectation suited me well.

Text: II Kings 2:4–15

A DOUBLE PORTION

Elisha had been the protégé of Elijah. He was familiar with and impressed by what Elijah had done. Elijah had faced the awesome power of King Ahab and had dared to pronounce in the presence of the royal court, the wickedness of the monarch. For Ahab had exercised the regal power of eminent domain and had confiscated the vineyard of a poor peasant. Elijah brought God's judgment into the royal court. In the presence of false prophets Elijah called upon his God for a sign of favor and vocation. And God set wet wood on fire.

Elijah was indeed a chosen one. But there was also the occasion when Elijah's enemies sought his life, and Elijah, giving in to despair, sat down and wept under the juniper tree. Yet, God cured Elijah's blues. God refreshed and revitalized the prophet, giving him renewed vigor and commitment. Surely, in their many days together these and other testimonies were shared with Elisha. But the time came when God called Elijah home from the battlefield.

Looking down upon the prophet whose days had been spent in the pursuit of justice and righteousness, God's voice rolled down the streets of Glory. Forth came a chariot of fire with flaming steeds, which had waited since creation for this moment. I can almost hear God saying, "I want you to go down to Jericho. I'm calling Elijah home. He's held fast to the gospel plow, now I'm calling him home. He's fought the good fight on the mountain and in the valley, now I'm calling him home. He has run the race, finished the course, and now it's time for him to receive his crown, I'm calling him home. He'll meet you at the Jordan River. Go and bring my servant home."

But before Elijah left for Glory, he turned to his friend Elisha and said, "Ask what I shall do for you before I am taken from you?" What can I do for you before I go? Out of all of the things for which Elisha could have asked, he chose this: "Let me inherit a double portion of your spirit." Whatever it was that put the truth on your tongue and righteousness in your heart, give me a double portion. Whatever it was that made justice your defense and love your way, give me a double portion of it. Elisha asked for a double portion, not because Elisha wanted to be twice as famous as Elijah, but because evil stalked the earth and plagued the human heart day and night.

Some of us may be familiar with the sermon that Martin Luther King, Jr., preached on the eve of his assassination. With the fire of divine inspiration in his eyes he said, "There are difficult days ahead . . . [but] I'm not worried about anything. I'm not fearing anyone. Mine eyes have seen the glory of the coming of the Lord. . . . I have been to the mountaintop, and I have looked over into the Promised Land." If there is one thing that we need today it is a double portion of Dr. King's spirit. Whatever it was that made him call the demons of racism, militarism, and oppression by name, we need a double portion. Whatever it was that made him stand up against fire hoses, billy clubs, physical and verbal abuse for righteousness sake, we need a double portion. A double portion, not because we want twice the notoriety of Martin Luther King, but because he has told us that there are difficult days ahead.

I suppose if Dr. King were here today he would respond to us in the way that Elijah responded to the request of Elisha: "You have asked me a hard thing," or "Do you know what that means? For along with the double portion comes more than your share of trouble. Are you ready to be rejected for no other cause than that your skin is black? Are you ready to be persecuted for no other cause than that you cry out for justice in behalf of the downtrodden? Are you prepared to go to battle against the forces of war with nothing but the weapons of peace? You are asking a hard thing." If we want a double portion of Dr. King's spirit today, we must be ready to accept all of its implications. The light of truth will not shine brightly until we name it. The power of justice will not cleanse us until we live it. The joy of righteousness will not be ours until we believe it.

SPIRITUAL INSIGHT

Elisha asked for a double portion of Elijah's spirit, but it was not completely within Elijah's power to grant the request. The spirit that Elijah had did not alter his physical makeup. It did not change the tonal quality of his voice. In fact, there was nothing about the prophetic spirit that was obvious to the casual observer. The only test that would answer Elisha's question was the possession of a spiritual insight. Elijah told him, "You have asked a hard thing; yet if you see me as I am being taken from you, it shall be so for you; but if you do not see me, it shall not be so."

Elisha may have already had his double portion, but in order to be sure, he had to see with the eyes of faith. We—you and I today—may already have our double portion, but to be certain we have to see with the eyes of faith. We have to be able to see in Afro-Americans the heritage of a noble African culture. But in order to see that we have to look with what the old folks call the spiritual eye.

For in the economic eye, Afro-Americans are simply surplus labor. In the political eye, Afro-Americans are simply surplus votes. In the social eye, Afro-Americans are merely a burden on society, but in the spiritual eye . . . in the spiritual eye these are they who have come up out of the great tribulation. In the spiritual eye, these are they who have formed mighty civilizations. In the spiritual eye, these are they upon whose blood this land is built. In the spiritual eye, these are they who are denied equal opportunity and the pursuit of happiness. In the spiritual eye, these are they who are destined for a place in God's house. We have to see with the spiritual eye.

We have to look behind the gleaming facade of corporate America and see persons consumed by their own greed. We have to see with the spiritual eye. We have to look beneath the manicured surface of American society and see people numbed by rampant apathy. We have to look beyond the attractive frontier of American military conquest and see a world in danger of nuclear annihilation. We need the spiritual eye! The spirit of prophecy is ineffective without the insight of faith. We cannot just cry out for justice but we need to have seen it from afar. We cannot just demand the righteousness but we must believe it. We cannot just pray for peace but we must be able to see the things that make peace possible.

In a speech that Martin Luther King delivered at the Riverside Church, he said, "A nation that continues year after year to spend more money on military defense than on programs of social uplift is approaching spiritual death. . . . Somehow this madness must cease." King saw with the spiritual eye the malaise of our country. If we want to redeem it, we need the spirit of prophecy and the eyes of faith.

PASS IT ON

Elisha was granted his wish. He received a double portion of the spirit of Elijah. The spirit of prophecy rested on him. And he was also endowed with spiritual insight with the eyes of faith. As the chariot of fire swung low he saw Elijah being taken up to heaven. He saw for himself the whirlwind that carried God's servant to his final and eternal reward. Elisha had the gift of prophecy and the eyes of faith, but the question still remained. Would he be able to pass it on? Would he be able to do for Israel what Elijah had done for him? Would he be able to pass on to the people the hope that had sustained Elijah?

Israel was the heir of a glorious history. Abraham had been summoned to be the founder of a great nation. Isaac prospered under God's favor. Jacob was blessed even when he did not deserve it. Joseph, sold by his brothers into Egyptian slavery became respected among the pharaohs. And when God delivered the Israelites from bondage in Egypt they took the bones of Joseph with them. In Israel's past lay her heritage and her hope. But something had happened to Israel. They forgot God's promise. They neglected God's command. They were unable to pass on to succeeding generations the liberating love that inspired their ancestors.

If there is one thing that has plagued black people, as well as many other religiously oriented people in America, it is the inability to consistently pass on our history. An inability to leave for future generations a heritage of hope and a legacy of love. It is a history held together by the demand for justice and a thirst after righteousness. In the lives and accomplishments of Nat Turner, Harriet Tubman, Richard Allen, Jarena Lee, Sojourner Truth, Augustus Tolton, Malcolm X, and all of the others, we can see the results of the prophetic call. The tragedy is that we have shown a disdain for our noble history and have failed to pass it on! The redemption of our race and our nation may rest on our ability to give to our children what we have received.

The Afro-American writer Toni Morrison in her novel, *Song of Solomon*, tells the story of an ex-slave whose farm embodies his heritage. The farm says, "Stop picking around the edges of the world. Take advantage, and if you can't take advantage, take disadvantage. . . . Grab this land! Take it, hold it, my brothers, make it, my sisters; shake it, squeeze it, turn it, twist it, beat it, kick it, kiss it, whip it, stomp it, dig it, plow it, seed it, reap it, rent it, buy it, sell it, own it, build it, multiply it, and pass it on—can you hear me? Pass it on!"

Elijah did not leave Elisha empty-handed, wondering whether or not he would be able to pass on to others the prophetic inheritance. No! As Elijah was being taken up, he looked over his shoulder and flung his mantle down toward Elisha. The mantle was a symbol of the prophetic vocation. It had no power in and of itself, but it served as a reminder of the God who protected him in danger, fed him when he was hungry, gave him drink when he was thirsty.

Martin Luther King, Jr., as he was being taken up to glory, in the midst of his eschatological joy, seeing our trepidation and fear, looked over his shoulder and flung down his mantle. He gave us his dream. A dream of justice and equality. The dream has no power in and of itself, but it is a reminder of the God who made a way out of no way, the God who has delivered us from bondage, the God who has opened doors that no one can close. No! Martin Luther King has not left us empty-handed but has given us something to hold on to. He has passed on to us his dream.

CONCLUSION

Elisha was left standing on the bank of the Jordan. He had in his hand Elijah's mantle. It was the same mantle with which Elijah had parted the waters. A mantle that was itself a reminder of the rod with which Moses had parted the Red Sea. But all of that was past and Elisha now faced the uncertain future. And the question that must have haunted his mind is, "Can we do it again? Can I part the water with Elijah's mantle?" As we face our uncertain future we may also be wondering whether or not we can weather the winter of persecution. Can we once again articulate a vision of the beloved community?

Elisha discovered that with the mantle of Elijah he could strike the waters of the Jordan and part them. With Dr. King's dream we can continue to work effectively for his beloved community, "where all God's children, black and white, Jews and Gentiles, Protestant and Catholic, will be able to join hands and sing the spiritual of old, 'Free at last! Free at last! Thank God almighty, we are free at last.'" We can part the Red Seas of the world again, we can defeat the pharaohs of this world again, we can dream again, because the power behind Elijah's mantle and dream has become flesh and dwelt among us.

Because the Child of God has taken the form of a slave, because Jesus came into the world of a lowly birth, because he ate with sinners and reprobates, we can dream. Because he befriended the outcasts, championed the cause of the downtrodden, proclaimed the release of the captives, because he has set at liberty those who are oppressed, we are able to act boldly as he did. Because Jesus died the death of a criminal, and assumed the keys of the kingdom, we are set free from sin and called to be disciples. Because Jesus Christ lived, died, and yet lives for us, we can take up Elijah's mantle, and we can live out the courageous spirit of liberation that makes this dream a reality of peace and mercy and justice for our world. We have received God's most precious gift, Liberating Love. Pick it up, take it up, hold it high, and pass it on!

THE PREACHER REFLECTS

I teach and preach as a Black Catholic woman professor and administrator in a historically Protestant seminary. The occasions when I was also able to exercise my preaching and teaching ministry at Immaculate Conception Parish allowed me the unique opportunity to profess in church what I regularly practice in the classroom as professor of education, society, and Black church studies.

My preaching is influenced greatly by the place where I teach. Martin Luther King, Jr., obtained his graduate theological education and substantial support for his ethical tradition of non-violence from the professors and the tradition of Crozer Theological Seminary. The spirit of Dr. King abides with us as a community of scholars and disciples and prophets and pastoral leaders and teachers. At the educational institution now known as Colgate Rochester Divinity School/Bexley Hall/Crozer Theological Seminary, we are daily challenged to hand on his teaching and tradition to those who come to us specifically for this purpose of gaining and growing from exposure to the legacy of Martin Luther King and other illustrious Afro-American alumni.

Theological and Homiletical Concerns

Moving back and forth between the context of the classroom and the context of the church, working both with pupils and parishioners who are in rich profusion a black–white, Protestant–Catholic, lay–ordained, youthful–aging, male–female mixture tends to make me stretch and reach and listen as well as speak. The theological and homiletical concerns that I have for bringing others along with me toward a greater experience of the biblical notion of shalom require that I find, articulate, and mark out the widest parameters of meaning and experience in order to be inclusive and insightful in preaching and teaching the gospel message. Subsequently, the theological and homiletical points of reference and exegetical range of meaning that I offer are almost always focused on how God is made manifest in a world of difference and dissonance.

The story of Elijah's mantle was not a familiar scriptural story to many members or visitors in our church community when I first began to prepare to preach this sermon. However, the experience of having hand-me-downs in clothing, in family traditions, in sayings and in doings from older relatives was something that the folks I was with could relate to very well, even though most of us had moved a bit beyond this personal and social reality, which signals neediness and poverty in status if not in spirit. As I worked with the metaphor of the mantle in relation to my own life, and together in class with a core discussion group of sermon preparation leaders, we collectively advanced and unpacked this idea; the basic prophetic and pastoral gospel imperative contained in the text began to come alive and to transform the middle-class reality and the middle-aged or middle-of-the road set of standards by which we tend to judge and to see others.

Martin Luther King, Howard Thurman, Mordecai Wyatt Johnson, and other notable Afro-American religious and educational mentors from the seminary made us mindful that to live up to their measure is to pick up their mantle. To pick up their mantle is to make efforts to master the message of the Gospel of Peace and Justice and to learn how to see with a spiritual eye. I know that this takes practice and that this demands a community of support and of faith in which one may share struggles and dreams. I am grateful that in my church and in my educational institution these things are available whenever I am willing to acknowledge that I have something to give as well as to receive.

However, in my own personal history it was not my church nor my school, but it was my grandmother who first taught me how to see with the spiritual eye. She taught me a great deal of what I know about effectively handing on my particular knowledge and expertise to others both through the pulpit and from the podium. My technical and formal training pale by contrast and comparison with what she instilled, although those components were indeed necessary to hone and polish my professional preparation and ongoing development. Her ability to combine a powerful prophetic stance toward life with a tender and peaceful posture toward those in need initially affirmed for me that I need not decide on only one vocation or direction in life, to the detriment of other gifts.

What I learned from my grandmother that is reflected in this sermon is that if one is given a double portion of grace, or when anyone feels the need of a second helping of courage in order to pass on what has been entrusted for the liberation of many, God does not abandon us when we respond to our callings. Both the teachers who have preceded me in my family and at the seminary and those who presently accompany me in the task of providing pastoral formation and religious education confirm this fact over and over again: If and when we know liberating love, we are called and compelled to pass it on to others. Whenever we engage in these activities with the intent of personal and social transformation as outcomes, our God does not leave us.

15. Learning to See

Isabel Carter Heyward

"Learning to See: An Epiphany Sermon" was preached at Christ (Episcopal) Church in Cambridge, Massachusetts, on February 8, 1987. In the fall of 1986, some lay leaders of Christ Church, a historic, predominantly white, affluent, and liberal parish with a large number of academics among its members, asked me to help design a six-week Sunday morning adult education program on liberation theology.

Since this was to be the introduction of this important, controversial movement in theology to the parish, the leaders and I agreed that the program should include both an overview of various liberation theological movements in the United States and elsewhere and an emphasis on the importance of studying our own lives in relation to the work of justice. As the design began to take shape, I was invited to make one of the six presentations, specifically on a historical and comparative study of basic themes in Black and feminist theologies in the United States.

Subsequently, the parish clergy asked if, as a means of embodying the connections between education and liturgy, I would be guest preacher on February 8, 1987, the Sunday on which the program was set to begin immediately following the service. This then was the context in which this sermon was presented.

Text: Habakkuk 3:2–6, 17–19; I Corinthians 2:1–11; Matthew 5:13–20

Epiphany is not merely a season of "showing forth," in which the meaning of Jesus is made manifest to those who seek him. The Epiphany of God's power, God's love and justice on the earth, in order to mean anything at all, requires that we see what in fact is revealed in Jesus. The Epiphany requires that we learn to see what is happening already around us, between us, within us in this world, that we learn to see what God is doing in the world and that we learn to understand what our lives, our commitments, and our work may involve if we intend to take seriously our vocation as people of God.

As we learn to see more clearly through the eyes of God, we will catch a glimpse of the Star of Bethlehem and see not only who lay in that manger two thousand years ago, but who lies there still, cast out of respectable inns and eating places; still, relegated to the margins of our religious institutions, society, and nation; still, the brunt of racist, sexist, homophobic, cruel, and demeaning jokes; still, the object of fear, scorn, and contempt; still, bound to be crucified. Still today, we crucify the daughters and sons of God, our sisters and brothers on this earth, because still today we liberal Christians fail more often than not actually to see what is happening and to believe not only in a God of justice and compassion, but also in ourselves as Her friends, compañeras and helpmates.

"O God, may we believe, with the psalmist, that we shall see your goodness in the land of the living. May we be strong. May our hearts take courage." For these are not easy days.

How then shall we learn to "see sacredly" so that we might believe? *First*, we must learn to look in unexpected places for the love and grace and power of God. Habakkuk, very much in keeping with the rest of the prophetic tradition of Israel, warns that even as God's glory covers the heavens, even as the earth is full of God's praises, even as the "brightness" of the divine—the splendor of the very power of Love itself—"flashes" among us, God will be veiling His power.

Now what is this all about? It is about the fact that God seldom takes the shape we expect. God rarely conforms to our expectations of what a God of power and might "should" look like. We are to look for God in the places we do not expect to find power or might on the earth, among the least of these, our brothers, sisters, and other earth creatures. There, and there only perhaps, are we likely to be encountered by the Holy One of Israel, whom Jesus called *abba* (daddy) and who, in truth, is also the Mother of us all, the Source of our Birth, the Wellspring of Love in History, the Root of all Justice—and Compassion; always veiled, hid from full view, perceptible only to eyes of faith. For only eyes of faith are able to see what Paul calls "the secret and ancient wisdom of God"—the fact that the Divine Presence seldom has much to do with the "good order" of religion and society. She has rather everything to do with the inclusion of those whom the custodians of good order have cast out because they are the wrong color, culture, creed, class; because they have the wrong nationality or wrong sexuality, because they have the wrong ideas or the wrong questions. As Paul noted in his letter to the people of Corinth, "None of the rulers of this age understand this secret, this wisdom, for if they had, they would not have crucified Jesus" (1 Cor. 2:8).

Still today, if the rulers of this nation understood this secret, they would not be killing the peasants of Nicaragua, the miners of South Africa, or the poor and destitute of our own land. If we understood that God's presence is hidden in this world among the least of our brothers and sisters (and in the places of our own lives that seem to us least important), we would not compute our worth by measuring our successes in relation to those who hold authority in the various institutions of our common life. Certainly, to the extent that we *are* those in authority, we would understand that our relation to God depends upon our willingness to risk losing our authority, our institutional power and privilege, in order to be faithful to the One who lives and moves most closely and intimately with those who are poor, marginalized, outcast in relation to our society and, too often, our churches.

So, we first must look in unexpected places if we are to see God's manifestations—places like mangers, prisons, AIDS wards, places other than church, religions other than Christianity, and even in the most unlikely places of our lives—our own shabby, secretive, scary closets.

Second, we must learn courage, how to see beyond the fear that impedes our capacity to know or love God.

Let me tell you a story. Eighteen months ago, along with twelve other U.S. theologians, I attended a ten-day seminar in Cuba, hosted by Cuban theologians, Episcopalians, Presbyterians, and Methodists. Having grown up with a fear of communist Cuba, a fear that is as American as the flag, I was shocked to learn that there are churches, and theologians, in Cuba. You would hardly guess it listening to the propaganda that the "free press" of the United States gives us about Cuba. In fact, while in Cuba, I attended several Episcopal churches and was invited to preach and preside at a Eucharist in the Cathedral in Havana. After the service, an old, bent-over woman approached me with a broad smile on her face, and her arms outstretched to hold me. In her Spanish and my "Spanglish," we managed to communicate! She was ninety-one years old, the only member of her family who had remained in Cuba after the 1959 Revolution.

"Now, my young priest and sister," she said, her eyes sparkling. "It is such a blessing to meet a person from the United States who is willing to see for herself what we have done. Now, I'm not a communist, I'm a Christian—a life-long Episcopalian! But I want you to know that twenty-five years ago, children lay dying out there on the street, sick and starving; women lay in brothels, exploited and abused; most people in Cuba could not read or write. Those were cruel and vicious times and the United States supported this cruelty and oppression. Today, in Cuba, this communist nation of ours, there are no children starving in the streets, and fewer women are exploited and abused in brothels, families, or business. Nearly everyone in Cuba today can read and write. Poverty has been eliminated, and this country has miraculously become a model of what can happen when wealth and power is shared. I believe that Cuba is a light to the nations! And now I ask you, one Christian to another, is this not the will of God? Is this not what Jesus would have us do? To feed the hungry, liberate the oppressed, offer hope to the exploited? Is this not the work of Jesus?"

Unless we can see through our well-learned fear, we are unable to hear the gospel truth in this wise old woman's words, or in the words of John Diamond, an Afro-American theologian in our delegation who preached in a Presbyterian church in Cuba. In his sermon, Dr. Diamond said, "I was terrified of coming here! In fact, I wouldn't have come if my seminary president hadn't insisted. I was terrified of communism, Marxist-Leninism, Cuba. I expected to be followed, bugged, and wired everywhere I went. But now I can tell you, God as my witness, that, having lived for six decades as a Black person in the United States, this week in Cuba is the first time in my life I've ever felt entirely free of the colorline—as if, here in Cuba, my being Black really doesn't make any difference. I am deeply, prayerfully grateful to have had this experience at least one time in my lifetime."

Through the eyes of fear, we see only those "gods" set before us by the rulers of our time. We cannot perceive the work of the Spirit that animated Jesus as long as we are blinded spiritually by the fear that makes us angry at beggars in the street rather than about an economic crisis that does indeed exist for the poor of this and every land. So, first, we learn to look for

God in unexpected places. Second, we learn to see, courageous-
ly, beyond the fear that impedes our efforts to know and do the
will of God.

Third, U.S. Christians must learn to see more deeply the fab-
ric of creation, the tapestry of liberation, and the designs of
God's blessing than we have learned as citizens of this well-
intentioned, but badly misguided, nation that most of us love.
The United States is, after all, for most of us, our home and, in
many ways, for most of us here I suspect, a good home. But,
my friends, that is not enough. We who are Christians in the
United States must learn to see beyond the libertarian . . . the
"I did it my way, it worked for me" brand of civil religion that
currently is so much in vogue and that has its twisted roots in
a badly mistaken doctrine of "freedom."

You may be watching the marvelous public broadcasting series on the civil rights movement, *Eyes on the Prize.* In last week's
segment, on the beginnings of the sit-ins in Nashville, Tennessee, in 1960, they showed an interview with a white woman
who said, "I really feel that these demonstrators are violating
my 'civil rights' to serve food only to those whom I want to.
This is, after all, a free country."

Now, this should not be heard as an anomaly, a strange statement by one racist Southern woman. This woman simply was
mouthing a mistaken, immoral tenet of U.S. society: That every
person—particularly every white, ostensibly heterosexual, affluent male—has a fundamental right to do whatever he wants
to do with *his* property, *his* family, *his* life, *his* nation, and that
he has no equally fundamental responsibility to act on behalf
of the well-being of others. Thus, to legislate justice for Blacks,
for women, for gays, for the poor, for Spanish-speaking citizens, for the sick, may well constitute an infringement upon *his*
"freedom."

Christians in the United States (especially we who are Anglo
and others who have acquired some access to economic or social
power) often fail to see that our fundamental identity is not as
individuals with "rights" but as members of one body, inter-

dependent and mutually responsible for one another. This is not simply a spiritual truth. It is literally true that as long as anyone is a slave, as long as anyone is in bondage, as long as anyone is cast out, marginalized, trivialized, all of us are profoundly diminished, broken people.

Theoretically, Anglicans should know this. We have a great theology of "participation," community and shared responsibility. Think of John Donne's "No man is an island" and of the lives and work of such Anglicans as William Temple, Pauli Murray, and Desmond Tutu. Too often, however, our vision falls short and we fail to see through the sham of the brouhaha and false patriotism on behalf of the "freedom" of every man to do pretty much as he pleases. As the old saying goes, "Here's to you and here's to me, in hopes that we don't disagree. But if in case we disagree, to hell with you and here's to me." Upon this irresponsible credo stands the popularity of our current president (Reagan).

We must learn to see through the fallacy of this perverted notion of freedom if we hope to see and recognize the face of God around us, or for that matter, in the mirror, for this selfishness breeds our own ugliness. It is all of us at our worst.

Finally, the Gospel of Matthew tells us something about what we must learn to see in ourselves. We must learn to see that we are empowered to act by the force of love itself, embodied among us, God incarnate.

If we spend our energies searching the "heavens" and "spiritual things," trying to rise above the clutter of our daily lives, we will not find the God whom Jesus loved. No. We must learn to see that to be the salt of the earth, flavorful and tasty; to be the light of the world, not hidden ourselves but rather illuminating God's presence in the world, is to be epiphanies ourselves. We are called in this season to be bright manifestations of the power of God in history. Our vocation is to join Jesus and many others in giving God a voice, giving God an embodied life on earth. By the power of the Spirit we witness in the life, death, and resurrection of Jesus, to be the salt of the earth, the light of the world is to be "in Christ," the active cooperative movement between divine and human being on this earth. This is what we must learn to see and it is where we are called to be.

Amen.

THE PREACHER REFLECTS

With ten other women, I was "irregularly" ordained an Episcopal priest in 1974 and banned immediately from functioning in the Episcopal church. The ban was lifted two years later when the denomination authorized the ordination of women, but the stigma of having been ordained in disorderly fashion remains to this day. I'm grateful for this "sacred stigma," which not only links me to other movements of resistance to injustice but also signals my ongoing "irregular" vocation in the praxis of a church and society that need as many deviants from business-as-usual as can be called forth.

In my own personal pilgrimage, I'm one of Gramsci's "organic intellectuals," though I doubt he had in mind theologians or women— much less a lesbian woman priest.

Theological and Homiletical Concerns

In 1979 I came out as a lesbian in order to work in a less intellectually and pastorally cluttered way in the context of a religious tradition that since the fourth century has put sexuality (often secretly) at the center of its doctrine, discipline, and worship. That same year, I began focusing on Christology in my scholarship. With other feminist theologians, I started making connections between what the Church historically has taught about Christ's *power-over* our lives and how "he" has been used to bludgeon self-respecting women and other sexual dissenters (for example, homosexuals) as well as Jews, Moslems, witches, and practitioners of other faith-traditions.

By the time Reagan ascended to the presidency in 1981, I had discovered that our civil and ecclesial institutions, from marriage to the military to the worship of Christ, are fastened in non-mutual power relations that are intrinsically abusive. These power dynamics have been secured in subsequent years, setting a troubling, critical agenda for justice-seeking folks in this nation and elsewhere.

During the past decade, trips to Cuba, Canada, Latin America, and Europe have helped sharpen my perspective on the United States in relation to the rest of the world. We are the most dangerous, arrogant, and self-preoccupied nation on earth, but there is hope for us just as there is for the rest of the world. Our hope stirs among those who will suffer oppression no more, not only elsewhere in the world but here among us.

Most of my current work is at the Episcopal Divinity School in Cambridge, Massachusetts, where I teach Anglican, systematic, feminist, and liberation theologies. In the seminary, I'm helping shape emergent degree programs in feminist liberation theology, in which we are studying together how to participate, gladly and for the long haul, in the struggle for justice.

16. No Bulls, No Lambs, No Goats

Leontine T. C. Kelly

"No Bulls, No Lambs, No Goats" was preached in a television studio without an audience/congregation present. "The Chicago Sunday Evening Club" is "the longest-running television series in the world." It is an ecumenical program that is telecast each Sunday evening from 5:00 to 6:00 P.M. over WTTW/Channel 11, Chicago's award-winning public television station. The broadcast is seen by several hundred thousand viewers.

Consequently, when Christ came into the world, he said, "Sacrifices and offerings thou hast not desired, but a body hast thou prepared for me; in burnt offerings and sin offerings thou hast taken no pleasure.

Then I said, 'Lo, I have come to do thy will, O God.' as it is written of me in the roll of the book."

When he said above, "Thou hast neither desired nor taken pleasure in sacrifices and offerings and burnt offerings and sin offerings" (these are offered according to the law), then he added, "Lo, I have come to do thy will." He abolishes the first in order to establish the second. And by that will we have been sanctified through the offering of the body of Jesus Christ once and for all.

—HEBREWS 10: 5–10

I have recently retired as a bishop of the United Methodist Church. We are bishops for life according to our polity, but there are age restrictions on the administration of episcopal areas. I enjoyed being an active bishop of the church, but there were some hard moments.

I recall an elderly woman approaching me on her cane. She was shaking with anger. "Bishop Kelly," she said, "if this decision is made I will see to it that the church does not receive the money my husband left in his will." Her body language as well as her words showed that SHE WAS INDEED a "Pillar of the Church!"

In another community a committee talked with me about pastoral leadership. In this instance the traditional white neighborhood had been "invaded" by people of another color and culture. The fear and anguish that was growing was expressed by a young father who tearfully stated that he had joined that particular church to, in his words, "keep my children pure" and, he added, "You might send us ANYBODY to be our pastor! (The implication was that as a bishop I might assign a member of an ethnic minority group or even a woman to that church, as the open itineracy position of our church encourages.)

In each instance I remembered the words spoken by a Caucasian friend of mine as the two of us shared a cup of coffee and discussed the racial tension within ours and other denominations, and in society in general.

"But, Teenie," she had exclaimed, "you can't mean that you think our churches ought to be integrated. That's all we've got left!" And she was serious! I asked her to repeat her statement very slowly three times and listen to what she was saying about the very nature of the Church of Jesus Christ. What a commentary on our times! What a misunderstanding of the "community of faith," the covenanted people of God. The fact that in each experience the sharing had been face to face with me, a Black woman, was indicative of the depth of fear present in our society. Perhaps our fear of one another is really deeper than our fear of nuclear conflict.

How does our biblical faith inform our ability to relate to one another and to all people as Children of God? What is the relationship between our "sacrificial" giving of time and substance to the Church and the growing divisiveness in this "One Nation Under God"? What is it we are afraid to confess, reluctant to repent of? How are our corporate and personal relationships interpretive of the reality of God's intervening, atoning act of salvation through Jesus Christ? Our money, our time, our talents are as inadequate as the sacrificial offerings of the early Hebrew believers.

"No bulls, no lambs, no goats", sounds strange to our ears, but it was not an unfamiliar warning to the community of Christians to whom the unknown author of the Letter to the Hebrews is written. Levitical sacrifices of animals had long been a part of their religious tradition. The law had confirmed burnt offerings as legitimate, liturgical worship. The biblical record shows, however, that in light of the sins of the people, such offerings were no appeasement to a God of Peace, a God of Love, a God of Justice and Righteousness. Symbolic worship without the accompaniment of obedient action was not acceptable to God. There was and is and probably always will be the Divine expectation that the quality of life within the community of faith and indeed in the world to be impacted by it will reflect the intentional goodwill of those who worship.

Both psalmist and prophet make clear this understanding:

Sacrifice and offering thou dost not desire; but thou hast given me an open ear.
Burnt offering and sin offering thou hast not required.
Then I said, "Lo, I come; in the roll of the book it is written of me;
I delight to do thy will, O my God; thy law is written within my heart."
—Psalm 40:6–8

I do not reprove you for your sacrifices; your burnt offerings are con-
tinually before me,
I will accept no bull from your houses, nor he-goat from your folds.
For every beast of the forest is mine, the cattle on a thousand hills.
I know all the birds of the air, and all that moves in the field is mine.

If I were hungry, I would not tell you;
for the world and all that is in it is mine.

Do I eat the flesh of bulls, or drink the blood of goats?
Offer to God a sacrifice of thanksgiving, and pay your vows to the
Most High;
And call upon me in the day of trouble;
I will deliver you and you shall glorify me.

—Psalm 50:8–15

Samuel says,"Has the Lord as great delight in burnt offerings
and sacrifices as in obeying the voice of the Lord? Behold to
obey is better than sacrifice, and to hearken than the fat of
rams"(1 Samuel 15:22).

No statement of God's purposeful will and call to specific
obedience is clearer than that recorded in the words of an early
Isaiah:

What to me is the multitude of your sacrifices? says the Lord,
I have had enough of burnt offerings of rams and the fat of fed beasts,
I do not delight in the blood of bulls, or of lambs, or of he-goats.

When you come to appear before me, who requires of you this tram-
pling of my courts?
Bring no more vain offerings; . . .
I cannot endure iniquity and solemn assembly.
Your new moons and your appointed feasts my soul hates;
they have become a burden to me, I am weary of bearing them.
When you spread forth your hands, I will hide my eyes from you;
even though you make many prayers, I will not listen;
your hands are full of blood.
Wash yourselves; make yourselves clean;
remove the evils of your doings from before my eyes;
cease to do evil, learn to do good;
seek justice, correct oppression;

defend the fatherless, plead for the widow.

Come now, let us reason together, says the Lord:
though your sins are like scarlet, they shall be as white as snow;
though they are red like crimson, they shall become like wool.
If you are willing and obedient, you shall eat the good of the land.
                                                    —Isaiah 1:11–19

The inability of human creatures to understand the prophetic word of God even as they sinfully refuse to do the will of God prompts the need for an all-sufficient sacrifice. The Letter to the Hebrews and our Christian faith affirms that Christ came into the world to be this sacrifice, this all-time sacrifice, thus freeing us to be obedient servants of God in a needy world. The act of Atonement, the bridging between the creature and the Creator, the suffering of Jesus on our behalf, is the only adequate sacrifice for the sins of the world. The complete forgiveness of sins was impossible in burnt offerings but was made possible by the One who accepted suffering and was "obedient unto death, even the death of the cross" (Philippians 2:8).

The Hebrew Christian community had grown weary of waiting for the return of Jesus. The period of waiting reveals their loss of initial enthusiasm for their faith. According to the biblical scholar Werner Kümmel, they had grown lethargic in their faith. They had a great fear of suffering, and there was lack of trust in the community.* We who call ourselves Christians today may well be endangered by the same weaknesses.

In the midst of a scientific, technologically astute culture we have become lethargic in our faith. Our lack of enthusiastic obedience to Christ and our absence of vital witness to our faith through action fails to address the global dimensions of God's love for all people. Scientific knowledge and technological capability without moral and ethical commitment to humanity makes questionable our ability to grasp the very nature of the God we claim to believe in. To believe in a God of Peace is to

---

* Werner Georg Kümmel, *Introduction to the New Testament* (Nashville, TN: Abingdon Press, 1975), 400.

be a people of peace, peace advocates and activists. To believe in a God of Love is to love all people of God whoever and wherever they are. To believe in a God of Justice is to work for that balance of life that is best expressed in the Hebrew concept of SHALOM, which is more than a mere absence from war. SHALOM is that harmony, wholeness in all relationships as birthed by God in Creation.

In a recent newspaper cartoon I was faced with the reality of our faithlessness. The cartoon showed a human skull on which were perched two insects. The skull was marked "America." One insect said to the other, "What happened to this great American culture? Was it nuclear war?" The other insect answered, "No, it was greed and pollution."

Our time and our talent and our monies, which we see as sacrifices to God, are as meaningless as the bulls, lambs, and goats of ancient days. We are motivated to meet together to protect our own exclusivity. Our native abilities and learned skills are devoted to proving false superiority, and our money builds temples too beautiful to embrace the homeless, or to minister to those with devastating diseases; too select to change attitudes and mores of our communities, or too closed to open to the organizations of people who are willing to confront the structures of our day with their own obedience to God's purposes. We identify people in our communities and our world as enemies, people who we take no time to even know.

Even so, we are called to love our enemies!

Obedience implies not only trust in God, but trust in one another. As racism deepens in our country and feminism continues to be the butt of our jokes, we fail to address major issues of our day. People who do not trust one another do not work out occasions to listen to one another. Dialogue never starts and those who would benefit most from constructive, workable solutions to problems in our society are victimized by our neglect.

We struggle with ways today of teaching our children to protect themselves in a violent society even as we seek to nurture them in trust. The answers we come up with lead to greater isolation rather than cooperative planning for safe neighbor-hoods. We invest more and more in security systems for our homes. Larger prisons that are never sufficient, more strin-gent controls on "the criminal element" and our ready admis-sion of the existence of "a permanent underclass" in this wealthy country assume a hopelessness in our ability to apply our Christian faith and be used of God to reestablish justice in the land.

When by the power of God's Spirit at Pentecost the Church of Christ was established it was not for the purpose of produc-ing fearful, timid, distrustful believers. It was for the purpose of preparing, nurturing, and developing persons of courageous faith who are willing to say with Christ and through Christ, "I have come, O Lord, to do your will."

Refrigerators have become the modern bulletin boards of our day. Small decorative magnets are a very marketable commod-ity to hold our children's drawings, our diet schedules, cut-outs from papers, meeting notices, and words of inspiration.

From a UNICEF poster on my refrigerator a young, poorly dressed girl smiles at the usual question, "What would you like to be when you grow up?" Her giggly answer is "Alive!"

Because we are not obedient disciples of Jesus Christ as we are called to be, others are being sacrificed. They are neither bulls, nor lambs, nor goats. They are children of God for whom the all-sufficient sacrifice has already been made. Their human-ity is their proven credibility.

Come now, let us reason together. Let us remove the evil of our lives before the eyes of God. Let us cease to do evil, let us strengthen one another to do good, let us seek justice and cor-rect oppression wherever it exists. We who are redeemed through the suffering of Christ are called to suffer. The promise of God is that we do not suffer alone. We are afraid to risk relationships because we fear the suffering change of mind and attitudes will bring. It is Paul who reminds us that our spiritual worship of God is defined by our transformation, not by our being "conformed to this world" (Romans 12:1-2). By the power of God's Holy Spirit we would come, O Lord, to do your will!

THE PREACHER REFLECTS

I was born and nurtured in Methodist parsonages. My parents, David DeWitt and Ila Marshall Turpeau, were persons of deep faith. Prayer was a constant in our lives for ourselves, for others, for conditions. Our beliefs were rooted in our understanding that we Black children were loved by God. All eight of us brothers and sisters and all others in the world were "Children of God." This assurance was contrary to the societal and cultural mores of our government, our communities, and the institutional church of which we were a part.

Preaching was celebration in our traditional Black churches. Like all of worship, it was celebration of life despite circumstances, because of God's love. My father's preaching and that of great visiting Black preachers interpreted the "Good News" of the gospel of Jesus Christ clearly to all who heard.

I sat on the front pews of my father's various churches with other children listening to the biblical stories, the experiential illustrations, the social implications of the gospel for those of us who lived in a segregated, racist society, and we responded with the adults appropriately. "Amen!" "Yes!" and "Preach!" gave support to the preacher and emotional outlet to the hearers. Preaching was a participatory event!

"Righteous indignation" against injustice was verbally expressed in both the sermon and the response of the hearers. It was not only acceptable but required action in community if we were truly committed to obedient discipleship of Jesus Christ. Faith did not permit acceptance of wrong though love, and forgiveness was expected. Unjust acts or laws were not the will of God. There was no dichotomy between social responsibility and personal piety. We prayed and studied the Word in order to be God's instruments to change the world. The power of the Spirit of God through the preacher and congregation in worship was the same power available to "do battle" against wrong. Jesus himself was the model of wholeness for us. He was crucified not for what he said, but for what he did. To choose to be a follower of Jesus Christ was to choose suffering.

The National Association for the Advancement of Colored People, the National Urban League, the Young Women's Christian Association, and other human rights organizations were extensions of the Church for us. Politics was necessarily a part of living out the faith and confronting unjust structures. Papa was not only a dramatic preacher, but he was a member of the Ohio Legislature seeking to assure civil rights legislation. Mama was not only a preacher's wife, but a dynamic speaker and inspiring elocutionist. We were trained at home to articulate clearly, in good English, and to speak in public. My personal shyness was overcome by congregational encouragement and family expectations.

My oldest brother became a preacher. I later married a preacher. Different preaching styles became evident to me early in life. When I gave up classroom teaching to enter the ordained ministry following my husband's death in 1969, I had been "speaking/preaching" long enough to know that my style was my own. I had been influenced by many, but my preaching came out of my own faith journey, my prayer and study, my joy and my suffering, my understanding of the Word of God, and my yearning to witness to the justice and love of God reflected in all of life. Preaching gave utterance to all of me and more as I experienced the dimension of spiritual presence in the preaching.

Television preaching, the form in which this particular sermon was delivered, felt contrary to my whole nurturing. The blank, dark, dead camera gave back nothing. The movement of the program director was not the spiritual movement of the Holy Spirit to which I am accustomed, but the mechanical precision of the technician he is required to be. In order to bridge the communication gap between myself and the thousands of viewers I found it necessary to dig deep inside myself and project the image of a single person to whom I was talking.

Theological and Homiletical Concerns

Preaching to an unseen audience, whether on radio or television, causes the preacher to have to generate his or her own "aliveness." The interaction between preacher and congregation enables a sensitivity to responsiveness. When this is absent the imagination of the speaker plays a great part in the delivery.

I was asked to avoid seasonal references because the messages are rerun at different times. As a lectionary preacher, I place importance on the Christian year in sermon development; however, under these circumstances, I chose a text that could be used at any time in the year.

I sought to develop the understanding that the requirement of God is not in sacrificial offerings, but in obedience. Jesus Christ is the all-sufficient sacrifice. I wanted to interpret this in light of the relationship of obedience to the solution for problems of justice and oppression. Submitting to the will of God, as Jesus does, becomes the task of the disciples of Jesus Christ.

17. A Powerful Gospel

Daisy L. Machado

"A Powerful Gospel" was written when I was asked to preach for the first time after we had arrived in Houston. The minister wanted me to share with the congregation why Ismael and I had come to Houston, to inform them about Hispanic ministry. I wanted to do more than just inform and wanted this sermon to let those people in the pews know that they, too, were our co-partners and more than that, they were also privy to that powerful and life-giving message that comes to humankind through the love of God in the person of Jesus. We had come to Houston, where we knew no one, had not one Hispanic name to look up and visit, so that in a very important way this sermon was also my public declaration of faith. As I stood facing the congregation on the morning of September 15, 1985, I knew God had to come through for us and as I began to preach I felt, no, I knew, that we would not be disappointed.

Text: Ezekiel 37:2–5; Acts 3:5–8

If I were asked to give two words that convey the essence of these two passages, I would answer: power and proclamation.* In each narrative it was God's power, made real by the proclamation of, first, the prophet Ezekiel and, second, by the apostles Peter and John, that caused the dead to be made living, and the hopeless to be made hopeful. And it would seem that without too much theologizing you and I have come upon what the gospel and the Church are all about—as taught to us in the words of God and as recorded in the Bible.

Listen to that again: "that the dead be made living and the hopeless be given new hope." Why is it necessary that we listen closely? Because the reality of today's Church demonstrates that so very many of us have forgotten or simply never discovered the essence of what we are called to believe, to live and to proclaim.

Do I sound harsh to you? Then let me share with you the opening line of the first sermon Jesus preached: "Repent; for the kingdom of heaven is at hand" (Matt. 4:17). I know that many people that go to church have problems with words like *repent, repentance,* or *conversion* and being *born again.* I feel this is so because examination of conscience is a difficult task. We want to look everywhere but to ourselves for the sources of our problems and the problems of others. Nations, individuals, and even the Church resist self-examination and fundamental change. But is this not the very meaning of the gospel? The coming of Christ always brings with it the call to repentance and to radical change. We are exposed for who we are, confronted by the claims of a sovereign Lord, and called to a complete redirection.

The Greek word for repentance is *metanoia,* which literally means to "change the form," to turn the mind around, to take on a new identity. It means a transformation of life that is more basic, deeper, and more far-reaching than our common understanding of the word *repentance.* We say the word with a sense

---

* Editor's note: The primary source for this sermon was Jim Wallis, *Agenda for Biblical People* (New York: Harper & Row, 1976).

of guilt and being sorry for something. In sharp contrast, Jesus uses this powerful word to describe the kind of change that must be undergone before one is prepared to enter into the Kingdom of God. This language of change is so strong and demanding because the coming of Christ heralds a new age, the coming of a new order in human affairs. What is occurring is that we are being taken from that valley of dried, dead bones into a new land from which flows milk and honey. We are having taken from us all that causes spiritual death so that we may receive life. And often we are afraid. We want to stay in the old order while we sing praises of the new. While we are not satisfied with the old order, we are not yet willing to give it up because we still have most of our securities there. And it is at this moment of indecision that we hear Jesus' call to his kingdom. A kingdom made up of all new things, including new disciples with new loyalties, new commitments, new priorities, new attitudes. A new kind of community, a new humanity united in Christ and empowered by the Holy Spirit to live according to the standing and character of that new order.

Dried bones, a valley of death—that image is what Ezekiel used to describe the people of Israel, taken forcibly from their homeland in the unwanted exile of a foreign oppressor. Israel lived surrounded by death: the death of their longings for freedom; the death of their power as a nation; the death of their soldiers as they battled to keep the enemy at bay. Death shatters hope and so God asked Ezekiel an important question: "Son of man, can these bones live?" (Ezek. 37:3). This question remains a very valid one. In a world dominated by death, can there be hope?

We too must answer the divine question. Today's world appears to be dominated by a cycle of injustice and violence; of exploitation and manipulation; of profit and power; of self-interest and competition; of hate and fear; of loneliness and brokenness; a cycle whose final meaning is death itself. My friends, can these bones live? The prophet was not sure his people would be liberated from their cycle of death, but God knew. Just as God knows right now that we need to be given life and given it in abundance. The answer is given in both narratives: in Ezekiel, "Dry bones, hear the word of the Lord!"; and in Acts: "Then Peter said: 'Silver or gold I do not have, but what I have I give you. In the name of Jesus Christ of Nazareth, walk.'"

My friends, there is power in God's Word, and the Bible tells us God's Word was made flesh in his son, Jesus. What I'm telling you is that the power of the cycle of death and hopelessness that holds men, women, and institutions captive and oppressed has been decisively broken by the cross and resurrection of God's only son, our savior Jesus Christ. That is what you and I must believe; that is what you and I must live; that is what you and I must proclaim. This world whose dominant cycle is one of hopelessness and death must hear the only proclamation of life and no one else can preach it but women and men who having experienced a true repentance have now pledged allegiance to a Kingdom, that unlike *all* that surrounds us, will *not* pass away.

The gospel we are needed to proclaim is much more than an attempted synthesis that combines a personal gospel with a social reform. The gospel we are needed to preach is the gospel of a new order and a new people. We are needed to proclaim, by our everyday living, that the cycle of hopelessness and death can indeed be broken, more—that it has already been broken in Jesus the Christ.

The New Testament sees the Christian community as the place where, by means of a shared common life, the cycle of the world begins to be broken. By rendering impotent the power of those things that oppress and divide people—the facts of race, class, sex—the Christian community demonstrates the victory of Christ. By showing the irrelevance of power, money, status; by the quality of their new style of life; by their active presence with the poor, the weak, the broken and unwanted; the Christian community can show that the cycle of death in the world need no longer have dominion over us. The Christian community can show that new possibilities of human life, a new fullness of living and loving can be achieved as we give our lives over to Christ and seek to obey his call. And what I say to you is not simple. It was difficult and painful for Jesus, it was no better for his disciples, it cost the lives of the early Christians and it will cost you as it will cost me. Death, hopelessness, and despair are formidable foes, but look, the empty cross and tomb remind us Christ has already won! We as the Church must never forget this, because a church whose life is lived in complicity and conformity to the world and its cycle of death can do nothing more than again nail Jesus to the cross.

The principal way the world system seeks to overcome the Church is by trying to squeeze the Church into its own mold, to reduce the Church to conformity. Therefore, the Church must resist the constant temptation to reduce the claims of Christ, soften the demands of the gospel, ease the tension between the Church and the world. If we truly believe that Jesus Christ has broken the authority and dominion of the powers of death in the world, then the life of the Church must demonstrate some signs and indications of that victory. We, the community of believers, must expect to find ourselves at variance with the social consensus, the political conformity, the popular wisdom of our society, for we are the witnesses to a whole new order. Our discipleship is tested throughout our lives by whether we love the things that are in the world and are anxious over the securities that most concern others, or by whether we abide in Christ and seek first the Kingdom.

The crippled beggar sitting at the temple gate was so oppressed by the hopelessness of his situation that a few coins, tossed at him by people who never really saw him, was what he was willing to settle for. Yet Peter and John were beyond money, beyond upholding the cycle of death. They asked the beggar to look up at them, quite symbolic for those who cannot see beyond their despair, and proclaimed the reality of the power of the Gospel of Jesus. And, "he jumped to his feet and began to walk" (Acts 3:8). There was power in John and Peter's proclamation because it had become incarnated in their practical, daily reality. They lived what they believed, and they believed what they lived. Because of this, they were able to change the lives of those lost in hopelessness and oppressed by death. It is clear to us that Peter and John understood the crucial difference between being in the world but not of the world.

We are challenged this day to go beyond what we have traditionally accepted as Christianity. It is essential that those in the world see clear signs and manifestations of what has occurred in the life of the believer. The disciple of Christ is a sign in history of what God has accomplished through his son. The follower of Christ must always seek to translate his or her conversion into actual forms of living. The cry of our society is for women and men who have been transformed through repentance and thereby filled with power to move in this world with surety and faith. The need is for us, as God's Church, to move so as to challenge the powers that only produce death—the power of racism, the power of fear, the power of doubt, the power of all those personal interests that take precedence over God's Kingdom.

Can these bones live? The Holy Spirit answers to our hearts: Yes they can!

THE PREACHER REFLECTS

I was born in the central province of Cuba, but moved to New York City with my parents when I was only three years old. As is the case for many immigrants, we left behind not only a homeland, but also the people who made that land a home. I suppose that is why when I think "church" I immediately also think "family." It was our church family that made this new country into a home.

I was educated in New York, earning my B.A. in sociology in 1974 from Brooklyn College, a master's in social work degree from Hunter

College School of Social Work in 1978, and a Master of Divinity degree from Union Theological Seminary in 1981. I served as associate minister at Iglesia Cristiana La Hermosa in Manhattan during my second year of seminary. From there I began to work as pastor of a fairly new congregation in Stamford, Connecticut, where I served for almost two years. When I graduated from seminary the Northeast Region (our church is divided into Regions) and the Hispanic Junta of Churches in the Metro-New York Area did not know what to do with me. I was the first Hispanic Disciples female to graduate from seminary and then request a full-time ministerial placement. It is very comforting to realize that God does indeed have to do with our call to the ministry and three months after my graduation from seminary a very daring church, Iglesia Cristiana Sinai in Brooklyn, New York, called me as their pastor. In 1981, I was ordained, surrounded by that church family that throughout my life had shared my joys and celebrations. The faces of this family at Sinai were all new, but the sense of community, the love, the feeling that we were part of a much larger whole, all these were still present. My four years as pastor of this congregation have shaped and reshaped my life, my faith, and my concept of ministry.

In 1984 I married a minister, Ismael Sànchez, who has since become an integral part of my life and my ministry. We were called in 1985 to the Southwest Region, specifically to Houston, to work as pastor-developers of what is now the first Hispanic Disciples congregation in the city. Our present congregation, Iglesia El Redentor, recently celebrated its third anniversary and we were filled with joy to see 106 people celebrate that special day with us. Our minds raced back to our first worship on September 27, 1985, when there were only four of us gathered around the Lord's Table.

Theological and Homiletical Concerns

Serving as pastor-developers in Texas has introduced us to a reality of life we were not familiar with in New York, the undocumented immigrants. We have learned firsthand that the Church, the gospel, does indeed have the power to touch those who are so despised, who live in the fringes. And in this touch we have seen the broken healed, the weak made strong, the despised feel welcomed, the lonely find a family, and we have seen shame exchanged for dignity.

We Hispanics are indeed a wandering nation. Unlike other immigrant groups whose influx into this country has lessened, now having third and fourth generations settled in the United States, we are a constantly moving human mass. Each one of us has left his or her particular Egypt but we often have found not the promised land, but the wilderness. I see this in the eyes, I hear this in the words of so many Hispanic refugees we have ministered to here in Texas. As an immigrant myself, often wondering how to fit in, my belief that the Church must be God's signpost to the Kingdom is strengthened daily. I suppose these personal experiences and convictions are reflected in this and other sermons I preach to non-Hispanic congregations. Experience has shown me that often our non-Hispanic congregations bear signposts warning to stay away, or they speak of fear of those they do not really understand. It was my intention to say that while it may be human to reject and to mistrust what is not familiar, through God's Spirit we are empowered to change.

18. Remember the Sabbath Day

Kim Mammedaty

"Remember the Sabbath Day" was preached during the morning worship service at the First American Baptist Church of Hobart, Oklahoma. The congregation is unique because it is 98 percent Indian. Most of the congregation comes from the Kiowa tribe although other tribal groups are represented. For example, the Comanche, Navaho, and Creek tribes are represented. The history of these peoples is rich and colorful, at times making one want to sing and dance. At other times, the history will move one to adorn sack cloth and ashes. Members of this congregation are direct descendants of great war chiefs. There is pride in carrying on the family name. Others are leaders in various warrior societies that give life to our culture in the now.

Another living historical reality that becomes a part of our community is governmental and religious paternalism. When conversion stories are shared in our church, we are reminded that our ancestors gave up all Indian ways to follow the Jesus way. These early converts are honored for the great sacrifices they made in order to embrace the Christian faith. Their stories are alive in the now.

It is understood that in spite of this paternalistic oppression and in spite of attempts to smother Indian expressions of self-identity, the cultural heritage remains alive and is the pulse of this congregation. The Kiowa language is spoken by the older members of our church. We have native speakers from both the Navaho and Comanche tribes. Kiowa Christian hymns are a part of every worship and frequently we include hymns from other tribes. It is important then to understand that the language, the songs, and the history are rooted in a spirituality of a great people who have known both triumphant victory and painful loss.

It becomes evident here that the preaching of the Word needs to be informed by the specific context of this community. If I were to say that the sermon must be *simple,* this could be misunderstood. Out of another context, this word might lead to assumptions regarding the intellectual abilities of the listeners. The assumption might lead to the notion that this congregation is limited intellectually. This is far from the truth. In this congregation, knowledge is gained from a world experience very different from that of the dominant culture. In this community, those most respected for their wisdom are those who have lived the longest, the elders. The elders know the language, the stories, and the complex extended family tree. They know the people, the lifestyle, and the culture. The sermon, then, is not "simple" or "primitive" in a pejorative sense. It moves out of the lived experience of this particular community.

The Word must be shared in a manner that bridges language barriers. There are members in this congregation for whom English is a second language. While English is the common language, Kiowa is used in hymns, prayers, and personal testimonies. In another sense, our thoughts are to a great extent organized by our language and experience.

One final note on context: The people of this community appreciate humor. Laughter and teasing are frequently a part of the whole worship experience. Perhaps it would be sufficient to say that laughter communicates a measure of love and understanding in situations where "logic" is impossible!

Remember the sabbath day, to keep it holy. Six days you shall labor, and do all your work; but the seventh day is a sabbath to the Lord your God; in it you shall not do any work, you, or your son, or your daughter, your manservant, or your maidservant, or your cattle, or the sojourner who is within your gates; for in six days the Lord made heaven and earth, the sea, and all that is in them, and rested the seventh day; therefore the Lord blessed the sabbath day and hallowed it.

—Exodus 20:8–11

F or many of us "remembering the sabbath day" carries with it a connotation of legalism; it is one of those "laws" that has become obsolete for our day. After all, Christ himself healed on the sabbath.

When we hear this commandment, we ask ourselves the question, "Does this mean I can't do *anything* on the sabbath?" We may also recall a familiar statement from childhood, "You must attend church every Sunday. The Lord commanded that we keep the sabbath day holy."

Very simply, sabbath means to desist, to abstain; for the Hebrews it became a special day to worship God; a time for both the community and the land to rest, gain renewed strength and refreshment.

Today I'm wondering how many of us take a sabbath day . . . and remember to keep it holy.

How many of us take a day to stop . . . rest . . . reflect . . . to be peaceful . . . ?

The trouble with taking a sabbath is that for many of us, it requires work.

We don't know how to be *still.* We don't know how to *rest.* Our world wants us to *work;* our culture *demands* that we keep moving and working.

Even our play becomes *work.*

We must work in order to buy the best equipment for hunting, fishing, golfing, climbing, running, camping. . . .

Then we must strive to be the best at our choice of recreation.

In our lives, there are so many things to *get done,* that if we stop doing—we begin to feel lazy or guilty. Modern technology has given us the ability to turn night into an eternal day—simply by flipping a switch. We even say to one another, "There aren't enough hours in a day!"

We may not have an 8-to-5 job, and yet we are busy.

We may ask someone, "What have you been doing this week?"

The response is, "I don't know, but I've been really busy!" We have a very difficult time just *being*—resting, reflecting, playing, taking leisure.

I read a meditation that said, "My life will not bear fruit unless I learn the art of lying fallow—the art of wasting time creatively."

My elders tell a story of an early missionary to the Kiowas of the Saddle Mountain area.

These people knew how to take a sabbath. It was within their culture to live as part of the natural cycle of creation: hunting, feasting, resting, playing, telling stories, moving camp. The way was good—life giving.

As the story goes, the missionary wanted the Kiowas to work the land; in this way, they would be allowed to own it, and the land would not be taken away. But the Kiowas were not accustomed to working from sunup to sundown. They came in from the field one day and refused to go back to work. They didn't understand why they had to work so hard every day. In response to the "strike" the missionary told them all to open their mouths; they were each to receive a heaping teaspoon of baking powder—because the baking powder would make them "rise up" to work!

Why is it so hard for us to truly observe a sabbath day?

My guess is that it has to do with fear. Fear of silence, fear of stillness, fear of God's revelation.

In our faith journey, it is necessary to take a sabbath day and set it apart from all other days.

It is necessary because powerful things happen in the stillness. We begin to see ourselves as we really are; our ugliness as well as our beauty. We learn that we have made ourselves much bigger than we really are; we learn that we take much more than we really need. We hear the voice of God.

It is necessary to take a sabbath because without it, our wellspring of the Spirit runs dry.
Remember the sabbath day, to keep it holy. Amen.

THE PREACHER REFLECTS

The story, as told to me by my parents, says that I was born on Thanksgiving Day. As a child this was a bit confusing as the calendar said that Thanksgiving was on one day and my birthday another. At any rate, the story of my birth and the sixty-mile trip home, was told and retold in a variety of ways, depending on which relatives were present. I suppose that my birth was an occasion for the making of a good story as I was the youngest of eleven children to which my mother gave birth.

As I grew older, this birth story became less a story about *me* and more a story about *us*, my family, my people—the Kiowas. When the telling of the story began, it was time to stop all else—and listen. It was much later when I realized more completely, the sacredness of those moments; the sacredness of that history.

Since that time as a young girl, I've heard many stories. They become animate in the moment. They soak up the context, the people, the place, the air of the now. They are (at once) connected to yesterday and tomorrow. The stories come to my ears from different directions with varying degrees of depth. As my life changes, the stories move to meet me where I am.

In 1978, I left my Indian environment. I crossed an important boundary. The telling of my story is recounted in years rather than in a community's retelling of a story. My community changed. I was changed. I entered Eastern College, in St. Davids, Pennsylvania, where I studied to receive a degree in psychology.

I grew both spiritually and intellectually. I learned a great deal. Emotionally, this was a painfully difficult time for me. I missed my Kiowa community. I was lonely. In my heart, I stayed connected to my people by running, praying, and walking. Outside, in the wind, I could feel the presence of my people. I knew the comfort of our God.

After graduating from Eastern, I continued my education at Colgate Rochester Divinity School in Rochester, New York. The distance and time away from my people grew. My knowledge and experience became more diverse. The loneliness of separation remained as it was. It was a reality that I coped with and moved through as God added depth and direction to my faith.

I did my field work in seminary at the Tuscarora Mission near Lockport, New York. It was within this Indian community that I preached my first sermon. Here, in this community, I grew in understanding that God was meeting me where I was as a Kiowa woman in the midst of a living gospel story. The stories of the Tuscarora community and the stories of the Kiowa community shaped my understanding of the world, of God's activity in the world. Finally, the stories of Indian people have a prominent place in the preaching of the Word.

Theological and Homiletical Concerns

"Remember the Sabbath Day" was preached as one sermon in a series on the Commandments. This series was developed as a means of addressing what I thought to be a problem in our faith community. The people have been taught to use the Ten Commandments as a kind of "measuring stick" for their faith. Christianity then becomes a religion with a set of rules that can not be followed on a day to day basis. Therefore, the attitudes prevail: "I am not good enough," "I am not acceptable." These attitudes perpetuate the notion that there are "cut and dry," "either-or" answers to very complicated issues and life experiences.

In taking a deeper look at the text in Exodus, we learn that the Ten Commandments also arose out of a historical context that needs to be explored before their significance for the Israelites can be understood. My concern is that the text be heard in a way that teaches my community about the context of the Jewish community. Then, I have given them an opportunity to decide for themselves whether or not the Commandments are to be used as "measuring sticks" and I have clarified the difference between Jewish values and the values of the dominant culture.

A central theological concern is that of liberation—liberation for the Indian community from paternalistic notions disguised in the rhetoric of the Christian faith, liberation from oppressive structures that perpetuate the idea that values from the dominant culture are a "measuring stick" for our faith. God's Word is a liberating word. It carries a message of freedom and hope rather than bondage and oppression. It is a message for the whole of God's people connecting tribe to tribe and culture to culture through inclusiveness rather than exclusiveness.

One way that liberation can happen is through empowerment and affirmation of Indian values. One example of this type of affirmation is found in this sermon. Work and leisure ethics are radically different in the Indian and dominant cultures. Indian people do not share the notions of working to "get ahead," working to rest, and using leisure activities for social prestige. Therefore, inherent in that particular example is an affirmation of how Indian people follow a more rational pattern of work and rest. The hope is that this congregation will experience affirmation from the expressed notions of a divine order in creation. The daylight for work and the night for resting. Also, the day set aside as a sabbath is named a sacred day. Indian people are well acquainted with sacred days and the necessity for periods of reflection.

The ideas of sacred days and divine order or creation are a part of Indian thinking. A choice to affirm these realities in our shared Christian story affirms these realities in Indian culture as well. The sermon seeks to affirm and empower the congregation.

Finally, the story of the early missionary works toward meeting three specific sermon goals. The first is to acknowledge the "saints" in our own history. It serves to honor the first converts and reaffirm their place in our present community. Second, it serves to say boldly our Indian history is alive and real. We have our own story. Finally, the use of humor adds to the cultural context and gives the congregation permission to be themselves.

When I reflect on the occasion and context of this specific sermon, I am reminded again of my own movement between two worlds, two cultures, two distinct "ways of thinking." It has been my goal to provide a few "simple" examples of how this sermon comes to life in our community. I am in the midst of the story myself so that I find myself trusting both God and you, the reader, to make connections with your stories in places where I might have been remiss.

19. The Stumbling Enemy

Ella Mitchell

"The Stumbling Enemy" was first preached on the second Sunday in Lent, at the Fifth Street Baptist Church in Richmond, Virginia, where I was a member. This church generally follows the Lectionary, and the psalm for that day was the Twenty-seventh. The passage is very familiar, especially to persons who are interested in choral music. There are few anthems that combine so much of beauty and the stirring of courage in the same selection, as does Frances Allitsen's version of this psalm. Then, there is a gospel song that is equally heroic in tone and yet beautiful, with radically different rhythm. These two have sealed the words of the Psalm in my memory, and sometimes they issue forth in my singing, as I work about the house or drive along in the car.

The verse chosen as the text was partly an effort to get off the beaten path, and partly the result of having heard the verse about the stumbling enemy preached during a spring convocation at Bishop College in Dallas, Texas. I cannot recall the name of the preacher, but I shall never forget his train of thought. It went something like this: "To be sure, there *are* enemies set against God's children, but they *will* stumble."

The second time I preached this sermon was years later, after what at the time was a crushing disappointment. There was a sense in which I was preaching it to myself, and in which I was able to hear this Word with great profit. This time, the setting was Ebenezer Baptist Church of Atlanta, to which I had moved my membership when I went to serve as dean of the Chapel at Spelman College. I had chosen this congregation because of its affiliation with the American Baptist Churches, on whose general board I served at the time. It is, of course, the church made famous by Dr. Martin Luther King, Jr.

The Lord is my light and my salvation; whom shall I fear? The Lord is the strength of my life; of whom shall I be afraid? When the wicked, even mine enemies and my foes, came upon me to eat up my flesh, they stumbled and fell.

—PSALM 27:1–2(KJV)

As I stand here, I see hundreds of pleasant, smiling faces. Does that mean that none of you has any troubles whatever? If you have nothing on earth that could be called trouble, and you're more than twenty-five years old, let me see your hand. Again how many of you are treated well by *every*body? Let me see *your* hands. It looks to me like *every*body is treated unkindly by *some*body, so *no*body is free of what David called "enemies." In fact, the more successful we are, the more envious enemies we have, and the more we smart from the unjust mistreatment we receive. But David had a way of dealing with this kind of pain. He was a gifted musician, and he put it in the words of a psalm he composed. We know it as the Twenty-seventh.

While there is much more to be said, David meant this all quite literally. He must have recalled with vividness the report he received that King Saul, who had stalked him like an animal, had fallen on his own sword intentionally. The very man who had sought to kill him had lost God's favor and ended up killing him*self*! *That* is awesome!

Then there was his own son Absalom, who had come very close to taking the throne away from his father. It looked like this kid was much too popular—that his aging Papa would either have to accept defeat in battle and surrender his crown, or die trying to keep it. But the young rebel was suddenly reported dead. He had been doing his usual swashbuckling horsemanship, when he forgot to look where he was going. His neck got caught in the fork of an oak branch, and he was hanged because his horse kept going.

When the wicked, even his enemies and his foes, came upon him to eat up his flesh they did *indeed* stumble and fall!

Let me not ask who tripped them up, but let it be well understood that this stumbling isn't unique to antiquity. I have seen it in my own three score and ten years.

Historians now say that if Marshall Rommel had kept going in the Battle of the Bulge in World War II, he could have won the war for Hitler and the Nazis. Never mind the slender line of support and supply; he *could* have ended it all right there, *but his mind stumbled*, and our Allied forces were able to catch their breath and reverse the battle. I can't help thinking that that "stumbling" was no accident—no mere happenstance. I trust *David's* God, and I suspect that my same Lord who allowed Saul and Absalom to lose their balance allowed an invisible block to ruin the reason of Rommel. And our democracy, imperfect as it is, was given another chance to survive and get better.

I call to remembrance one of the smoothest rascals who ever held a major church office—a man who thought nothing of taking a church to court. He kept up his mischievous plays with power even when his health was failing. He maintained his harassment until one day he stumbled into an almost unmourned grave. You know, sooner or later, God allows those who wickedly persecute the seekers after righteousness to lose their balance and fall!

When the wicked, even mine enemies and my foes came upon me to eat up my flesh, they *stumbled* and *fell!* Love wishes no evil on even its enemies. David *mourned* the death of Absalom. And Sojourner Truth cried in pain when those who enslaved her son met horrible ends. We too may even grieve rather than rejoice at their fall. But *God* in justice limits their mischief by letting them get tripped up, I tell you.

And that reminds me to move on and put this whole business into larger theological context. This psalm is *more* than a treatise on unjust enmity and its inevitable consequences; it is a peon of *praise* to that just and righteous heavenly Ruler, who gives us freedom, but sets *limits* to our mischief. Evil can neither succeed nor even survive indefinitely. Our slave forebears had it well in mind when they sang, "I'm so glad trouble don't last always. Oh my Lord!"

David phrased it well, "The Lord is my light and my salvation; whom shall I fear? The Lord is the strength of my life; of whom shall I be afraid?" When he least expected it, and in ways that he could never have dreamed, the Salvation and sure Protector of the faithful was at work. How would he *ever* have guessed that big, strong, impressive Saul would actually take his own life? And who ever heard of a skillful horseman getting his neck broken in the fork of a tree, because he just didn't look where he was going?

In connection with the grand rascal mentioned, you should know also that his pastor could sincerely grieve over his brother's demise. It was in part because all the while the mischief was going on, that pastor and family were cared for and loved as they had never been. Some of the happiest days of their lives together were spent while they were literally and legally excluded from the sanctuary of a congregation from which they had received a strong call. There were guards with uniforms and sidearms to keep them off of the premises, based on a strange court order lasting six months! They had moved over two hundred miles, with four children in school, two of them in college. But there are *no* scars, because in even this bizarre situation, God was their light and their salvation. Whom on earth did they need to fear? As they had never seen it before, that Lord was the strength of their lives; of whom then should they have been afraid?

This experience was not unique to the pastor and family mentioned. The problem is that most of us forget these blessings when another trial comes. So I suspect we all may have needed to hear something like that too. I don't know about you, but every now and then I get upset about the way somebody treats me. Do you ever do that? Do you ever come to a point where you feel that you have wicked enemies, and what hurts is the fact that they seem to be getting away with it? It seems almost as if God isn't watching or doesn't care. We wouldn't *say* it out loud, but that's the way we feel?

Well, let's face it: It's altogether natural or normal, but it isn't necessary for a believer. All such upset feelings and anxieties are born of *fear*, and who is there to be afraid of? Whom shall I fear? NO enemy deserves the honor of seeming to overpower God in *my* mind and heart!

Even if I fail to trust as I should, all I have to do is to remember that clear across history, NO enemy of God has ever succeeded. Martin King loved Lowell's poem that said:

> Though the cause of evil prosper,
> And 'tis truth that stands alone;
> Truth forever on the scaffold,
> Wrong forever on the throne.
> Yet that scaffold sways the future,
> And, behind the dim unknown,
> Standeth God within the shadow
> Keeping watch above his own.
> WHOM THEN SHALL I FEAR?

The life of faith is lived *above* the flux and flakiness of fear. There is something better. As David sang along, he said it this way: "One thing have I desired of the Lord, and that will I seek after; that I may dwell in the house of the Lord all the days of my life, to behold the beauty of the Lord, and to inquire in his temple."

In the house and presence of the Lord . . .

We can even *help* our enemies. Of course we needn't tempt them by the exposure of an unprotected back. But dwelling in the house and presence of the Lord, we can *afford* to be gracious and magnanimous.

We can treat *every*body the same.

We can deeply accept and understand our enemies and grieve sincerely for our own Sauls and Absaloms.
We can keep a calm and pleasant spirit.
We don't have to be vexed and paranoid.

Yes, there are enemies. Yes, there are illwishers and holediggers. God *knows* there are those who would do us in, but Thou preparest a table before us in the very presence of these enemies.

And when we desire only to dwell in the house and presence of the Lord, our cup runneth over and surely, surely, surely goodness and mercy shall follow us all the days of our lives, and we shall dwell, just like we asked for—we shall dwell, just as our souls seek—we shall dwell in the house of the Lord forever.
AMEN AND AMEN!

THE PREACHER REFLECTS

I was born in a Presbyterian parsonage in Charleston, South Carolina, as the third of four daughters of the late Reverend Dr. and Mrs. Joseph R. Pearson, who served at Olivet Presbyterian Church in Charleston for thirty-eight years.

My husband, Dr. Henry H. Mitchell, and I met in seminary and have been married for forty-four years. We have three living children: Muriel, Elizabeth, and Kenneth. Our son Henry was lost to leukemia at age twenty-six, after exposure to radiation during atomic physics research.

My educational and professional careers are varied. I am a graduate of Avery Institute in Charleston; Talladega College in Alabama; Columbia University and Union Theological in New York; and the School of Theology in Claremont, California, where I earned the Doctor of Ministry. My professional experience has been as a Sunday school missionary in South Carolina; a member of the staff of the Church of the Master in Harlem; teacher at Berkeley Baptist Divinity School in Berkeley; professor of Christian education at the School of Theology at Virginia Union University; and, after retirement, dean of Sisters Chapel at Spelman College. I now teach courses with my husband at Interdenominational Theological Center (ITC) in Atlanta.

My "retirement" is quite busy. In addition to teaching at ITC, I am also engaged in writing, speaking, and being a wife and grandmother. My first book, *Those Preachin' Women*, was released by Judson Press in May 1985, and is now in its third printing. Volume Two of *Those Preachin' Women* was released in March of 1988. I am also working on a book, *Black Nurture*, a chapter of which appeared in the Winter 1986 issue of the journal *Religious Education*, and in the book *Black Church Life-styles* (1986).

As far as "The Stumbling Enemy" is concerned, it is easy to see how my life experiences influenced the content of this sermon, since it contains an illustration taken directly from that experience. This would normally be most indiscreet, but the person mentioned has long since passed, and the harassment he dealt to us was a matter of public, legal record.

This single incident was handled with ease because of a long standing core belief in our family. And this belief was validated by experience many times. We held and hold that God works in everything for good. Our professional careers have seemed stymied repeatedly by racism, sexism, and just plain Black-on-Black pettiness. However, the enemies have not been able to close all the doors, so that when they slam one, God seems to open another. Meanwhile, we have lived to see more enemies stumble than just the one mentioned in the sermon. The problem is that of remembering all of this when one is under stress, and so it was good to have to preach the sermon the second time, just to remind me.

Theological and Homiletical Concerns

Our family's favorite verse for generations has been Romans 8:28. My husband's entire book, *Soul Theology*, has as its central focus this one verse, about how God works in everything for good. He recalls (on pages 169 and 170) our son Hank's mischievous yet deeply spiritual remembrance of this verse as he lay dying of leukemia, "'Didn't you guys used to tell me, God works in everything for good?' Then he would smile in mock triumph as he tried to keep all three of us from tears, and he would say, 'Surely we aren't going to give up on that now, are we?'" The fact is that he never did.

The implications of this theological base for dealing with enemies had healing influences on all of our children. Unlike many PKs (Preacher's Kids), they never did become bitter at the mistreatment of their parents.

My husband and I are presently team-teaching a course on the preached Word as healing. It amounts to trying to give people core beliefs in just such verses as Romans 8:28, in order that they may cope with stress and trials. It has been both surprising and instructive to find that some of our students were deficient in these core beliefs themselves. This kind of gut faith comes much more by contagion than by cerebration. To stimulate faith one has first to have it.

The weakness of some of our students' gut belief is referred to as surprising, perhaps because the faith of the psalms, so much of it expressed under persecution, is part and parcel of Black culture and worldview, even outside the churches. The word *is* may have to be changed to *was*, but there is indeed hope, and a resurrection of preaching in the Black churches these days.

20. Let Pharaoh Go

Nancy Hastings Sehested

I first preached "Let Pharaoh Go" at Oakhurst Baptist Church in Decatur, Georgia. I was serving this Southern Baptist Church (SBC) as associate minister at the time. The church is a vibrant, multiracial, multiclass congregation with a membership of 450. It is located about five miles from downtown Atlanta. In the 1960s, this seventy-five-year-old church decided to keep its doors open to all people. Loss of membership occurred, which resulted in the relinquishment of the congregation's building program for a new sanctuary and educational building. Staying in the old building, the congregation was forced to ask the question, "What does it mean to be a church, if it doesn't mean bigger buildings and bigger membership?" They answered by giving their lives to mission endeavors. By the 1980s the church had mission groups sheltering the homeless, tutoring neighborhood children, establishing a group home for mentally handicapped adults, giving support and care to persons with AIDS, and ministering to Cuban prisoners.

In the early 1970s, the church began ordaining women as deacons. They were among the first of Southern Baptist churches to ordain women to the ministry. The church has been willing to risk and bear witness in many controversial areas. Consequently, the church has felt outside the mainstream of Southern Baptist life. In recent years, the church has understood its place in the SBC as "missionaries" to the denomination, bearing light in the darkness of roaring controversy. Since 1978, Fundamentalist leaders have held the power in the convention. This has made it difficult for Oakhurst and other like-minded SBC churches. The SBC "pharaohs" have been clear about who is wanted and unwanted, with overt firings and tightening controls occurring on all levels of SBC life.

Oakhurst has also articulated its witness in opposition to national "pharaohs" of militarism, sexism, racism, and classism. This stance brings up methodological questions, such as: Do we work to change the minds of our leaders or do we just go on with our mission endeavors? The answer has usually been to respond in both ways, rather than with an either/or policy.

Text: Exodus 1:8–22; Hebrews 11:32–34, 12:1–2

Shiphrah and Puah, not exactly household names. Some of us who have read the Bible all our lives have never even heard of them. And I am surprised that the Southern Baptists haven't at least named an offering after these women. Shiphrah and Puah were ordinary women who did extraordinary things. They had no power. They were considered weak. But they showed enormous courage—playing a large role in the redemptive history of Israel. Let me remind you of their story.

Once upon a time there was a pharaoh in Egypt who started having trouble sleeping at night, worrying that he didn't have enough to worry about. So he turned his worry on the people of Israel who had done nothing wrong to the Egyptians. But Pharaoh was worried about control—or loss of it. He started playing the "what if?" game:

"What if these Hebrews were to start birthing babies like rabbits?"

"What if these Hebrews were to join our enemies and start a war against us?"

"What if these Hebrews escaped from our country and our control over them?"

Boy Scout Pharaoh wanted to be prepared. Nothing wrong with that. Interests had to be protected, you know. National security depended on it. Build the house upon a rock so floods don't wash it away. Pharaoh was making a wise investment in the future by planning ahead. And he showed skill as a politician by naming the possible risks and dangers to his people and enlisting their help in the plan of action. "Let us . . . " said Pharaoh. "Let us together build a safe future for our children." The Egyptians couldn't say no to such a worthy call to action.

Plan #1 was instituted with slave labor inflicted on the Hebrews. Pretty soon whips were cracked and commands were barked to keep the Hebrews bending over bricks for buildings and bending over fields for planting. Bent backs were intended to decrease the expanding numbers of Hebrews. But bent backs only served to increase the bitterness.

With Plan #1 failing, Pharaoh decided to try Plan #2. He called in the Hebrew midwives for this one: Shiphrah and Puah. On call day or night. Always ready at a moment's notice. Dependable. Assuring. Years of experience left them having seen it all—the long labors, the stillbirths, the death of mothers in childbirth, the deformities. But the midwives were always there, always ready—wiping the brows of the straining and sweating women, whispering words of encouragement, never leaving their side, weeping with them over the tragedies, rejoicing with them over the miracles, lifting up the baby for momma to see and hear and touch, and watching momma weep tears of joy for having survived with a newborn squalling baby to hold.

Now Pharaoh explained to the two midwives that for the good of the nation and for the security of the children of Egypt, he wanted them to be part of a secret and daring mission to kill all the boy Hebrew babies. And the midwives were asked to do this at the moment the boy babies were born.

Pharaoh had no idea what he was asking. How does a midwife, whose very vocation is grounded on the hope of assisting in bringing life, drop the vocation with a stab wound of death in the birthing room?

Pharaoh had no idea what he was asking. All he could see was his precious and imagined threat to Egyptian national security. All he could see were two ordinary women who had no power, whom he considered weak, and who would certainly obey him.

But Shiphrah and Puah knew who they were. They knew their vocation meant assisting in life, not death. They knew they had no power before Pharaoh. So they let Pharaoh go—to think his own thoughts—to go his own way—while they followed their way assisting in life.

It didn't take long for Pharaoh to get news of their defiance. Hebrew mommas were strolling boy babies up and down the streets showing them off, proud to have a son. The midwives were called in for the scolding. "Can't practice civil disobedience in this country,"said Pharaoh.

The midwives looked Pharaoh straight in the eye and told him a cockamamy story about the Hebrew women delivering their babies so much more vigorously than Egyptian women that the babies were already being burped for their first feeding by the time the midwives arrived. Shiphrah and Puah must have surely thought that such a noble lie could easily pass by Pharaoh. After all, what did he know about birthing babies?

Who are our pharaohs? They are slavemasters who want to convince us that there are no hungry in this land, only the lazy and irresponsible. Have you ever tried to hand that word of comfort from Pharaoh to the mother working two jobs at minimum wage to support her three children? Have you ever tried to hand that word of encouragement from Pharaoh to those standing in the soup line? Have you ever tried to hand that word of hope to the forgotten elderly living on meager fixed incomes?

Who are our pharaohs? They are national pharaohs who want to convince us that being held hostage in the greatest terrorist act in human history, with the whole human family targeted for destruction, is for our security. Have you ever tried to explain the billions for bombs to our children?

Who are our pharaohs? They are Southern Baptist slavemasters who want to convince us that some people in our convention should be included and some excluded, depending on one's doctrine or one's sex. They are church growth specialists who want to persuade us that our churches need a pastor who is a benevolent dictator. How do we explain this—when Baptist bedrock is planted firmly on the priesthood of all believers—with all of us equal before God in our call to be disciples?

Who are our pharaohs? Look in the mirror. Perhaps you will see controlling fears in the guise of words like:

"I can't possibly make a difference in the world."

"I can't possibly live a life transformed."

"I'm stuck with accepting the miserable fix I'm in."

Or perhaps your pharaoh is the flip side of "I can't" Pharaoh, relying on your *own* power to pull things off. Is self-sufficiency your pharaoh?

Who are our pharaohs? Sometimes Pharaoh is almost imperceptible, because we do not have militaristic fascism that makes our subjection of life to other controlling values completely clear.

But we live under powerful forces that run through our lives that tell us how we should live—and what we need to live. We live under a creed of power with phrases like: "growth at any price," "profit at any price," "competition at any price," "limited liability," "charity," "controls."

Our institutions exist for the life and health of the institution—where once they existed for the life and health of the people in them: the children, the sick, the elderly. We are living under Pharaoh's rule, under Caesar's ways, under the *Pax Romana*.

Who are our pharaohs? Any institution or any person who rules or controls our lives. Anyone or anything that stands in our way of claiming our high calling from God.

Our pharaohs expect us to slave away in brickyards without asking value questions, or caring questions, or authority questions. Slavemasters don't expect, want, or permit their slaves to grow or change. They want to keep things in their control.

How do we let these pharaohs go to follow our God of life? We are surrounded by a cloud of witnesses, like Hebrews 11 talks about, like Shiphrah and Puah, who have boldly and defiantly resisted the injustice of the powerful through the ages.

Our defiant cloud of witnesses includes people like: Harriet Tubman, who let Pharaoh go to lead Black slaves to freedom on the underground railway. Like Rosa Parks, who let Pharaoh go to refuse to move to the back of the bus. Ordinary people who did extraordinary things.

We Baptists are people of the Reformation. We wrote the handbook on defiance. There are our Anabaptist ancestors who let Pharaoh go to defy the injustice of the state in the face of enormous resistance and persecution. There are Southern Baptist churches like this one and institutions who let Pharaoh go— to hire women and ordain women as deacons, as pastors and professors, giving women opportunities to use all their God-given abilities in the face of great controversy and threatened funds.

There are churches around our country today, who let Pharaoh go—to care for the forgotten and broken in our land, regardless of the current government policies, giving up the seduction of giant church buildings and big business, success-model number games.

Pharaoh stands at the barricaded door and demands that we sign death certificates. He has no idea what he is asking of us. For we know who we are. For we are the people who follow the life-bearing God. We are the people who follow one God.

Surrounded by a cloud of witnesses, such as Shiphrah and Puah and Harriet and Rosa, we are invited, expected, and urged to move away from Pharaoh and his oppressive ways— to enter another door with the sign "Birthing Room" in bold letters across it. And in that birthing room are the neglected, the broken, the wounded, groaning in travail with the whole of creation. The God who holds that door open for us does not look at our degrees or ask for our resume. This God bends down and whispers in our ears "a secret and hidden wisdom, one decreed before the ages for our glorification" as Paul says in First Corinthians: "None of the [pharaohs] or rulers of the age understood this, for if they had, they would not have crucified the Lord" (1 Cor. 2:8).

But we know to step into that room alive with the hope that: "What no eye has seen nor ear heard nor the heart of people conceived what God has prepared for those who love God" (1 Cor. 2:9). We know the grandeur and courage of people who follow our God. We know the remarkable resources available to us when we let Pharaoh go.

Our story in Exodus ends with Pharaoh's decree to throw boy babies into the Nile. The power of the Evil One remains strong. But Pharaoh has no idea what he is asking of us. For we know who we are. We are the people who follow the one God. We are the people who follow the life-bearing God.

(Read Hebrews 11:32–34, 12:1–2.)

And time would fail me to tell of Sarah and Ruth and Deborah, of Mary and Priscilla and Aquila. And what more shall I say? For time would fail me to tell of each of you. People who know who you are. The weak who confound the strong. Ordinary people who do extraordinary things through the power and the spirit of our life-bearing God.

THE PREACHER REFLECTS

This story of Shiphrah and Puah is a story that I claim as my story, too. I graduated from Union Theological Seminary, in New York City, in 1978. My husband and I moved to Atlanta with our young daughter in hopes of finding a position on a church staff in a Baptist church. Ken joined the staff of Seeds, a world-hunger ministry of Oakhurst Church. I continued to search for a church position. Three years passed before a church offered me a job. In the interim, I worked as a community organizer, and blamed myself for not being able to find a pastoral position. I grew up in Dallas, Texas, the middle child of five children. My dad and granddad were Southern Baptist ministers. This makes me a full-blooded Southern Baptist. It is my family name. As I answered my call to pastor, I realized I was part of a denominational family that no longer wanted me. To stay in the denomination meant to stay within a very narrow range of approved roles. Pastoring was definitely not one on the approval list. I began looking into the possibility of changing denominations. I let go of blaming myself, and began to examine the "powers and principalities" at work in my SBC family that blocked me from exercising my call. It became clear to me that the SBC would not only refuse to affirm me, but that they would do all they could to exterminate our tiny species of female ministers. Just at the time I was ready to leave the SBC, Oakhurst Baptist Church called me as associate minister.

After six years at Oakhurst, and in spite of considerable opposition from other Southern Baptist churches in the Memphis area, I was called to serve as pastor of the Prescott Memorial Baptist Church in Memphis. Prescott is a dually aligned Southern Baptist and American Baptist church. I was installed as pastor on November 1, 1987, as the first woman pastor in the church's seventy-one-year history. I am also the first woman pastor in Tennessee, and one of ten women pastors of Southern Baptist Convention churches.

Theological and Homiletical Concerns

I have wrestled with many questions on this faith journey: "How does a woman get out of being a victim when the oppressors are so strong?" "How do I live in a system that demands I give my allegiance to denominational policies?" "How does change occur?" "What power do I have?" "If the denomination does not grant me their 'good housekeeping seal of approval,' then where does my power and authority come from?" "Does strength come through weakness?" These are the questions I was personally struggling with as I examined the Shiphrah and Puah story.

In preparing the sermon, I was aware of how powerful, ironic, and engaging the story from Exodus 1 is. I wanted to find a way for the story itself to speak its prophetic word without first killing it with too much interpretation. I chose to begin the sermon with a retelling of the story, using a bit of creative imagination as a vehicle for communication. The theological concerns popped out immediately: "What is God's word to victims of oppression?" "What is a liberating course of action against an oppressive regime?" "What is our God-given vocation that threatens the oppressor?" "What does this story say about God's ways of empowering the weak and the powerless?"

I began to answer these questions through a communal effort. First, I gleaned from biblical scholars through commentaries, word studies, and historical considerations. Then I led a Bible study on the passage with a group of church members. For this particular sermon, I invited a group of women to my home for study and reflection on the passage. Then in an adult Sunday school class of men and women, I asked questions such as: "Who are your pharaohs?" "Where do you see evidence of people acting like Shiphrah and Puah?" "How are you, how is our church, following Shiphrah and Puah?" A primary homiletical concern—that my preaching grow out of the community—was realized in this process.

21. The Redemptive Songs We Sing

Christine Marie Smith

"The Redemptive Songs We Sing" was originally created as a part of a four-sermon series I was preaching at the Ohio School for Ministry of the United Methodist Church 1987. This school is held annually and involves a week of continuing education experiences for both western and eastern Ohio conferences. The school is primarily for ordained clergy, diaconal ministers, and local pastors, attended by several hundred people each summer. All four sermons addressed the issue of what it means to be a hope-filled people.

Text: Psalm 137:1–6

The Baltimore United Methodist Clergywomen in Maryland sing a song called "Zion's Song." The chorus goes like this:

> Bring your battered spirit
> Bring your broken dreams

Bring your clouded visions
We will sing Restore . . . Redeem!
Zion's Songs are meant for Babylon
Zion's Songs are meant for Babylon
Zion's Songs are meant for Babylon.

How do we enable ourselves and others to *know* that Zion's songs are meant for Babylon? When will we fully understand that all people need to *sing* to know who they are?

The psalmist describes the plight of our ancestors in the faith, a lament, a moment of bitter weeping from their time in exile. The writer of this lament recalls a painful moment in our forbears' history, a moment when they had decided to hang up their lyres on the willow trees, intentionally silencing the songs of their lives in this foreign and hostile land. Their decision to silence their voices was in direct response to the taunting encouragement of their captors to sing and entertain them with "songs of Zion." To sing in such an environment would have been a violation of their faith and their loyalty to their creator, for a song was often sung as an offering to God, a worshipful, celebrative moment. To remain silent in this foreign oppressive place was an act of faithfulness. Yet, even so, the overwhelming impact of the psalmist's words focuses on the deep sorrow, and the very honest anger, of a people who for a time lost their song. The psalmist speaks a truth our ancestors in the faith knew, and a truth we must never forget as well, *that we must sing to know who we are. Songs of Zion are in fact meant for Babylon.*

The people of God have often sung in praise and thanksgiving for God's abundance and goodness, yet at times we are hauntingly silent during periods of struggle, oppression, and suffering. But if I understand our calling as God's people, we are not only those commissioned to sing during moments of joy and fulfillment, but during moments when life's penetrating pain threatens to muffle our spirits and our songs. To sing during abundance is an act of celebration, to sing during moments of despair is a sheer act of faith. Yvonne Delk in *Those Preachin' Women* says:

Black people know about singing God's song in a strange and foreign land because Black American's spirituality was born in the context of the struggle for justice. We sang our songs on boats called *Jesus* that brought us to America. We sang our songs on auction blocks—"Over my head I hear music in the air; there must be a God somewhere." We sang our songs on plantations—"Walk together children, don't you get weary; there is a camp meeting in the promised land." We sang our songs on picket lines—"Ain't gonna let nobody turn me around, I'm gonna keep on marching, keep on praying, keep on singing, moving to the freedom land." We have sung our songs as we moved through the past 367 years.*

The ability to sing God's song in a foreign land is rooted in our willingness and our capacity to embrace life in all its complexity and celebrate it in all its paradox. This capacity to say "yes" to all of life, just the way it comes to us, is shaped by the clarity we have about who we are in this world as the faithful people of God. Ultimately singing God's song in a foreign land asks hard questions of us in terms of our Christian vocation and identity, questions that demand of us a hope-filled and faithful response at every turn of our lives. The psalmist prods us with the relentless question of our own lives, "How shall we sing God's song in a foreign land? If I forgot you, O Jerusalem, let my right hand wither! Let my tongue cleave to the roof of my mouth, if I do not remember you, if I do not set Jerusalem above my highest joy!" *What is our song? What is the message we sing with our voices and our lives in order to know who we are? What essence of faith compels us to know that Zion's songs are meant for Babylon?*

These are not only questions we ask of ourselves as individuals, but we ask these hard questions of ourselves as a Christian community, as a people. The people of God do not

---

* Quoted from: Yvonne Delk, "Singing the Lord's Song" *Those Preachin' Women: Sermons by Black Women Preachers*, ed. Ella Mitchell (Valley Forge, PA: Judson Press, 1985): 58.

choose to sing in isolation. We sing best in solidarity with other members of God's family who share a common vision of justice and hope, a common cup of suffering, a common bond of spiritual perseverance. Our ancestors were a *people,* united in suffering and in vision, and it was out of that communal and collective power and reality that they sang their songs.

One of the first places in my life that I consciously realized the power of "singing our songs" to know who we are was at Lakeside, Ohio. The first time I attended the West Ohio Annual Conference of the United Methodist Church, I was a teenager, and we stood to sing the opening hymn "And Are We Yet Alive." I was absolutely overwhelmed with the collective power and spirit of God among us as we sang this song in one united voice. *We do sing to know who we are.* And after the trials and tribulations of a year of ministry, one knows all too well *that Zion's songs are meant for Babylon.* . . .

There are places and people around the globe that we might also look to in order to understand more fully what it means *to sing to know who we are.* . . .

Three years ago when I was in Nairobi for the United Nation's Decade For Women Conference, a group of us visited a village several hours away. We had the opportunity to witness a nutrition project, a water project, and an agricultural project begun by Catholic Relief Services. The water project is what I remember most. The women were using hoes and picks to dig a kind of reservoir hole in the ground to catch rain water. They would shovel clods of dirt into burlap bags and carry them up a hill to build up a kind of dam around the hole. It was backbreaking work, done by about twenty women. We gathered in a circle with our interpreter to talk with the women for a few moments. At the end of the conversation they presented our group with a bag full of fresh eggs, a token of friendship and hospitality. And then they began to dance and sing. All the way back to our van the women escorted us with their powerful chanting, singing, and dancing. By the time we reached the van, there were few dry eyes. It was a moment not to be forgotten.

I saw Kenyan women dance and sing in response to the essence of life itself. It seemed to me looking on *that they sing to know who they are.* When they sing they proclaim with their bodies, their voices, and their spirits, that their lives are rooted in a spiritual dimension that permeates their hard labors and their most oppressive situations. Their singing affirms in ways that simple spoken words could never do that they share deep bonds of solidarity with each other in *mutual* work, *Black, African identity,* and a unity of persevering spirit. During their singing, it's as if they reach up into the willow trees of poverty—starving children . . . blistering work—claiming the lyres of their songs in a land that is still not fully their own. *Zion's songs are meant for Babylon?*

Have we a song of faith that threads through our lives like the song of spirit of the Kenyan women? Have we a dance of solidarity and power, a dance of common Christian identity that roots our lives in hope and perseverance, a song that renews our spirits?

We turn to another part of our globe. In Latin America the people have an amazing affirmation of life and faith. When in public gatherings the names and stories of sisters and brothers who have been killed are called forth, the community responds ¡*Presente!* ¡*Presente!* In a very real sense during those moments, those who have been killed are present and alive, a cloud of witnesses forming anew before the people. There is a commitment to keep the spirit and life of those who have given *all* in the struggle for freedom, and those who have been innocent victims, very much alive and real in their cultural and community life. They chant ¡*Presente!* to know who they are. It's as if the people of Latin America reach up into the willow trees of terrorism . . . invisibility, and fear, claiming the lyres of their songs in a land where to remember is an act of redemption. *Zion's songs are meant for Babylon!*

Have we a song of remembrance that undergirds our faith like the chant of our Latin American sisters and brothers? Have we a ¡*Presente! of redemption, a song that transforms death into living presence?*

In Jewish communities, and all communities committed to remembering, each spring there is a special day, *Yom Hashoa*, Holocaust Remembrance Day. It is a time to remember and recall the stories of a people, those who survived and those who died. It is a time to rehearse the stories of human alienation and tragedy revealed in the Holocaust, our human story. The magnitude of this remembering leaves us momentarily without speech or song. And yet on that day candles are lighted around the globe *to remember who we are*, God's human family, a painful blend of oppressed and oppressor. On this day of remembrance it's as if Jewish people reach up into the willows of annihilation, global amnesia, and immobilizing anger, claiming the lyres of their songs in a land where to forget is to lose one's humanity. *Zion's songs are meant for Babylon!*

Have we a song that continually penetrates our forgetfulness like the songs of Yom Hashoa? *Have we a candle of renewed awakening?*

We do not have to be women of Kenya, people of Latin America, or men and women of Jewish culture and faith, to know that we need to *sing to know who we are*. Our lives of faith only flourish when we are attentive to rituals, symbols, affirmations, and actions that powerfully remind us of our Christian identity, songs that compel us to be who we are called to be. To be people of faith in this world of ours, we need to constantly reach up into the willows of human despair and injustice, claiming the songs of our Christian heritage that tell us who we are as the feet, and hands, hearts, and arms of God in this world.

It is so obvious, yet so mysterious, that each of us will sing *Zion's songs in Babylon* in our own distinctive ways, with our own particular voices and lives, each in our own time and way. I would be bold enough to suggest, however, that all our singing must be about two things in this troubled and broken world in which we live. Singing God's songs in a foreign land has always demanded of us that we be *bearers of hope* and *proclaimers of liberation*. We are those who are to bring healing, comfort, and a word of good news to the human community, but we also are called to confront and transform our world into a radically more just and liberating place for all. When we only sing a word of security and comfort we reduce our faith to pious individual spirituality and oversimplified answers. When we sing only a prophetic word of confrontation we reduce Christian faith to social action without the undergirding care and unconditional love of God that will sustain during moments of despair and failure. The two must be sung together, *bearers of hope* and *proclaimers of liberation*. *We know who we are when we sing songs of hope and liberation, eternally* claiming Zion's songs for the land of Babylon.

When we sing God's song as Bearers of Hope and Proclaimers of Liberation it's as if we:

reach into the willows of broken relationships and claim the lyres of strengthened and transformed spirits,

reach into the willows of suffering, and claim the lyres of life lived at new depths and meaning,

reach into the willows of human difference, and claim the lyres of reconciliation,

reach into the willows of betrayal, and claim the lyres of forgiveness,

reach into the willows of dominating power, and claim the lyres of mutuality,

reach into the willows of death, and claim the lyres of the essence of life renewed.

> Bring your battered spirit . . . bring your
> broken dreams. . . .

bring your clouded visions . . . we will
   sing Restore . . . Redeem.

Zion's Songs Are Meant For Babylon. . . .
Zion's Songs Are Meant For Babylon. . . .
Zion's Songs Are Meant For Babylon.

Amen!

THE PREACHER REFLECTS

I was born in Portsmouth, Ohio, and grew up a United Methodist. I have a B.S. degree in sociology and speech from Ohio University. I earned two degrees at the Methodist Theological School in Ohio: the Master of Divinity and the Master of Arts in Christian education. In 1987, I completed the Ph.D. in Religion/Theology and the Arts with emphasis in Liturgy and Proclamation at the Graduate Theological Union (GTU) in Berkeley, California. I am now on the faculty of Princeton Theological Seminary.

Many of my interests and commitments are reflected in this sermon. For example, I am deeply interested in the spiritual expressions of peoples of different races and cultures. Some of this overtly surfaces in the sermon. One interest that influences me a great deal but that is not overtly present in the sermon is my study of native American spirituality. My time at GTU gave me opportunity to explore that in some depth. Another area of commitment for me is feminism and the whole area of women's contributions to ministry and preaching. My dissertation grew out of this commitment. A book has now evolved from the dissertation; *Weaving the Sermon* was published by Westminster in the spring of 1989.

During the years I have had numerous experiences that helped me develop a certain discipline in sermon preparation. The more than five years I served in parish ministry are especially important. Of equal importance to me is my growing understanding of preaching as a theological act.

Theological and Homiletical Concerns

I believe that preaching is first and foremost a theological act. In this sermon I attempted to address the fundamental theological issue in the Christian faith of redemption. The sermon seeks to challenge the contemporary hearer to engage in redemptive activity in the world, for it is in the midst of this redemptive activity that we know who we are as God's people, and we know whose we are.

My preaching, as theologican and pastor, is primarily rooted in liberation theology. Following the principles of liberation theology, that one always begins with the real life experiences of the marginalized and oppressed, I develop the sermon around the experience of our ancient ancestors' exile, and three contemporary experiences of exile from our present world. The sermon suggests that each time people sing in the midst of suffering; each time people reclaim their power and dignity; each time people will not be silenced, therein is redemptive activity and moral agency. The Christian community is called into this saving activity and is called to remember who it is at every turn in its collective life.

As demonstrated by the sermon structure, I am very drawn to a repetitive style in preaching. The repeated line, "Zion's songs are meant for Babylon," becomes the structural and theological thread that weaves the sermon together from beginning to end. I am indebted to the witness of Black preachers for my exposure to the power and possibility of repetition.

I made a significant hermeneutical decision in my exegetical work, and in the crafting of the sermon. The psalm suggests that our ancestors' silence was in fact a faithful response to the experience of exile, and the humiliation of taunting captors. Yet, a hermeneutics of suspicion grounded again in liberation theology, compels us to look behind the text, underneath the text, and through the text to seek what might not be so obvious. In a day when many marginalized and oppressed people are silenced, I do not believe that the final word of this text to our lives is to remain silent. Rather, I chose to explore imaginatively what our ancestors' experience of silence revealed to them about the significance and centrality of their own faithful songs. This is a clear hermeneutical leap, but I think it is one that does not violate the integrity of the text and offers new insight to us about religious identity and redemptive activity.

The sermon begins with the plight of our ancestors in the faith, and ends with us, the contemporary church. The sermon ends not with utter mystery, nor with subtle confrontation, but with a very clear challenge. It is a challenge that has specificity and particularity. The most powerful challenges to the Christian community come in the form of invitations, not mandates. Thus, the sermon invites us all to claim our role in God's ongoing redemption, ultimately suggesting not just what we might do, but who we might be.

22. What Is Our Place?

Barbara Brown Zikmund

"What Is Our Place?" was preached in my home church on August 31, 1986. First Congregational Church (United Church of Christ) of Berkeley, California, is a large congregation with a mix of university people and long-time Berkeley residents. It is an affluent church and a socially committed church. I decided to preach this sermon that Sunday for two reasons: first, I was overflowing with the experiences of my recent travels in Africa and I needed to share. Regardless of where I might have preached that Sunday, I would have begun with Africa. But, in the second place, I know that the people in that congregation try to bring their commitment to Christianity and their involvement in the world together. During the summer months many of them also travel. The beginning of a new school year was a good time to challenge them all to integrate their summer travels with the rest of their lives.

The congregation at FCCB, as the church is known, is a well-educated and thoughtful community and I wanted to show how I had found a new way to relate my Christianity to other religious traditions. I wanted to invite them to be more than tolerant (which most of them are already), and suggest that their faith can be strengthened by approaching other religious faiths with real openness to dialogue. I know that they want to be informed intellectually. They want to be nourished spiritually. They want something to take away and think about. Some congregations might have found this sermon too "logical," but for that church it was consistent with their expectations.

Text: Ezekiel 18:1–9, 25–29; Hebrews 13:1–8; Luke 14:1, 7–14

As many of you know, one month ago I returned from a four-week trip to West Africa. I was attending a World Council of Churches meeting on the future of theological education in Africa. I had an opportunity to learn a great deal about the people and culture of Africa—visiting churches, sharing groundnut soup, rice, and conversation with many African people.

West Africa is not a place for tourists. It is mostly a tropical rainforest, and travel is difficult. I did not see any elephants or the open country Americans associate with African safaris. Hotels and restaurants are very modest. The economies of these relatively new nations are fragile and subject to the trauma of military coups and the whims of world markets. As an American, I found living with these people a humbling experience. Materially we have so much, and they have so little.

Early in my trip I wrote a poem to capture some of my emotions. I want to share it with you this morning.

"MY NOSE KNOWS"

White noses have forgotten how to smell.
Perfume and disinfectant deodorize my world
So I see and hear without my nose.
But Africa invites my nose to grow in understanding.
Because Africa is . . .
the salty air of ocean spray along the beach
smoked fish riding by on a woman's head
the smell of wet rain dripping off zinc roofs
the scent of flowers on trees and shrubs

the presence of warm bodies untamed by deodorant
the sour smell of latex tapped from stately trees
the pleasant aroma of roasting peanuts
a breeze covering everything with red dust
the smoke of burning garbage in city streets
the whiff of cold beer on a warm afternoon
the smoldering rice fields cleared for new planting
the smell of urine on old stone walls
the black exhaust of buses promising "Jesus Saves"
browning ears of corn on a charcoal fire
the stench of sewage in ditches crossed to shop
the chemical warfare of insect repellant
the musty odor of mattresses in wet weather
the chocolate steam from a cup of cocoa
the burned wood smell of newfired charcoal
the tangy sweetness of fresh pineapple
My nose knows the African story
My heart is sad and glad.

When I turned to the Scripture lessons assigned for today I could not help but read them in the light of my African experience. I invite you to reflect with me about the ways in which these texts call us to consider our place in the world—particularly our place as affluent, mostly white, Christians in a world increasingly dominated by poor people of color who worship God in very different ways.

All three of the Scripture lessons deal with God's justice and the human situation in relationship to God's justice. Ezekiel rejects the ancient proverb that because the ancestors ate sour grapes the children's teeth will be set on edge. No, says Ezekiel, it is not what our ancestors did that will determine our situation, but what we do. God holds us accountable. God is just. It is our waywardness that distorts divine justice, not our ancestors' actions, and certainly not God.

The letter to the Hebrews follows the same theme. If we do the right thing, God can be trusted. We are reminded that showing hospitality to strangers, going beyond selfish motives, may provide new blessings. We may be entertaining angels unawares.

And finally, in the Gospel of Luke there are two short parables about the human tendency to rank and prioritize God's people and purposes. Jesus says that we cannot presume to know who ought to have the place of honor at a banquet. We are told that as guests it is better for us to sit at the lowest place, rather than exalt ourselves.

A second parable stretches our assumptions about who ought to be invited to God's banquet anyway. When we are hosts, as well as guests, we are chided not to invite those who are like us, those who will be able to return the invitation. No, we are told to invite the poor, the lame, the maimed, and the blind. The banquet is for all. God's justice is not for those who are like us, or for those who are worthy. God's justice is for all. Each person, each community IN ITS PLACE is an important part of God's creation.

There is an old Yoruba proverb told among the indigenous tribes of Nigeria in West Africa that expresses the same message: "The hand of a child cannot reach the ledge; the hand of the elder cannot enter the gourd: both the young and the old have what each can do for the other."

All of these texts lead me to reflect upon the nature of God's justice in our world and the varieties of religious convictions we hold. How can peoples from developing nations give us what we need, and how do we invite them to the banquet? When we consider Christianity next to traditional African religiosity, what is our mission? What is our place?

I have decided that God's justice will be done in this world only when we (the white, affluent citizens of Christendom) find new ways of expressing what it means to be a Christian AMONG the world's religious peoples. I invite you to think with me about the ways we relate to the millions of people in this world who are not Christian and probably never will be Christian.

One approach is to divide the whole world into Christians and non-Christians. Christians have the truth. Everyone else is pagan or heathen. Because the pagans and heathens are lost, Christians need to send out missionaries and share the saving truth concerning Jesus Christ.

It is becoming increasingly difficult, however, to make such negative judgments about other religions. We have a hunch that truth and error are not that simple. As the author to Hebrews put it, we never know when we might be "entertaining angels unawares." So, it has become the better part of valor to be tolerant.

Even in our tolerance, however, we do make value judgments about other religions. In Africa, I became painfully aware of these habits.

First of all, we rank the religions of the world according to our biases. Most of us believe that monotheism is better than polytheism. Hence we have a special appreciation for the faith and practice of Jews and Muslims. Or, we are impressed with the history and philosophy of the "great historic religions" of Asia (Hinduism, Buddhism, and Confucianism). We rank them above what have been called "primitive, animistic, tribal religions." We operate with unexamined assumptions that religions can be ordered from "lower" to "higher" forms.

In Africa this summer these intellectual habits were challenged. I am coming to believe that there is really no justification for taking some religions more seriously than others. When a religious tradition provides a meaningful worldview and makes sense to its followers, it must be taken as seriously as the most sophisticated Christian theology. I have not only been pressed to consider my place in the global economic and political picture, I have had my loyalty to Christianity challenged. What is the place of Christianity in this world and why do I invite others to confess Jesus as Lord? What kind of theological imperialism do we perpetuate when we share our faith by depreciating and even destroying the faith of others?

In Christian theology many people answer these questions like the great Swiss theologian, Karl Barth. He insisted that Christianity is totally "unique." As a "religion of grace" it is discontinuous with all other religions. The act of faith in Christ is the essence of religious life and nothing else is true religion. For Barth, and many of the world's Christians, all creation remains unredeemed, except through Christ.

But what about the people who lived before Jesus, the Jews, or those who never learn about Jesus Christ, through no fault of their own? Are they saved? Some Christian theologians throughout the centuries have argued, "yes, they are." It has been argued that Christ was and is an expression of the eternal Word of God, the "logos." Although Christians believe that Jesus was the Word made flesh in first-century Palestine, through Christ all peoples in all times and places have been saved by God's gracious love. This is true even when they do not know it.

Roman Catholic theology since Vatican II has built upon the "logos tradition." Catholics have argued that Christians can uphold the exclusive redemptive action of God in Christ AND recognize God's saving action at work in other religions, "insofar as those religions conform to Christian faith and morals." Ecumenical relations and interfaith dialogue are possible because of a belief that God's redemptive work in Christ is never limited by human knowledge and efforts.

As we live with the pluralism of the world's religions, however, both of these approaches to other faith communities is problematic. Greater knowledge of the traditional religiosity of peoples in Africa and Asia challenges our Christocentric assumptions. I confess that my trip to Africa has forced me to look at questions of evangelism, mission, ecumenism, and interfaith dialogue with new eyes My religious worldview has been shaken.

One contemporary writer, John Hick, has compared this shift to the scientific revolution of the late Middle Ages. It is a "Copernican revolution." Instead of thinking of Christ at the center of religious reality, with all of the world's religions understood in relationship to Christianity; we are called to place God at the center of the universe, with all of the world's religions providing various means to salvation. This is a radical new way of thinking about religious reality.*

Obviously, in order to live with the pluralism of the contemporary world many people are open to such a shift. They develop a "balance of power" mentality, which tries to be a "good neighbor" to persons of all faiths. And because there is no way to "prove" that one religion is "better" than another, everyone is tolerant, defending each neighbor's right (literally) to "go to hell in his or her own way." Such tolerance tempers the arrogance and hate that has justified past religious prejudice and persecution.

Drawing upon my African experience this summer, however, I believe that we are asked to do more. The West African proverb I quoted earlier and the Scripture lessons for the day suggest that mutuality and enrichment, not just coexistence, are possible. If we are truly sensitive to the religious experience of people of other living faiths, the result is more than tolerance. "The hand of the child cannot reach the ledge, and the hand of the elder cannot enter the gourd: the young and the old have what each can do for the other." They do not just continue along living with their limitations, they help each other out.

Jesus reminds us that we cannot presume to know where our place is at God's banquet, so we dare not exalt ourselves. We must wait until the other invites us to move to a new seat. Furthermore, when we are the hosts (as affluent Christians often are in the global context) we are reminded not only to invite those who are like us (who can pay us back in kind), but to extend our invitation to the poor and the lesser valued parts of God's creation. We may be called to include at our table those

---

* See K. A. Dickson, *Theology in Africa* (New York: Orbis, 1984).

people called pagan and heathen. And we may be entertaining angels unawares.

In a world where it is possible to know more and more about the religious beliefs and practices of peoples and cultures far from home, I am convinced that learning about other religions simply in order to be more tolerant is not enough. Rather, through genuine dialogue we who follow Jesus Christ have an opportunity to develop new understandings and insights about our OWN faith (not just about the other faiths). In true mutuality we discover that each has something we can do for the other. When this happens, our Christian faith is not shaken, but enriched.

There are times, however, when the values and practices of one religious tradition seem to come into direct conflict with another tradition. What do we do then?

Let me illustrate with one example from the African context— polygamy. As an American Christian woman I find the idea of polygamy repugnant, violating the integrity of women and compromising my understanding of human commitments. In African tribal society, however, both women and men always understand themselves in community. One African writer notes that whereas Western philosophy builds upon Descartes's statement, "I think, therefore I am," Africans define selfhood in relationship to community. An African philosopher would say, "I am because we are, and since we are, therefore I am."*

Polygamy is an expression of community. When Christianity enters a village and demands that a man get rid of all of his wives in order to become a Christian, it is insensitive to the African context. Indeed, an African woman unconnected to a family group or clan is an outcast. In such cases, the gospel is not "good news" for women; but keeps women from the freedom and stature they enjoy in a polygamous family. African

---

* See John S. Pobee, and Carl F. Hallencreutz, eds., *Variations in Christian Theology in Africa* (Nairobi: Uzima, 1986).

Christians are struggling to develop a theology of marriage appropriate to their situation. In the process they are enriching and expanding everyone's understanding of the gospel. Some churches have decided that Christians in that context need not be monogamous.

As open as we may want to be on some of these things, there will be times when faithful people of different traditions and different faiths will disagree. This is to be expected, because religion is a powerful force. In these situations, however, we are reminded that OUR PLACE is always a human place. We can never speak as God. Even as I state my convictions and take moral action to correct what I name as evil, I do so always aware that the actions and convictions of others are not merely tolerable, they may contribute to my own faith. My place in mutuality with my neighbor does not release me from the obligation to act out of my faith, but my place in mutuality with my neighbor allows me to appreciate and be ready to accept what we can do for each other.

May God give us the grace to understand differences, to allow our neighbor to be different AND to benefit from that difference.

Amen.

THE PREACHER REFLECTS

My denomination, the United Church of Christ, has been ordaining women for over one hundred years. However, when I was ordained in 1964, I had heard very few women preachers. In high school I competed in "interpretive reading," and through seminary courses in preaching I learned how to handle biblical material. Only in recent years, however, have I become self-conscious about the ways in which I, and other women, bring some special gifts to the preaching task.

At present I am a professor of Church history and the dean at Pacific School of Religion in Berkeley, California. In my work in theological education I have seen increasing numbers of women students. Today more and more women are openly claiming their call to preaching and pastoral ministries. I celebrate the fact that women ꞏlergy are doing some of the most creative preaching today.

In the 1950s, I attended a large urban high school in Detroit, Michigan. Most of my friends were Jewish. In fact, it was my personal desire to explain why I followed Jesus Christ to my friends and myself that drew me into the youth program at a nearby Congregational church. I needed to defend my Christian witness *and*, at the same time, I wanted to take other religions seriously. My search led me to seminary and ordained ministry. In later years, I did doctoral work at Duke University and taught history in undergraduate colleges and seminaries. My "apologetic" agenda persisted. For me a primary faith question remains: "How do I confess my faith in a pluralistic world and respect the faith and practice of my neighbor?"

I have just completed a term as the first woman president of the Association of Theological Schools. The globalization of theological education has been a primary agenda item for the Association of Theological Schools during this entire decade.

At present I am one of three North Americans on the Programme on Theological Education, a sub-unit of the World Council of Churches that deals with the concerns of theological education around the world. PTE, as it is called, is a small group of educators involved in universities, seminaries, Bible schools, and extension education preparing persons for religious leadership. Every time we convene, we hold our meetings in different regions of the world so that we can personally experience the diversity of theological education. Since the Vancouver assembly of the World Council, we have gathered in Mexico, Ghana, Fiji, and Czechoslovakia.

Theological and Homiletical Concerns

Theologically, I believe that most Christians want to be tolerant, but they also want to hold on to their belief that there is something unique in Christianity. There is no question that Africa shook my "religious worldview" and also, to some degree, my theological concerns. It forced me to look at questions of evangelism, mission, ecumenism, and interfaith dialogue with new eyes.

My conviction is that context shapes all theological and moral choices. We need to ask, "How do we hold to Christian principles and acknowledge cultural differences?" Pluralism does not need to weaken our faith.

Initial homiletical questions for me are: "What do I want people to take away?" "What message is embodied in this experience for me and how can I make it useful for others?" In my understanding of preaching, a sermon is always grounded in Scripture. People need to know how the insights of Scripture connect in real life. Although preachers can preach thematic or topical sermons, they must link those themes to the biblical word one way or another. We dare not assume that modern listeners know the Bible.

Personally, I find it important to end most sermons on a note of humility. In the end, all that we say and do as Christians is limited by our human condition. We may feel strongly about something, and believe that it is suggested by Scripture, but we must remember that we are not God. We forever state our convictions and make our ethical decisions in the shadow of divine perfection. God is bigger than all of our theologies, confessions, creeds, and laws. God is God.

The good news is that God finds many ways to nurture the world's peoples. I may not even understand what they are, but as a Christian I encounter God through Jesus Christ and I am witness to that redemptive joy.

Notes

Part I Introduction

I. Barbara Brown Zikmund, "The Struggle for the Right tó Preach," in vol. 1 of *Women and Religion in America* (San Francisco: Harper & Row Publishers, 1981), 193–94.
2. Rosemary Skinner Keller, "Ideology and Experience in First Generation Puritanism," in vol. 2 of *Women and Religion in America* (San Francisco: Harper & Row, 1983), 139.
3. Helen Auger, *An American Jezebel* (New York: Brentano's, 1930), 127.
4. Ibid., 207.
5. Howard Brinton, *Friends for Three Hundred Years* (New York: Harper Brothers, 1952), 89–90.
6. R. R. Ruether, and C. M. Prelinger, "Women in Sectarian and Utopian Groups," in vol. 2 of *Women and Religion in America* (San Francisco: Harper & Row, 1983), 261.
7. Alice Matthews, "The Religious Experience of Southern Women," in vol. 2 of *Women and Religion in America* (San Francisco: Harper & Row, 1983), 194.
8. Martha Tomhave Blauvelt, and Rosemary Skinner Keller, "Women and Revivalism: The Puritan and Wesleyan Traditions," in vol. 2 of *Women and Religion in America* (San Francisco: Harper & Row, 1983), 318.
9. Ruth Tucker, and Walter Liefield, *Daughters of the Church* (Grand Rapids, MI: Zondervan, 1987), 258.
10. Ibid., 259.
11. Ibid.
12. E. Glenn Hinson, "The Church: Liberator or Opressor of Women?" *Review and Expositor* 72, no. 1 (Winter 1975): 25.
13. Ibid., p.26. See also Georgia Harkness, *Women in Church and Society* (Nashville: Abingdon, 1972), 95–98.
14. Tucker and Liefield, *Daughters of the Church*, 258.
15. Ibid., 261, 285.
16. Janette Hassey, *No Time for Silence* (Grand Rapids, MI: Zondervan, 1986), 97–98.
17. "Sawdust trail" is a phrase associated with revivalistic tent meetings. The ground inside a tent (or other shelter) where services took place would be covered with sawdust. Persons who preached from meeting to meeting were sometimes described as being "on" the sawdust trail.
18. Tucker and Liefield, *Daughters of the Church*, 269.
19. Hugh T. Kerr, and John T. Mulder, eds., *Conversions* (Grand Rapids, MI: Eerdman's, 1983): 113.
20. Tucker and Liefield, *Daughters of the Church*, 270.
21. Hinson, *The Church: Liberator or Oppressor?*, 27.

22. Hassey, *No Time for Silence*, 53.
23. Ibid., 101.
24. Tucker and Liefield, *Daughters of the Church*, 279.
25. Hassey, *No Time for Silence*, 76.
26. Tucker and Liefield, 286–87.
27. Ibid., 71.
28. Ibid., 61, 231.
29. Tucker and Liefield, 287.
30. Ibid., 53.
31. Harkness, *Women in Church and Society*, 129.
32. Ibid., 130.

1. A Golden Chain

1. Quoted in *The Shakers and the World's People* by Flo Morse (New York: Dodd, Mead & Co., 1980), 3.
2. A celibate community governed by two women and two men (elders) as to spiritual affairs and two women and men (deacons) as to administrative affairs wherein each person had well-defined responsibilities for work and worship.
3. Morse, 93.
4. Frances A. Carr, "Lucy Wright: The First Mother in the Revelation and Order of the First Organized Church," *The Shaker Quarterly*, vol. 15, Fall 1987, 94–95.
5. Ibid., 98.
6. Ibid., 94.
7. Edward Deming Andrews, *The People Called Shakers* (New York: Dover Publications, 1963), 56.
8. Ibid., 96–97.

2. The Path Is Plain

1. Rosemary Radford Ruether, and Rosemary Skinner Keller, *Women and Religion in America*, vol. 1 (New York: Harper & Row, 1981), 307.
2. Frances E. Willard, and Mary A. Livermore, eds., *American Women*, vol. 2 (Detroit: Gale Research, 1973), 649.

3. Baptism

1. So Georgia Harkness, *Women in Church and Society* (Nashville, TN: Abingdon, 1972), 113.
2. Ibid.

4. Like a Tree Planted

1. In "Helen Barrett Montgomery: A Labor of Love," *The American Baptist*, 185:4 (July/August 1987): 15.
2. Frank T. Hoadley and Benjamin P. Browne, *Baptists Who Dared* (Valley Forge, PA: Judson Press, 1980), 90.
3. Helen Barrett Montgomery, *The Preaching Value of Missions* (Philadelphia: Judson Press, 1931), 8–9, 15.

5. Live Wire—Beware!

1. William G. McLoughlin, "McPherson, Aimee Semple," *Notable American Women 1607–1950*, vol. 2, ed. Edward T. James, Janet Wilson James, Paul S. Boyer (Cambridge: The Belknap Press of Harvard University Press, 1971), 478.
2. Aimee Semple McPherson, *The Story of My Life* (Waco, TX: Word Books, 1973), 111–12.
3. Quoted in Robert Bahr, *Least Of All Saints: The Story of Aimee Semple McPherson* (Englewood Cliffs: Prentice-Hall, 1979), 292.

6. God Is Love

1. Herbert A. Wisbey, Jr., "Booth, Evangeline Cory," *Notable American Women 1607–1955*, vol. 1, ed. Edward James, Janet Wilson James, and Paul S. Boyer (Cambridge: The Belknap Press of Harvard University Press, 1971), 205–7.
2. "General Evangeline Booth," a brief biography included in the order of service at her funeral.
3. Wisbey, 205–7.
4. Edward H. McKinley, *Marching to Glory* (San Francisco: Harper & Row, 1980), 94–95.

7. The Imperishable Jewel

1. Georgia Harkness, "A Spiritual Pilgrimage," *The Christian Century* 56:11 (March 15,1939):348–49.
2. Ibid., 349.
3. Georgia Harkness, *The Dark Night of the Soul* (New York: Abingdon-Cokesbury, 1945), 177–78.
4. Georgia Harkness, *The Gospel and Our World* (New York: Abingdon-Cokesbury, 1949), 9.
5. Georgia Harkness, *Women in Church and Society* (Nashville, TN: Abingdon, 1972), 33.

Part II Introduction

1. Carol Gilligan, *In a Different Voice* (Cambridge: Harvard University Press, 1982).
2. Edwina Hunter, "Preaching: An Examination of Contemporary Influences and Current Movements." *Prism* (United Church of Christ) vol. 3, no. 2 (Winter 1988-89), 112.
3. Don Wardlaw, ed., *Learning Preaching: Understanding and Participating in the Process* (Lincoln: Lincoln Seminary Press, 1989). (Contributors include Fred Baumer, Donald Chatfield, Joan Delaplane, O. C. Edwards, James Forbes, Edwina Hunter, and Thomas Troeger.)
4. Myrna F. Tuttle, "Four Women's Sermons: A Critique from a Feminist Theological Perspective." Paper submitted for reading course with Edwina Hunter, Pacific School of Religion, Berkeley, December 1988.
5. Nancy A. Hardesty, *Women Called to Witness: Evangelical Feminism in the Nineteenth Century* (Nashville: Abingdon, 1984), 115.
6. The Mudflower Collective, *God's Fierce Whimsy* (New York: The Pilgrim Press, 1985), 135.
7. Ibid.
8. Christine Smith, *Weaving the Sermon* (Louisville, KY: The Westminster/John Knox Press, 1989), 19–20.

Source Bibliography

The following is a list of sources consulted in writing the historical biographies of each of the women preachers presented in part I of this book.

1. *A Golden Chain* by Lucy Wright

Andrews, Edward Deming. "Lucy Wright," in *Notable American Women 1607–1950*, ed. Edward T. James, Janet Wilson James, and Paul S. Boyer, vol. 3. Cambridge: Belknap Press of Harvard University, 1971.
———. *The People Called the Shakers*. New York: Dover Publications, 1963.
Carr, Frances A. "Lucy Wright: The First Mother in the Revelation and Order of the First Organized Church," *The Shaker Quarterly* 15:3 (Fall 1987): 93–100, and 15:4 (Winter 1987): 128–31.
Morse, Flo. *The Shakers and the World's People*. New York: Dodd, Mead & Co., 1980.

2. *The Path Is Plain* by Anna Howard Shaw

Harkness, Georgia. *Women in Church and Society*. Nashville, TN: Abingdon Press, 1972.
de Swarte Gifford, Carolyn. "Women in Social Reform Movements," in *Women and Region in American*, ed. Rosemary Radford Ruether, and Rosemary Skinner Keller, vol. 1. New York: Harper & Row, 1981.
Thomas, Hilah F., and Rosemary Skinner Keller, eds. *Women in New Worlds*. Nashville, TN: Abingdon Press, 1981. Willard, Frances E., and Mary A. Livermore, eds. *American Women*, vol. 2. Detroit, MI: Gale Research, 1973.

3. *Baptism* by Olympia Brown

Graves, Lawrence L. "Olympia Brown," in *Notable American Women, 1607–1950*, ed. Edward T. James, Janet Wilson James, and Paul

S. Boyer, vol. 1. Cambridge: Belknap Press of Harvard University, 1971.

Harkness, Georgia. *Women in Church and Society.* Nashville, TN: Abingdon Press, 1972.

Hinson, E. Glenn. "The Church: Liberator or Oppressor of Women?" *Review and Expositor* 72:1 (Winter 1975).

4. *Like a Tree Planted* by Helen Barrett Montgomery

Hoadley, Frank T., and Benjamin P. Browne. *Baptists Who Dared.* Valley Forge, PA: Judson Press, 1980.

Hudson, Winthrop S."Helen Barrett Montgomery," in *Notable American Women, 1607–1950,* ed. Edward T. James, Janet Wilson James, and Paul S. Boyer, vol. 2. Cambridge: Belknap Press of Harvard University, 1971.

"Helen Barrett Montgomery: A Labor of Love," *The American Baptist* 185:4 (July/August 1987):15.

Montgomery, Helen Barrett. *The Preaching Value of Missions.* Philadelphia: Judson Press, 1931.

5. *Live Wire—Beware!* by Aimee Semple McPherson

Bahr, Robert. *Least of All Saints: The Story of Aimee Semple McPherson.* Englewood Cliffs, NJ: Prentice-Hall, 1979.

McLoughlin, William G. "Aimee Semple McPherson," *Notable American Women 1607–1950,* ed. Edward T. James, Janet Wilson James, and Paul S. Boyer, vol. 2. Cambridge: Belknap Press of Harvard University, 1971.

McPherson, Aimee Semple. *The Story of My Life.* Waco, TX: Word Books, 1973.

6. *God Is Love* by Evangeline C. Booth

"General Evangeline Booth" (biographical information included in the order of service for her funeral furnished by the Archives of the Salvation Army).

McKinley, Edward H. *Marching to Glory.* San Francisco: Harper & Row, 1980.

Wisbey, Herbert A., Jr. "Evangeline Cory Booth," in *Notable American Women, 1607–1950,* ed. Edward T. James, Janet Wilson James, and Paul S. Boyer, vol. 1. Cambridge: Belknap Press of Harvard University, 1971.

7. The Imperishable Jewel by Georgia E. Harkness

Bass, Dorthy C. "Georgia Elma Harkness," in *Notable American Women: The Modern Period*, ed. Barbara Sicherman, and Carol Hurd Green. Cambridge: Belknap Press of Harvard University, 1980.

Frakes, Margaret. "Theology Is Her Province," *The Christian Century* 69:39 (24 September 1952):1088–91.

"Georgia Harkness Dies," *The Christian Century* 91:30 (4 September 1974):815.

Harkness, Georgia. "A Spiritual Pilgrimage," *The Christian Century* 56:11 (15 March 1939):348–51.

_____. *Women in Church and Society*. Nashville, TN: Abingdon Press, 1972.